CONVERGENCE

CONVERGENCE

Why Jesus needs to be more than our

Lord and Savior for the church

to thrive in a post Christian world.

Jon Thompson

Author Photo by Matthew Robin, matthewrobin.com

Use of curriculum template and cover designs retained by Lifetogether Ministries.

Interior design by Dana Boll.

ISBN 978-1-790607-95-2

To my wife Joanna,

who has always stood beside me,

pushed me and prayed for me.

So thankful that you are the one

on this journey with me.

To the amazing staff, leaders, and congregation of Sanctus,

thank you for your continued openness

as we walk with Jesus in this together.

TABLE OF CONTENTS

Introduction

Think of this book as a picture, a snap shot of a group of people on an amazing journey. You will read about the present reality of a church that's the result of a 19-year journey. Change is ongoing. In fact, by the time you read this we will have changed even more. Yet in the most important ways we will always remain the same. In one sense, this book is about the things that must remain constant in a church in order for change to be meaningful rather than chaotic. Hebrews 13:8 says, "Jesus Christ is the same yesterday and today and forever." But Jesus' church continues to change day by day. How these two truths miraculously work together is part of what convergence is all about.

My name is Jonathan Thompson, and I currently help lead a church with a 32-year history that today is known as Sanctus. I joined this church when I was 15, served as a volunteer, became youth pastor, and then suddenly, at age 30 became the senior leader of a church hovering around 1,000 with no vision, no self-examination, and unsure of next steps. Eleven years later we have 2,600 in attendance and now meet in a multi-venue, multi-service experience in a cultural setting where growth is extremely difficult.

My 17 years of pastoral leadership, including my 11 years in senior leadership, have been full of high highs, clinically low lows, boredom, anger, sadness, joy, and hope. I've learned the difference between mission, vision, and strategy and how to make sure you have the right people in the right seats on the bus. And much of it, if not most of it, has come through trial and error. I've come to understand how competence, character, culture, and calling all come into play and why none of them can be ignored. It's about seeing that God designs us for certain roles and none of us can do it all. Putting these truths into play in the constantly changing flow of congregational life has been more than just a challenge—it borders on the impossible. Yet we worship a God who relishes doing impossible things with improbable people to the amazement of the watching world.

Like every church, our church doesn't function in a vacuum but a web of relationships in the near and far environment which require constant oversight and decision-making. This challenges us to wrestle with rapid and challenging cultural shifts, social justice in the suburbs, and moving traditional missions giving to mutual life-giving partnerships. Plus there is the question of charismatic empowerment and the positions of women in ministry, to round out the situations we've navigated in the somewhat conservative church I lead.

I must first provide a bit more history as a foundation for our study of convergence. The leadership transition when I began my tenure created repercussions and expectations that have taken a long time to work through in our church. The former senior pastor, a beloved, 22-year veteran, was gifted as an evangelist, a pragmatic entrepreneur, driven by core values, and a topical preacher. He grew the church from 50 to around 1,000— making an indelible impression on many people's lives, including mine. By contrast, I am a small "c" charismatic, small "c" Calvinist, expository preaching theologian, and visionary. We were as different as leaders could be. The transition of leadership between us is an amazing and incredible success story.

But in transitions, all that has lain dormant–great, good, bad, and evil– seems to suddenly spring to life to fight for the soul of a church. Following our transition there was personal pain as many chose to leave the church, including many friends. At times I felt like I was living in a perpetual state of divorce. In my eleven years there have been three significant groups to leave our church body: one over theology, another over vision, and one over implementation of vision.

Yet in the middle of this 11-year journey I can clearly see how God has moved, how God has done a new thing, how God has been faithful. Our church has grown by 34% in 4 years. During that period we have baptized 100 people per year in the last four years, and this in Canada! What's even more amazing is that in 2011-2015 our giving went up 34.5%! And! What's behind all this is something I know to be deeply true: convergence.

There are so many lessons we as a church have learned from history and re-learned as we have applied them to our own time and place, that I'm convinced would benefit other groups of Christ-followers. When I have introduced these themes and told our story in public, I've found the response to be immediate and encouraging. My hope is that you and I can have a conversation about convergence that is based firmly on the Bible and guided by an unflinching honesty about our traditions, thinking, and experiences. I have tried to include the kinds of questions we asked or that others have asked as we navigated waters that often felt uncharted but have turned out to be the sea-lanes of our spiritual grandparents.

Convergence is something new, but it's comprised of something old, tried, and true. We follow the One who doesn't hesitate to claim He can make all things new, but who is also described as the same yesterday, today, and forever. We are discovering the mystery I now call convergence. I hope you discover it too. It's God at work again as He has always worked.

Chapter One:
The World as We Know It

We live in a post Christian, Post Modern yet modern, multicultural, radically globalized, fully mobile, highly personal world. One of the great paradoxes of today's life is an ever-increasing level of connectedness, paralleled by increasing levels of fracturing. Social media offers the hope of bringing us all together but is often the instrument for tearing us apart. The long held assumption that an increased awareness of diversity would easily lead to understanding and unity now seems to be morphing culture into something reminiscent of the ominous situation described at the end of the book of Judges: *"In those days Israel had no king; everyone did as they saw fit"* (Judges 21:25).

I happen to live in Toronto, Canada, one of the most global cities on earth. The fourth largest city in North America, it's rated as one of the top 5 most multicultural cities in the world, with over 300 languages spoken every day. It's an amazing place to live. Our city can be seen as a microcosm of the world and we are trying to grow the church right in the middle of it.

But here in Canada, as in much of the West, Christians find themselves more and more at the edge of society, not the center. Along with marginalization, we now experience increased hostility and intolerance toward expressions of a Christian worldview. There is a storm brewing around us.

On one hand we have a very militant, secular, sexual revolution that involves all parts of society, and on the other hand we have the global rise of dangerous religious fundamentalism. The sexual revolution calls Christians hateful, backwards, and medieval while the religious fundamentalists call us compromised, untruthful, and secular. In the middle, we stand with Jesus and Scripture, calling for grace and truth, pointing to life and rejecting legalism, hate, and violence, while at the same time saying no to ungodly, self-centered licentious living. Make no mistake, as biblical, orthodox, historic Christians we are caught in the clash of two massive global revolutions, both of which loudly claim to have the answers. And we stand, saying humbly, "You are both wrong." As much as we dislike the discomfort, we're right where God wants us to be. We have discovered that Jesus wasn't speaking in hyperbole when He said, *"I have told you these things, so that in me you may have peace. In this world you will have trouble. But take heart! I have overcome the world"* (John 16:33). Or as Peter wrote, *"Dear friends, do not be surprised at the fiery ordeal that has come on you to test you, as though something strange is happening to you"* (1 Peter 4:12).

So how do we stand, love, and see the Church not just survive, but thrive in this storm? What can we do? What do faithful followers of Jesus Christ look like and act like at this time in history?

Are you part of the "we" I'm addressing? "We" are people who hold that there is a core to the Christian faith that must be maintained even while there is significant diversity in the Church. Though I'm most familiar with the church I help lead and other churches in Ontario, when I have described our situation and discoveries across both Canada and the United States, I've found hundreds of local churches of various sizes that face the same issues and struggle to find faithful answers. "We" are people increasingly under pressure to compromise our core beliefs under the guise of adaptation.

This pressure is not new. Every generation of Christ-followers has faced the challenge to live in the world without becoming part of it. Believers in some ages have done better with this than others. None of us succeeds completely. The tension between the reality of our identity as sin-centered creatures attempting to be faithful to a gracious and forgiving God ought to keep us ever alert to our tendency to drift into compromise, even as we try to adapt in a new environment for the sake of the message we seek to present. This is the ongoing challenge for the Church in every age all over the world.

Like it or not, the Church is constantly adapting. We are faced with both proactive and reactive approaches. This is partly because the Church is not an organization. It's an organism. It's alive. That's one of the reasons it's called the Body of Christ. As an organism, it instinctively as well as intentionally adapts to its environment. Because having an impact in the world is the Church's grandest purpose for existence, change and adaptation are unavoidable.

Some of our efforts to change wisely have succeeded while others have failed, sometimes accompanied by pain and disappointment. Some of our efforts to remain unchanged have also failed. As a church we have sought to worship and obey the unchanging God while making it a priority not to raise change or stasis to a place of idolatry.

The concept of Convergence conveys a remarkable and adaptable core that has managed to be ever new through the centuries. In this we see the hand of God moving and His sovereignty exercised over the Church He calls His own. Despite our obvious and frequent shortcomings, our church has discovered that the closer we come to certain proven practices, the more God blesses our efforts. And though our story is neither unique nor are we the only church to experience these results, a very real part of our story is seeing new life in very hard soil. I've said frequently to my Christian friends across the border to the south that

Canada is nearly two decades ahead of American society in adopting a hostile outlook toward Christianity. In such an environment, what God is doing brings Him glory.

It's a story worth telling for at least two reasons: it bears witness to the power of God and may also help others who will face the same challenges in the years to come. Our story includes such factors as re-visioning, significant growth, moving to a multi-site strategy, and biblical revival. But our story really boils down to just one word: *convergence*. The core of our church change has unfolded between prompting and planning, the high value of spiritual gifts, spiritual disciplines, personal brokenness, and the unusual proximity of God's palpable presence. All of these feel remarkably new, yet are recognized as classic characteristics of the living Church through the centuries.

Over the last half-century, attempts at adaptation by local churches have focused on changing organizational models and finding the right leader, strategies that are both good and needed. Yes to right leaders, yes to being honest about personality and ability, yes to strategic planning, and yes to defined process and knowing the felt needs of a neighborhood or city. But these are not the key. Models will always have a shelf life; all pastors and leaders are truly "interim".

If the standard we use to develop these models revolves around the idea of finding what will work in today's world, we will be limited and controlled by cultural and political factors alone. It is our ability to adapt while keeping a concrete core to build on that we will think about, pray about, and walk through together during this book.

What Is Convergence?

Let me illustrate with a story from when I was an eighth grader. I said to my pastor, "Where's all the cool stuff?" He answered, "What are you talking about?"

I tried to explain to him that as I read the New Testament I realized even at my age that the amazing stories on the pages were not replicated in ways I could see around me among Christians. Jesus and his followers had all these cool things happen around them. I wanted to know where all the cool stuff was today!

He then said, "Jon, Jesus was God; you're not God. Your expectations have to change." I had already accepted the fact that Jesus was God, so I reluctantly changed my expectations. Years later, I understood why he responded the way he did, but I came to realize that though his basic statement was true, it didn't go far enough. And his conclusion didn't really follow from his assertion. As God came in the flesh, Jesus isn't just our Savior and our Lord; he is also our model.

That might not sound all that earth-shattering to you, but I believe you'll realize as you read this book that Jesus' role as our model should have just as much impact on our lives as the fact that He is Lord and Savior. This is because Jesus, though always God, deliberately chose to limit His divine attributes and power in order to not only show us who God is, but also to demonstrate for us what the normal Christian life should look like. Jesus used spiritual disciplines to walk with the Father, and develop and learn as we do: *"Jesus grew in wisdom and stature and in favor with God and man"* (Luke 2:52). Jesus also used spiritual gifts (not His inherent power) to actually carry out His ministry while on earth. And He used the promptings He received from the Father and the Spirit to lead His disciples into moments of revival. His life is the ultimate example of convergence.

You see, convergence is when three unexpected things come together. Spiritual gifts, spiritual disciplines (or practices), and unusual works of the Spirit (revival) converge to form the authentic Christian life. What we will explore in this book is how Jesus modeled these three factors in convergence. They are signs of the living Church; the one Jesus founded and that He promised would prevail even against the gates of hell.

Many of us live out our spiritual lives in settings where those three things aren't taught or practiced. Churches tend to focus on one of these and exclude or minimize the others. One church makes spiritual practices the central point of discipleship. Another emphasizes spiritual gifts as the main thing. And some churches long for revival. Convergence describes believers determined to see all three come together. If Jesus provided that model, it should fit every single local church on the face of the earth, no matter how we might differ in other ways.

Though spiritual gifts are normal and assigned, and though the spiritual disciplines are normal and should be practiced by everyone, we've found that during times of revival/renewal there is a greater openness to what God is doing. This has led to heightened awareness and prayer on the part of leaders to recognize and encourage gifts that have not been seen before. It's not about the giving of the gifts, but fanning them into flame. This pattern of seeing dormant or ignored gifts become active started early in the convergence process in our church and has continued to expand along the way.

Remember when Jesus talked about wineskins? Many attempts at adaptation by local churches have focused only on changing models, but Jesus said, "*And no one after drinking old wine wants the new for they say, 'The old is better'*"(Luke 5:39).

Convergence recognizes the usefulness of new "wineskins" and new "wine" but doesn't lose sight of the "old wine." If it's hard for you to imagine what I'm describing in today's setting, here's how I'd put it: If we could get Tim Keller, John Wimber, Dallas Willard, and J.I. Packer to take turns speaking, while we sing Bethel and Hillsong worship music and celebrate communion like Anglicans, we would be very pleased with that model at Sanctus! There's no scarcity of fine "old wine" and very good "new wine" too. Those apparent contradictions are evidence of the convergence I am talking about and that we in a mega-church context are experiencing today.

Understanding the goal of convergence is an important part of getting there. We've found that certain presuppositions must be shared or efforts toward convergence are doomed from the start. You see, the various "streams" of old and new traditions I just mentioned seldom come together in one place—but they should.

The significant presuppositions we hold about models and reality from a Christian perspective at Sanctus have proved effective as we face the increasingly complex puzzle of today's world. Interestingly enough, they tend to have something to do with communication: the way God communicates with us, the way we communicate to one another within a shared faith, and the way we communicate with those who don't share our worldview.

Common Script

Let's begin with the matter of language, which I sometimes call common script. This is more than using the same vocabulary, which often leads people to have long and contentious arguments without ever acknowledging that they are using the same terminology but with significantly different meaning behind the words. An effective common script implies both shared vocabulary *and* agreed meanings.

This is the hidden key to unity. If you are a pastor in today's world, you are keenly aware of the porous nature of congregations and the semi-collapse of denominations, with people continuously on the move. We deal with spiritual nomads in our worship services every week. Often they are not aware of the backgrounds of those seated in the row with them. At Sanctus it would not be unusual to have a Reformed, a Pentecostal, and a Baptist sitting next to each other, taking in and responding to what's happening from their particular point of view. I've experienced the outworking of such cases when individuals like these have approached me after a message and offered me their responses. The Baptist might say, "Pastor, that was really a powerful *word* today." This is followed by the Pentecostal's "Brother, you were anointed today—fire from heaven and angels on high!" These two people are speaking about the same exact thing with different terms.

So we have people who use the same words to talk about different things and different words to talk about the same thing. But we need to communicate clearly. As a result, we have identified the values we hold most highly in our life as a church—spiritual gifts and spiritual disciplines—and worked very hard by continual reference and patient explanation to help everyone understand exactly what we mean, so that increasingly we all mean the same thing, use the same words, and walk through shared experiences.

Let me add that the language your church uses is, almost by history and necessity, unique to your church culture. The issue here is to make sure that within your relational circle you are doing all you can to communicate with each other clearly and consistently. Take time to clarify, and invite questions. This is not an easy task and it will generate both heat and light as you undertake it. But the unity that comes from a common script will make the struggle to achieve it worthwhile.

Normative and Regulative Scriptures

Another huge issue is the tension over how the Scriptures are used to define who we are as the church in a certain time and place. At Sanctus we acknowledge a normative, not just a regulative, view of Scripture.

By *normative* I mean a robust, orthodox doctrine of the Bible alongside a significant level of freedom in application. In other words, if we find it in Scripture, we should do it; if we don't find it, but it doesn't violate the letter or spirit of the Scriptures, we can do it too. Contrast this with the *regulative* position, which says, "If you find something in the Bible to do, you must do it; if you don't find it in Scripture, you shouldn't do it." One way to clarify this is to ask: Does God's Word tell us everything we as the church should do and not do?

Does the Bible present a restrictive collection of directives that we must obey in detail without falling short or going beyond in any way? Or does God's Word give us reliable frameworks, limits, direction, and examples that provide ultimate guidance but don't necessarily prescribe every specific step to be taken?

For many committed Christians, the assumption is that faithfulness and obedience are determined by how closely we see the Bible as regulative. Evangelicals in particular have often tried to make this the cornerstone of their self-descriptions. In practice, however, all of us handle the Word of God in more or less a normative way, though we often hesitate to admit it or don't even realize we're doing it. This becomes obvious when we come up against a church practice or experience that is unfamiliar to us and which doesn't immediately bring a Bible passage or verse to mind. When we say, "I don't see that in Scripture," we reveal a regulative view. This objection is not saying, "If I can't see it, it isn't there," rather, "My internal review of the Bible has yielded no instances where something like that is either mentioned specifically or commanded, so it shouldn't be done." This is all well and good until we actually examine our own practices and apply the same standard.

Regardless of our church tradition, we conduct our spiritual lives almost entirely in ways that rise from previous normative uses of Scripture that now *seem* regulative because they have become part of our tradition. We treat the familiar as an exact replication of biblical instruction even though we may not be able to put our finger on where and how our practices relate to any specific texts. When encountering someone who insists on the "If I don't see it in Scripture, it can't be accepted" approach, I usually respond with, "Show me in the New Testament a church worship service that sets out the pattern your church uses every Sunday? How many items, including the bulletin, would remain in the service or in their current form if the criteria for inclusion were a specific biblical command? Please show me small groups, drama, worship teams, children's ministry, church architecture, and a mind-boggling assortment of other "must have" and "must do" parts of church life that actually can't be found in Scripture." There's nothing necessarily wrong with any of these; but we shouldn't present them as "Thus says the Lord" parts of our church life. The answer, "But this is what we've *always* done" is not the same as "This is what the Bible tells us to do."

I think Jesus Himself handled the Bible like this. His continual conflict with the Pharisees of His day was *not* over the divine nature of the Scriptures. Both Jesus and the Pharisees believed the Old Testament canon to be God's Word. But each side interpreted and applied the Scriptures in very different ways. For example, note the running argument during Jesus' last week that is reported in the Gospels (Matthew 21:23—22:46; Mark 11:27—12:37; Luke 20:1-44). The bulk of these passages describe the religious leaders trying to formulate "gotcha" questions for Jesus that would trick Him into a statement they could use to condemn Him. Both sides in this confrontation used Scripture. But the climax comes in a telling statement in Mark 12:32, made by the one Pharisee who asked an honest and personal question, *"Of all the commandments, which is the most important?"* (v.28). When he heard Jesus' answer he said, *"Well said, teacher . . . You are right . . ."* (v.32). They were in agreement.

Jesus understood and applied the regulatory aspects of the Scriptures, but he also frequently used them normatively. He ended that meeting of the minds with that Pharisee by making His haunting observation, *"You are not far from the kingdom of God"* (Mark 12:34). In other words, knowing what you should do is not the same as doing it. It doesn't address what you should do when you discover that you're unable to do what you should do. By "not far from the kingdom of God" did Jesus mean the proximity of the Pharisee to correct belief, or the proximity of the Pharisee to the Kingdom embodied in the King who was standing before him, or both?

The Sadducees reduced the Word of God primarily to the Torah and were adept at sidestepping the spirit of the law while insisting everyone else stand squarely on their self-exempting applications of the law to the minutia of life. In the hostile press conference mentioned above, Jesus made very clear what the Sadducees' problem was: *"Is not this the reason you are wrong, because you know neither the Scriptures nor the power of God?"* (Mark 12:25). He shattered their shallow dilemma over which of seven brothers would be married in heaven to the woman who had outlived all their marriages. They had taken a regulative view of God's instructions regarding levirate marriages (Deuteronomy 25:5), but expanded it in unwise normative ways to the point where they undermined the truth and practicality of God's Word with a silly argument based on an error of interpretation and a failure to appreciate the wisdom and power of God. Jesus' appeal to both the Scriptures and the power of God are highly significant and will come up again and again in our discussion.

Again, where the Scriptures are specific, we want to be specifically obedient. In many cases God's Word is clear. By accepting the broader normative role of Scripture, we actually allow it to speak more clearly into our practices, not only by honoring the letter of the Law, but also by freely pursuing matters not specified that are part of our response to God's leading and general direction. This understanding is critical and foundational to convergence.

The Scriptures and Three Points

A big part of the conversation over normative and regulatory uses of Scripture comes back to the way we read and interpret God's Word. Picture a diamond shape in your mind. At the top we place Scripture. The other diamond points are reason, experience, and tradition (also commonly known as the Wesleyan Quadrilateral). Scripture is on top as the ultimate source, it's the Supreme Court, but it's not our only source of authority or direction. It has final say, not the only say. Why is this true? Because the Bible itself tells us there are other places where we see, hear, and encounter God.

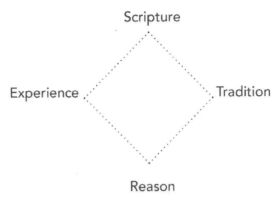

The next point of the diamond is tradition. It's easy and sometimes popular to malign tradition. But from the point of view of convergence, one of the repeated lessons of history is the rediscovery that our spiritual great grandparents got a lot of things right. There's a place for tradition. If we categorically deny a vote to two millennia of accumulated Christian experience and pretend we have developed something new and unfettered by the past, we delude ourselves and fail to learn from either their mistakes or their excellence. G. K. Chesterton wisely described tradition as allowing our ancestors to have a vote.[1] The application of this point is the call to know Church history. There is very little we face today that hasn't confronted the Church in the past. The fact that Christ's Church has prevailed ought to be a clue to us that they figured some things out. Let's practice greater humility about the generations that have gone before us.

Not all Church history speaks with equal clarity or helpful application. I appreciate Luther and Calvin for their immeasurable help with doctrine, but they also lived in Europe when everyone was considered a Christian. That's why I read the Church fathers more and more; they lived faithfully in a highly sexualized, pervasively violent, aggressively pluralistic environment. Today I live in Rome and Corinth, not Wittenberg and Geneva.

Reason, the next diamond point, is more complicated because the Scriptures make clear that sin infects us through and through. Our reason is fallen, so it can't be trusted absolutely. The claim that we can simply reason ourselves unaided to God is foolhardy. But reason is also God's gift and used with humility is essential to read, understand, interpret, and apply Scripture. To acknowledge the importance of the input and thinking of others is a guard against trusting my own reasoning capacity as infallible.

The next point of the diamond is experience, and oh yes, we do live in an age of exalted personal experience. We almost deify our feelings and awareness. Still, experience is significant. All of life is tied to experience. I find so many pastors who are deeply suspicious or outright against using experience as a filter to interpret God's Word. Instead, compare it to a plug in a wall outlet; its value is a question of source. Where is the experience coming from? The idea that some spiritual experiences seem weird or outside the box doesn't actually tell us what's really happening. As Christian leaders, we should never dismiss experience or deny it, but help interpret it. The whole Christian life is to know God, not in the Greek sense "to know *about*," but in the Hebrew sense "to intellectually and experientially know." That's why the Bible uses the word *know* to describe the role of sex in marriage. To know your spouse is not merely an intellectual exercise, it is experience at the deepest level! This is key to see churches come back to life. Too few of us who get up to preach stop to consider that we stand before a virtual ocean of spiritual experiences in the lives of our congregations, some evil and some from God. But if we never acknowledge those experiences, we confirm in people's minds that they have experienced something they shouldn't, or that their experiences have little or nothing to offer the believers around them (including the preacher).

As crucial as it is to recognize the supremacy of God's Word, if we ignore or invalidate any of these other points in the diamond (tradition, reason, and experience), our capacity to correctly respond to God's Word will be limited.

Another major assumption we might have is the necessity to view the incarnation of Jesus as the foundation for any models. In the next chapter, we will explore the identity of Jesus in greater detail; here I simply want to emphasize that the way Jesus operated while He was here on earth was much more than just as a divine being cruising through His creation on a visit to see firsthand how we were doing in our messed up state. The fact that He was really and truly one of us from the moment of conception made Him not only worthy to be our Savior, but also the ultimate model for living humanly in relation to God. It's unfortunate that the question "What would Jesus do?" has become a cliché in our times, because it remains so valid. The glib reply that the question is meaningless because none of us is Christ betrays a profound misunderstanding of a major part of Jesus' purpose in becoming one of us.

Jesus' incarnation is one of the reasons why church models do change, can change, and must change. Jesus was a 30-year old Jewish man who grew up and lived fully in His own community. Later, as more and more people from different backgrounds became followers, they took His Spirit and His Word, but the style, look, and emphasis of the early church began to change and become different and varied.

My current assignment is a large mega-church in the suburbs of Toronto in the twenty-first century. So, of course it can feel like Wal-Mart or Starbucks to a degree. I don't expect that our style of church will be around in 100 years and that's the point. The key is not to theologically enshrine our temporal church culture but to admit that our current iteration is only a model that can and must change. When we understand the difference between timeless and timely, we will see the convergence that can be found across all times and missional efforts.

The Three-Legged Stool

I remember sitting in a class when my professor pointed to a three-legged stool and changed my life forever.[2] He said, "See that stool? Take away one leg and what happens? If you're sitting on it, you'll fall over." That is what's happening in churches all over the world. Having a clear view of Jesus doesn't in itself ensure personal discipleship. We can know a lot of truth about Christ and still live ineffective, disobedient, and powerless lives. Let's see how the three-legged stool analogy can help us keep our balance.

The first leg of the stool represents allegiance, primarily faith in Christ as Lord and Savior. This is faith as an active verb as well as a body of belief. It is a growing trust that allows God to do His saving work on our behalf completed in Christ on the cross and continued by the Holy Spirit daily. This matches up with Jesus' claim in John 14:6 to be the Way.

The second leg represents truth. This is the teaching of the whole counsel of God, continuously displacing lies and training followers of Jesus to greater understanding of God's will and God's ways. Though we come across truth and insight continuously throughout life, the Scriptures, as stated, are the Supreme Court in our quest for truth and present the final word. Jesus told us in John 16:13 that the one He would plant within us would guide us into all truth. That is why, in Acts 2, the first description of the early church starts with the Apostles teaching. It's also why Paul wrote in 2 Timothy 3: 16, *"All Scripture is God-breathed and is useful for teaching, rebuking, correcting and training in righteousness."* Jesus also called Himself the Truth (John 14:6).

The third leg of the stool represents spiritual power. Because every single one of us is a part of the fallen human race and can be under the influence and power of the devil, it is crucial that we depend on the power made available to us by Jesus and the Father sending the Holy Spirit to indwell His people. We are not just talking about the correct doctrine of the Holy Spirit as the third person in the Trinity, but also the active, immediate, promised, and experienced work of the Holy Spirit in this messed up place we call the world. Asserting the power of the Holy Spirit as a line in the Apostles' Creed is not quite the same as relying on and seeing the Holy Spirit very much at work in a myriad of ways in people's lives, much as we see happen in the pages of Scripture. This matches up with Jesus' claim in John 14:6 to be the life.

LEG 1:
ALLEGIANCE

LEG 3:
POWER

LEG 2:
TRUTH

In fact, reading through the Gospels makes it abundantly clear that Jesus emphasized allegiance, truth, and power continuously. Luke's final quote from Jesus is found in Acts 1:8, *"But you will receive power when the Holy Spirit comes on you; and you will be my witnesses in Jerusalem, and in all Judea and Samaria, and to the ends of the earth."* This passage is almost exclusively used to urge missions and evangelism rather than application to the whole life of the church, which includes evangelism. As our church has engaged in a concerted emphasis on faithfulness to Christ, we've been struck with our own tendency to downplay the spiritual power leg of the stool that supports everything we do. We have been led time and time again back to the reality that without the power Christ has made available to us in the Holy Spirit, we try to maintain a sense of allegiance and proclamation of the truth that relies on our own means rather than those provided by God.

We're convinced it's a lesson God wants to teach His Church in every generation. If you sit on a stool with only one leg or two legs, you're likely to fall over. Many churches talk about allegiance and meeting Jesus personally but then what happens next? Other conservative churches are all about truth, believing we just need to preach more truth and everything will be okay. But then what about the lost and why do so many people sit under great preaching yet experience so little life change? Still other churches are all about power, signs, and wonders, but where is the teaching, the balance? It's an all or nothing deal. As we are about to see in Jesus, He practiced all of them in the best way for our salvation, and to model for you and your church what a normal Christian life could and should be.

Let me summarize the stool analogy this way. Only wrong allegiance is replaced by right allegiance. For example, "I was once a Buddhist; now I'm a Christ-follower. I was a self-sufficient agnostic; now I rely totally on Jesus." Only lies are replaced by truth. For example, many of us who know Christ still struggle with all sorts of lies and distortions from our past that our enemy constantly whispers, because we still need to integrate all God has given us in His Word—an ongoing, life-long process. And only unholy power can be overcome and replaced by holy power. For example, faith in Christ and knowledge of biblical truth doesn't necessarily prepare us for the immense power that evil can still bring to bear in our lives. We have an underlying problem as long as we think we can balance on one or two legs of the stool and deal with all three needs.[3]

Convergence

You might still be wondering, Is Convergence a label or a brand? Is it merely another way to attempt distinction among competing views of the Church? Or is convergence simply a description of the way God always works to ensure that the gates of hell will not prevail against His people? Is Convergence about old wine or is Convergence about new wineskins?

It's about all of the above. Convergence, as you are about to see, embraces the solid core of biblical truth that is non-negotiable while at the same time moving boldly into areas where we act in trust, and depend on God's power, areas currently under the power of evil to bring the freedom Christ desires for His people and to those who still wait to know Him.

Chapter Two:
The Trinity as Foundation; Jesus as Our Model

Models for church growth are good, and much of the leadership and vision in our churches is focused on trying to refine or develop new models–our preferred futures. If we are to not just survive but thrive in the future, we must humbly look for something that transcends all missional and incarnational models throughout history and is still found today. Rather than seek new leadership models as a magic bullet to help us thrive, I suggest we look to what every generation of Jesus followers in multiple cultures have in common.

Convergence is a name we can give to the historic default setting that God established for His Church. At any one time, the church exists as a mind-boggling variety of forms with many emphases, and this has been God's plan all along. When Jesus prayed in John 17:22, *"That they may be one as we are one,"* he had diversity in mind as much as unity. If we step back and view the church across the centuries, we can see the repeated convergence of certain central characteristics that have always determined the orthodoxy and faithfulness of the Church that belongs to Jesus Christ.

We can see this same convergence in Jesus Christ Himself. In fact, as I will say repeatedly, Jesus is not only our model in the things He taught and did; *He is our model in the way He lived*, particularly as it relates to His relationship with His Father and the Holy Spirit during His time on earth. Hebrews 13:8 says, *"Jesus Christ is the same yesterday and today and forever."* This verse does more than shut down the ongoing deluge of newly discovered modern versions of Jesus that regularly appear in books and magazines. Of greater importance is the way we actually apply it and think about Jesus' sameness. If you think this verse in Hebrews is an isolated statement, think for a bit about what he said in John 8:58, *"'Very truly I tell you,' Jesus answered, 'before Abraham was born, I am!'"* We need to take into account the unchanging sameness of Jesus in our thinking about the church and our efforts to obey Him as Lord.

Jesus As God *and* Man

Serious thinking about the claims and character of Jesus leads us to think about God. In particular, the revelation of God as the three Persons-in-One God, Father, Son, and Holy Spirit; whom we call the Trinity. I am thoroughly Trinitarian and would gladly submit that everything in this book is true to the way God has revealed Himself to us. As Karl Barth said, "The doctrine of the Trinity is what basically distinguished the Christian doctrine of God as Christian"[1] Marshall Shelley wrote, "Within his own mysterious being God is Father, Son, and Holy Spirit. The designations are just ways in which God is God. Within the Godhead there are three 'persons' who are neither three Gods nor three parts of God, but co-equally and co-eternally God."[2]

Think about it. Outside of time and space, God the Father, the Son, and the Holy Spirit coexist equally. But when God Himself enters time and space, in creation, in salvation, the unity of the Trinity never changes but the persons take on different roles, and it is here, where so much insight and freedom is available but sometimes missed in our churches.

Let's consider the familiar words of John 1:1-14.

In the beginning was the Word, and the Word was with God, and the Word was God. He was with God in the beginning. Through him all things were made; without him nothing was made that has been made. In him was life, and that life was the light of all mankind. The light shines in the darkness, and the darkness has not overcome it. There was a man sent from God whose name was John. He came as a witness to testify concerning that light, so that through him all might believe. He himself was not the light; he came only as a witness to the light. The true light that gives light to everyone was coming into the world. He was in the world, and though the world was made through him, the world did not recognize him. He came to that which was his own, but his own did not receive him. Yet to all who did receive him, to those who believed in his name, he gave the right to become children of God— children born not of natural descent, nor of human decision or a husband's will, but born of God. The Word became flesh and made his dwelling among us. We have seen his glory, the glory of the one and only Son, who came from the Father, full of grace and truth. (John 1:1-14)

This passage introduces us to God and the Word, and identifies them further as God the Father and God the Son in verse 14. The passage not only claims that the Word is/was God, it also demonstrates that the Word did many things (like making everything that was made) that only God can do. John's short phrases manage to convey with clarity the mystery that is one God who is also three. Although this passage is not overtly Trinitarian, there's no particular reason to exclude God the Holy Spirit from verse 13 as the divine person directly instrumental in making us children of God, born of God (see John 3:5). Verse one speaks of the Word's constant, eternal existence that leads to His temporal experience of becoming flesh and living among us (v.14). Yet as verse 14 concludes, Jesus' dwelling among us in flesh did not diminish His glory or His Sonship.

That little phrase, *"The Word became flesh"* (v.14) is both the foundation of our salvation and a stumbling block for all who fail to understand the unique and awesome role of Jesus Christ, God's Son. The phrase summarizes the results of *kenosis*, a word Paul uses in Philippians 2:7 to describe the way the Son of God transformed Himself into one of us, never ceasing to be God but setting aside His privilege and power as God to fully take on the limitations of being truly human. Paul wrote, *"He made himself nothing by taking the very nature of a servant, being made in human likeness"* (Philippians 2:7). Jesus became flesh and is now physically resurrected, and in that state we will meet Him face to face and spend eternity with Him.

That word *kenosis* (translated *"made himself nothing"* above) has been the foundation for orthodoxy and the spark for heresy since New Testament times. In English, the word has been translated *to empty, to pour out,* and *to make oneself nothing.* The Church has held councils in which the exact meaning and implications of this term were thoroughly debated. In particular, the Council of Nicaea in 325 (which settled the full deity of Christ) and the Council of Chalcedon in 451 (which settled the full humanity of Christ) are the prime examples of our forbearers painstakingly working through all that God's Word reveals to us about God the Word, who became flesh.

Understanding Jesus, His relationship with the Holy Spirit, and Their (the Son and Spirit) ongoing relationship with us is the key to spiritual power for thriving churches. Let's be clear from the outset that speaking in the present age about a relationship with God through Jesus Christ that deliberately or accidentally leaves out the immediate, essential, and unavoidable participation by the Holy Spirit is to ignore a significant body of clear teaching by Jesus Himself during the Last Supper (John 13-17) about His coming physical absence and the role the Holy Spirit would carry forward into the future (where we come in).

As God in the flesh, Jesus is at one and the same time our savior, our Lord, our judge, our model, our shepherd, our teacher, and our friend, to name a few of His roles. But to understand the roots of convergence we need to look at the context of *kenosis* in Philippians 2:5-11. Paul is writing about how our lives should imitate Jesus, but his foundation for this is the key to understanding the significance of the way Jesus lived when He was on earth: *"Your attitude should be the same as that of Christ Jesus: Who, being in very nature God, did not consider equality with God something to be grasped,"* (Philippians 2:5-6).

"Being in very nature God": these 5 words are ground breaking. Paul here starts with Christ's pre-existence before the manger. He was the form (*morphe*), the very nature of God Himself, which means Jesus was God. You cannot have the nature of God and not *be* God, for there is only one who has the nature, the DNA, the personhood of God, and that's God Himself. This is *not* to say He was *like* God but not really God; it *is* to say that Jesus of Nazareth, born more than 2,000 years ago who walked this earth for 33 years, was the Creator, God in flesh! Both John 1:3 and Colossians 1:16 emphasize the role of Jesus as the agent of Creation.

Then Paul wrote that Jesus *"did not consider equality with God something to be grasped:"* (Philippians 2:6). This is really central to understand Jesus and the idea of spiritual power. The phrase tells us that Jesus, though He was fully God, chose not to grasp, to be selfish, or to hold on to the reality of who He was. He rejected the common and popular view of power but instead deliberately chose to pour Himself out, to be humble, and to be submissive. He didn't stop being God or become something other than God. He simply and firmly chose not to seize or take advantage of what was His by divine nature. As Gordon Fee commented, "Jesus did not empty himself of anything but simply emptied himself, poured himself out."[3] The *Message* paraphrase got it right: *"Jesus had equal status with God but didn't think so much of himself that he had to cling to the advantages of that status no matter what. Not at all"* (Philippians 2:6).[4]

How did Jesus do this? This ancient song gives us the answer: *"but made himself nothing, taking the very nature of a servant, being made in human likeness. And being found in appearance as a man, he humbled himself and became obedient to death—even death on a cross!"* (v.7-8). God took on flesh, the incarnation we celebrate at Christmas, and then lived a perfect life, died a death we all deserved, and ultimately overcame the grave. The point Paul emphasizes here is that Jesus' life was one of humility. As N.T. Wright wrote, "The real humiliation of the incarnation and the cross is that one who himself is God and never during the whole process stopped being God, could embrace such a vocation."[5] The result is what has given the world and many of us the personal hope we have in our Christian faith.

Paul assumes the resurrection and moves directly to the eternal results of Jesus' actions: *"Therefore God exalted him to the highest place and gave him the name that is above every name, that at the name of Jesus every knee should bow, in heaven and on earth and under the earth, and every tongue confess that Jesus Christ is Lord, to the glory of God the Father"* (vv. 9-11). Notice this is a full picture of Jesus: His pre-existence, His incarnation, His death on a cross, and His exaltation, not only from the grave but also to the pinnacle of heaven for all eternity.

What happened during Jesus' thirty-three years and *how* it happened matters. It might come as a shock to many of us to realize that we often speak of Jesus as if we were actually Apollinarians, who believed Jesus was not fully human; He had a human body, but a divine mind. We too can treat Jesus' life as extraordinary, but not as a human life, rather, a human life that relied on His own power as God to perform activities like miracles and unrivaled teaching. We will come back to this because it shapes in a fundamental way our understanding of everything that it means to follow Jesus.

At the heart and start of Jesus' ministry life was His baptism at the hands of John, described in the first three Gospels (Matthew 3:13-17; Mark 1:9-11; Luke 3:21-22) and implied in John 1:6-8. We accept the fact of Jesus' baptism, but we are somewhat uncomfortable with the implications. John preached and practiced a baptism of repentance and we wonder, but often don't ask, *why would God need to repent and be baptized? What was the sinless God doing in the water? And how does the response of the Trinity factor in to our understanding of everything about Jesus?*

There are three reasons why Jesus wanted to be baptized. First, as R.T. France wrote, "Jesus intended to identify himself with John's message and with the revival movement it had created to enroll as a member of the purified and prepared people for God, it is this rather than forgiveness."[6]

Secondly, and even more importantly, Jesus wanted to be connected to us fallen sinful humans. He wanted to show solidarity with all of us who are separated from Him. It's the first glimpse of the gospel that says, though Jesus was perfect, He came to take on our sin and alter us through God's power. Later Paul would write these history-changing words in 2 Corinthians 5: 21, *"God made Jesus who had no sin to be sin for us, so that in him we might become the righteousness of God."*

But thirdly, only when we pair Philippians 2:5-11 and Jesus' baptism do we start to get a clear picture of His divine power at work in the human context. At this point we see how Jesus continued not to grasp His deity even between His baptism and His death. The *kenosis* wasn't a momentary choice that allowed Him to become flesh; it was a continual choice that allowed Him to live life as we live it, with limitations. The gospels fill in the blanks between Christmas and Easter with the account of Jesus, fully human while remaining God, accepting the limitations of humanity in order to show us how we could truly follow in His footsteps and rely on the power He relied on every moment of every day.

We need to get to the place where we actually believe Jesus when He said, *"I tell you the truth, anyone who has faith in me will do what I have been doing. He will do even greater things than these, because I am going to the Father"* (John 14:12). And we won't believe it if we harbor a secret assumption that Jesus was able to do everything He did simply because He was God. Resolving this dilemma takes us back to His baptism:

> *"When all the people were being baptized, Jesus was baptized too. And as he was praying, heaven was opened and the Holy Spirit descended on him in bodily form like a dove. And a voice came from heaven: 'You are my Son, whom I love; with you I am well pleased'"* (Luke 3:21-22).

"Heaven was opened": it was immediate, it was straightaway, and His coming up out of the water was answered by a coming down from heaven itself. Heaven now speaks; heaven's will is now being done on earth, and the words spoken over 740 years earlier by Isaiah finally happen, *"O that you would tear open the heavens and come down"* (Isaiah 64:1).

Don't miss that in almost every image and actual historical occurrence, these words and signs all point to the life, ministry, murder, death, resurrection, and ascension of Jesus. In Mark's account he reports that Jesus *"saw heaven being torn open and the Spirit descending"* (Mark 1:10). Some three years later, when Jesus died, the huge carpet-like curtain that prevented people from going into the Holy of Holies, the very presence of God within the Temple, was torn in two. The beginning and conclusion of Jesus' ministry are bookends of great tearing that would change the fabric of human existence and allow messed up, alienated people like us to know God again in a face-to-face relationship. The writer of Hebrews spells this out in Hebrews 9 as part of an explanation of Jesus' unique ministry as our eternal high priest.

Out of the torn heavens comes the *"Spirit descending on him like a dove"*: this is of huge significance when you remember the historic acts of God in the Old Testament. The Spirit of God was first seen at the beginning of creation. *"Now the earth was formless and empty, darkness was over the surface of the deep, and the Spirit of God was hovering over the waters"* (Genesis 1:2). The image of the dove over water was also seen in the days of Noah. As Alan Cole commented, "The Spirit is seen here in two lights. He is the gentle dove hovering over the waters of baptism as Noah's dove had hovered over the ark of salvation and the waters of judgment, but he is also the mighty Spirit of creation, hovering over the baptismal waters out of which God will call his new creation, in terms of new-made men and women."[7]

The Spirit alights on Jesus for two reasons. The first is seen in what heaven declares, *"And a voice came from heaven: "You are my Son, whom I love; with you I am well pleased"* (v.11). The Spirit is present/sent to affirm Jesus' identity so His ministry, death, resurrection, and ascension would be valid. Here we see God in His fullness: the Father's voice, the Son of God in flesh, and the Spirit in the form of a dove. Father and Spirit authenticate the divine nature of the Son. In this we see the reality of the Trinity.

The second reason reveals convergence. Not only did the Spirit's appearance confirm Jesus' identity, the Holy Spirit was also given to empower Jesus. His reliance on His Father was real, not pretended. His emptying left Him in our same position of need for God's power and direction. One of the clearest statements of this is Hebrews 4:15, *"For we do not have a high priest who is unable to empathize with our weaknesses, but we have one who has been tempted in every way, just as we are—yet he did not sin."* The God/man remains a mystery to us, but always to our benefit, since both these aspects of His incarnation were for our good and God's glory. Think about it; in all of Jesus' life to this point, He never healed, never cast out demons, and He did not teach in public. Only once at age 12 did He speak at the Temple, yet no one followed after Him. It was only after the Holy Spirit came on Him at His baptism that His ministry began.

The third person of the Trinity empowered Jesus who was sent by the Father. Without the power of the Spirit, Jesus, out of choice alone, would not have been able to bring the good news. In this way He did not grasp the power or privilege of deity: he did only what the Father wanted by the power the Holy Spirit. Jesus did not perform ministry out of his deity but only under the power of the Holy Spirit.

Charles Kraft wrote:

We read in Philippians 2:5-8 that Jesus laid aside the use of his divinity and worked totally as a human being in the power of the Holy Spirit while he was on earth. He did nothing to indicate to the world, including the people of his hometown, Nazareth, that he was, in fact, God incarnate until after his baptism. Then, functioning wholly as a human being under the leading of the Father (Jn. 5:19) and the power of the Holy Spirit (Lk. 4:14), he began to set people free from captivity to the enemy as evidenced by sickness, lameness, blindness, demonization and the like. Jesus worked in the authority and power given him by the Father, never once using his own divinity while on earth.

Jesus did all this to demonstrate God's love (a relational thing), to teach us what God and the Christian life are all about (knowledge/truth things), to free people from Satan (a power thing). Thus he showed us how we should go about our lives as participants in the Kingdom of God that Jesus planted in the middle of Satan's kingdom. He gave to us the same Holy Spirit under whom he worked, saying that whoever has faith in him will do the same things he did, and more (Jn. 14.12). Since today, as in Jesus' day, the enemy is doing power things, Jesus gave us his authority and power (Lk. 9.1) to carry on the freedom-giving activities of Kingdom builders.[8]

You could miss a crucial detail if you read this too quickly. It says in Mark 1:12, *"At once the Spirit sent him out into the wilderness."* Jesus, fully God was now sent out by the Spirit. But the word *sent* means *driven,* or *pushed.* Jesus' expulsion by the Holy Spirit is real and it matters to you and your church. So the heavens tear open, the Spirit comes down, a heavenly voice announces, John points, the crowd wonders, and we who are reading in amazement think things will now get better and easier. The stage is set and the star of the show has been revealed. There should be a great big victory party. Instead, Jesus is led into battle in a hostile place. As Luke writes, *"Jesus, full of the Holy Spirit, returned from the Jordan and was led by the Spirit in the desert, where for forty days he was tempted by the devil"* (Luke 4:1-2).

Why would Luke include the "forty days" detail here? Does it matter? Yes, because it parallels a pattern we see in the Old Testament. Moses fasted for 40 days and nights when he received the Ten Commandments (Ex. 34:28), Elijah, running for his life, wandered for 40 days and nights to meet God (1 Kings 19:8), and Israel wandered for 40 years in the desert before they were let into the Promised Land.

Why should we pay attention to all these historic precedents? Luke wants us to know that Jesus is God come as servant, greater than Moses, greater than Elijah, and unlike Israel—who wandered, disobeyed, and failed God. As the ultimate servant He is acting on God's orders. He will travel and suffer in the wilderness but will not give into Satan. He will successfully live the life and witness that Israel was supposed to give to the world.

There is further significance to Jesus' desert experience. Right after Jesus' identity is given and exactly when He is empowered for ministry, the first thing that happens is a clash between the leader of the kingdom of darkness and the leader of the kingdom of light (Colossians 1:12-14) coming to destroy it. There's a pattern here. As we can see in the book of Acts and other places in Scripture, when God moves, there is a demonic attempt to stop God and His people every time. The slaughter of the children in Bethlehem following Jesus' birth was not only about an earthly ruler threatened by a new king; this was the kingdom of darkness realizing it had been invaded. We run the risk of being blindsided in our world today if we overlook the power behind Jesus' ministry and the resisting, evil context in which He moved.

After Jesus was baptized, affirmed, empowered, and overcame Satan, He started His public ministry under the power of the Holy Spirit by declaring that freedom through godly power was about to come!

"Jesus returned to Galilee in the power of the Spirit, and news about him spread through the whole countryside. He taught in their synagogues, and everyone praised him. He went to Nazareth, where he had been brought up, and on the Sabbath day he went into the synagogue, as was his custom. And he stood up to read. The scroll of the prophet Isaiah was handed to him. Unrolling it, he found the place where it is written: "The Spirit of the Lord is on me, because he has anointed me to preach good news to the poor. He has sent me to proclaim freedom for the prisoners and recovery of sight for the blind, to release the oppressed, to proclaim the year of the Lord's favor" (Luke 4:14-19).

There is so much to unpack in this powerful summary of why God entered the world to win us back to Himself. Never forget that the poor not only include those in bondage caused by lack of education, gender, family, religious purity, vocation, or economics, but also the heart of every single person sentenced to the poverty of sin, and of death, and the poverty of living under the dominion of Satan. We are called to love, to help, and to advocate for the widow and orphan, but the fundamental issue remains a poverty of spirit that can only be dealt with by the person, the truth, and the power of Jesus the Christ.

When Luke concludes his summary with the words, *"Jesus returned to Galilee in the power of the Spirit"* (v.14), he makes clear that Jesus would not use His own power or carry out His own plans. Everything Jesus said and did He did in surrender and under the power of the Holy Spirit. Luke's phrase is not just a transition statement to bridge Jesus' time in the wilderness and the launch of His ministry.

Jesus Our Example

Our view of Jesus' ministry changes significantly when we ask the question: If Jesus didn't teach, or cast out demons, or heal because He was God but did all these amazing things under the Holy Spirit's power and direction, what does that look like today? How does His way of life and ministry intersect with ours? Jesus operated under the Holy Spirit's power, not His own (which He had set aside). Jesus used spiritual gifts to serve and He clearly had the gifts of teaching, miracles, healing, and discernment, to name a few. The Holy Spirit provided what He needed to carry out the Father's purposes on earth. Do you see the connection? If we have the same indwelling Holy Spirit Jesus had, and the church universal has the same spiritual gifts He used, together we can do what Jesus did.

We can and should give great attention to all the ways that Jesus is different from us and therefore worthy of our worship and obedience. He is and always was our Savior and Lord, the second person of the Trinity. But He chose to become one *of* us and one *with* us, for very important reasons that go beyond His priceless act of substitution on the cross. He not only made our eternal life possible; He made our life *now* possible by demonstrating as a human being how to live as people empowered by the Holy Spirit. In fact, since the time of Jesus, every generation of believers has had to re-learn this truth, that the authentic life of a Christ-follower must be a Spirit-filled life. The Holy Spirit whom Jesus promised and described during the Last Supper (John 13-17) isn't an add-on to the spiritual life but the driving force behind everything God wants to accomplish in us and through us. Where Jesus went first, we the Church now go.

Jesus provides a pattern for us personally and together. Remember that the Bible calls the church the Body of Christ; we (corporately) are Jesus on earth. Everything He did in his earthly life and ministry, we are able to do together as His representatives on earth. We are called into His life by using the practices He used and we are called together to use the gifts He used to serve the Church and the world. Watch this; our walk with God is just like Jesus' walk:

- We are all baptized in the Spirit when we become Christians and enter the relationship with the Father that Jesus had: *"So it is with Christ. For we were all baptized by one Spirit into one body—whether Jews or Greeks, slave or free—and we were all given the one Spirit to drink"* (1 Corinthians 12:12-13).

- We are all spiritually marked or sealed by the Holy Spirit at the time of our conversion: *"And you also were included in Christ when you heard the message of truth, the gospel of your salvation. When you believed, you were marked in him with a seal, the promised Holy Spirit, who is a deposit guaranteeing our inheritance until the redemption of those who are God's possession—to the praise of his glory"* (Ephesians 1:13-14).

- We are all called to ask God to produce in us the same character that Jesus had, which was the fruit of the Spirit: *"But the fruit of the Spirit is love, joy, peace, patience, kindness, goodness, faithfulness, gentleness and self-control"* (Galatians 5:22-23).

- We are all called to walk in the spiritual practices that Jesus walked in. It is here we are transformed, learn to hear God's voice, and are challenged to move to the deeper places in our walk personally and together. Notice that each practice is open to all of us. Every Christian is invited into these practices to be truly transformed, and as we move in them over a long period of time we will continually become more like Jesus.

- We are all called to walk in the power of the Holy Spirit by using the gifts of the Holy Spirit. As a church we will have all the gifts, while personally we may only have one or more. You personally will not have all 21! That's the difference between the practices and the gifts. The practices are open to all; God gives the gifts as He wills. The result is that we can never say, "Well, we will never see all that Jesus did again because He was God and we are not." No, like Jesus, the Spirit is given to affirm that we are children of God and to empower us.

Jesus laid aside the privilege of deity and was filled by the Spirit and perfectly did the will of the Father. So when we are baptized in the Spirit, and filled by the Spirit, and when we follow Jesus in His practices, and recognize our spiritual gifts as undergirded by the fruit of the Spirit, we, like Jesus, can and will do greater things.

We have the same access to the Father that Jesus had. We have the same Holy Spirit living in each one of us that Jesus had. We have the same power that He had and the same character traits offered to us that He had. We have the same gifts He had and we have the same practices that He followed. If spiritual gifts are a guaranteed source of power, then spiritual practices for the believer are a guaranteed source of transformation!

We will see in the chapters to come that spiritual practices and spiritual gifts were the inner and outer life of Jesus and they ought to be the inner and outer life of each of His devoted followers. They are the glue in our relationship with God and others. Jesus used spiritual disciplines to hear and walk with the Father, because these holy habits are guaranteed places of personal change. Jesus used spiritual gifts to demonstrate submission and service because they are the only heaven-guaranteed place of power. They are the sanctioned and empowered means God has provided to us to accomplish His purposes and bring Him glory.

With Jesus as our model, let me emphasize a key verse that puts Jesus firmly where we live each day: *"Jesus gave them this answer: 'Very truly I tell you, the Son can do nothing by himself; he can do only what he sees his Father doing, because whatever the Father does the Son also does'"* (John 5:19). The Gospel of John presents in Jesus the pattern of submissive empowerment and permission-based action that should characterize our lives. This obliterates the assumption we often make that Jesus' actions can only be explained because He was the Son of God. We therefore conclude that we couldn't be part of such demonstration of God's power because we're *not* the Son of God. But throughout His life here among us, Jesus, as He said above, could *"do nothing by himself."* In His humanity He was completely dependent on His Father and the Holy Spirit for permission, direction, and empowerment. That Jesus expects us to imitate Him is a foundational idea introduced in John 5:19 and repeated in John 14:12, *"I tell you the truth, anyone who has faith in me will do what I have been doing. He will do even greater things than these, because I am going to the Father."* It comes as no surprise then that Jesus is the original Spirit-baptized, Spirit-filled, Spirit-empowered person in every sense of the term. And He wants each of us to follow in His steps. So now, welcome to Convergence.

Chapter Three:
Spiritual Disciplines

The last decade in our church has been saturated with lessons about the essential role of spiritual power in our lives as Christians. God has made available everything we need to live the Christian life, while also reminding us constantly that we can't live that life in our own power and means. So let's think together about the way God's Spirit did His work through Jesus and does His work through the Church.

There are four empowering factors:

1. natural talents and abilities,
2. spiritual disciplines or practices,
3. spiritual gifts, and
4. spiritual results or fruit.

Much of the remainder of this book will be devoted to understanding the role of the second (Spiritual Disciplines) and third (Spiritual Gifts) items on the list as they create convergence, but it will be helpful to differentiate them all here at the start.

I will continue to state what our church has discovered firsthand; that spiritual gifts are the only guaranteed place of power to do ministry, and that spiritual practices, when engaged as a Christian, are a guaranteed place of communion, transformation, and healing.

Having used the word "guaranteed," let me hurry to emphasize that spiritual practices do not make you a Christian. Spiritual disciplines do not get you a relationship with God. They do not impress God. But spiritual practices are the very things that can place us in His presence so we can be transformed and hear what we are called to do. They bring health to the relationship we are already in. Spiritual practices help complete the picture of salvation presented by Paul in Ephesians 2:8-10, *"For it is by grace you have been saved, through faith—and this is not from yourselves, it is the gift of God—not by works, so that no one can boast. For we are God's handiwork, created in Christ Jesus to do good works, which God prepared in advance for us to do."* We Evangelicals, so insistent on the centrality of faith and salvation by God's grace alone, have often been guilty of downplaying the role of "works" in God's plan for us post-salvation. Just because we can't do anything to save ourselves doesn't mean God doesn't have a whole list of "good works" for us to do once we are saved. The spiritual disciplines don't save, but they are what saved people practice. They are the very life skills Jesus practiced.

Here's how I differentiate spiritual practices from the three other categories mentioned above:

- Natural talents and abilities[1] – By way of genetics and God's participation in "knitting you together in your mother's womb" (Psalm 139), you are a "fearfully and wonderfully" made creature. As an original work of divine art, you have been created with an amazing collection of capacities, abilities, and native skills that you have had from the start.

  Contrary to motivational speakers, not everyone can become a world-class athlete or a piano virtuoso based solely on personal discipline. But it's also true that natural talents and abilities can be improved and honed through training.

The story of David's sling is an interesting example of raw talent improved by training and use. By the time David went up against Goliath in a duel to the death, young David had a burning confidence in God and a significant certainty in his ability to hit what he aimed at with his sling. The muscle memory created through thousands of stone casts came to play as David faced his opponent. In an important sense, while others looked at the giant Goliath as an opponent too big to defeat, David saw him simply as a target too big to miss!

At the heart of the Christian life is our willingness to place everything God has given to us by way of talents and abilities at His disposal. He made us the way He made us for a reason, and His plans for us will include making use of His designed gifts along the way, often in ways that may surprise us. David honed his skill with the sling for the practical purpose of defending the flock from marauding wild animals, not because He expected to face a giant on the battlefield. But the skill developed in one place became useful in another. I would be surprised if you can't think of examples in your life where a skill you learned or developed early in life has been used in unexpected ways later in life. But those are not guaranteed sources of power to do ministry.

▪ Spiritual Disciplines/Holy Habits – Spiritual practices/disciplines/habits (all capable of continual improvement) help us walk with God and each other in order to be changed and hear what God wants us to do. They are activities that place you in the presence of God so you can continually grow in your faith. They include acts like fasting, solitude, silence, corporate worship, prayer, service, confession, and study, among others. To become like Jesus, the same Spirit that was on Him and in Him must fill us, and we must incorporate the disciplines He used in His relationship with the Father.

Again, Spiritual practices are for walking with God in order to be changed and hear what God wants us to do. By way of brief distinction, spiritual disciplines primarily strengthen individuals while the spiritual gifts are used to serve or strengthen others.

- Spiritual Gifts– When the Holy Spirit enters our lives at the moment of conversion, He comes bearing a gift or gifts. While we are invited to practice any and all the spiritual disciplines, the spiritual gifts are at the sole discretion of the Holy Spirit. He gives as He wills. We do not choose our spiritual gifts, though we can possess them in ignorance, unaware of the power God has given to us for His use. We may hesitate, not understand, recognize, or refuse to use a gift that has been given to us.

As a divinely guaranteed place of power for ministry in our lives, the spiritual gifts are at the heart of what it means to be a faithful disciple of Jesus Christ. Because the spiritual gifts have to do with power, they are the recognizable though not always acknowledged explanation for the effective work of the Church. Later I will describe the twenty-one spiritual gifts, which can be identified in Scripture. Along with the spiritual practices, spiritual gifts are a consistent feature throughout Christian history, a sign of convergence. In every generation, the faithful Church has been made up of people through whom God's Holy Spirit worked, and He did that work through the gifts in His people.

Beginning within the events recorded about the Church in the New Testament, the natural abilities, motivation, and dedication of the early followers of Jesus are simply not enough to explain the explosive growth of the Church. What Jesus promised would happen in Acts 1:8 did in fact happen and continues to happen—God empowers His people by His Spirit to do His work.

- Spiritual fruit– The last area we need to talk about is the fruit of the Spirit. Paul speaks of these in Galatians 5:22-23, *"But the fruit of the Spirit is love, joy, peace, forbearance, kindness, goodness, faithfulness, gentleness and self-control. Against such things there is no law."* These qualities and character traits are increasingly present in those who are day by day being transformed into the likeness of Christ by the Holy Spirit. This ever-growing character allows us to faithfully steward the power God has given and is evidence of our times with God in the spiritual disciplines.

Here's a little aside for fellow pastors. I realize we live in an age that measures results by numbers and size. The assumption is that a Spirit-empowered ministry, accompanied by faithful spiritual practices will inevitably yield an ever-growing circle of influence or a larger church. When this view is extrapolated, it means that God's perfect plan must be to have a Willow Creek-size church in every city. This distorted measurement of faithfulness and blessing has a deadly undermining effect. It misses the mark of holy dissatisfaction (a growing conviction about our inadequacy and humility in light of what God is doing in and through us) by focusing instead on disappointment that God hasn't given us more recognition and fame (couched in spiritual language, of course). You and I can pray along with Jabez, *"Oh, that you would bless me and enlarge my territory!"* (1 Chronicles 4:10), but if we fail to consider all that Jesus meant when he said, *"From everyone who has been given much, much will be demanded; and from the one who has been entrusted with much, much more will be asked"* (Luke 12:48), we may well miss what God actually has in mind for us to do while we are secretly envious of what He has called someone else to do.

All three: the gifts of the Spirit, the fruit of the Spirit and spiritual disciplines form a nexus for ministry that is needed and necessary for effective ministry.

Where Credit is Due

In our lifetime, God has used various authors to revive the central emphasis on spiritual practices for many of us. For me, Richard Foster (*Celebration of Discipline*)[2] and Dallas Willard (*The Spirit of the Disciplines*)[3] have been key. While many have since reflected and expanded on their work, they are both amazing examples of the disciplines conversation: that God's ways of working with us don't change, though one generation may become so forgetful that an explanation of God's ways ends up sounding like radical new ideas. The survey and notes on spiritual disciplines included in this chapter will display an obvious debt I owe to them and many others for the study, application, and explanation of the spiritual practices that they have made a major part of their ministry. They would be the first to claim no originality, but an effort to echo the lessons passed on from previous generations.

My purpose in this chapter is not to duplicate their many other excellent and thorough works, but to emphasize how Jesus used spiritual practices as a model so we can do the same. I will consider my effort successful if you are driven to dive deeply into the amazing and challenging life that can be shaped by the spiritual disciplines. Along with God's Word, the two books I just mentioned would be valuable launch points for you.

How Jesus Functioned

I have claimed and experienced that the spiritual disciplines and spiritual gifts are divinely guaranteed means of spiritual transformation, hearing, and empowerment. We can be encouraged in this discovery when we trace Jesus' ministry through the Gospels and realize that His life was a continual model for us of what it means to conduct our lives by the exercise of these disciplines and gifts. He talked continually to his Father and walked constantly by the Spirit. Jesus did it and so can we. We have His word on it: *"Very truly I tell you, whoever believes in me will do the works I have been doing, and they will do even greater things than these, because I am going to the Father"* (John 14:12). Notice the way Jesus moved from this promise to telling His disciples about the Holy Spirit He and His Father would send. To put it another way, we often say that spiritual practices and gifts are the outer and inner life of a fully devoted follower of Jesus, serving as the glue in our relationship with God and others.

Don't miss the weight of this: before we can think seriously about becoming like Christ, we have to think seriously about how He was like us. He willingly placed himself in the same position to God the Father that we have. We read in John 5:19, *"Jesus gave them this answer: 'Very truly I tell you, the Son can do nothing by himself; he can do only what he sees his Father doing, because whatever the Father does the Son also does.'"* First, don't overlook the context of this statement. Jesus was under attack for doing miracles on the Sabbath and "breaking" the holy Law in other ways. Second, He also called God, "Father," which his opponents correctly understood as a claim to divinity. But notice how Jesus managed to combine divine unity between Father and Son alongside obedient submission by the Son to the Father. Jesus was doing what God does because He let God do it. Every time Jesus was alone praying, He was getting permission for what to do next.[4] How did Jesus hear, learn, and see what the Father was doing? The answer is, He used spiritual practices. He prayed without ceasing and He memorized, studied, and applied God's Word as starting points. When we say we want to be like Jesus, are we imitating His practices?

I love what Dallas Willard wrote, "My central claim is that we can become like Christ by doing one thing—following Him in the overall style of life He chose for Himself.... What activities did Jesus practice? Such things as solitude and silence, prayer, simple and sacrificial living, intense study and meditation upon God's Word and God's ways, and service to others."[5] When we encourage one another to become more like Jesus, part of what that means is imitating His use of spiritual practices. I'll say this over and over: Jesus didn't put the spiritual disciplines into practice because He was God; He did it because He was like us—He needed them. His life, moment by moment, remained "emptied" of His personal, vast spiritual power, in order to depend on His Father and allow His Father to direct Him as a human. It's the kind of life He wants us to live and He showed us it can be done with His Father's help. But don't forget; the spiritual disciplines are one part of convergence, not the whole story.

As we struggle to imitate Jesus in the use of spiritual practices, let's keep in mind Matthew 11:28-30, *"Come to me, all you who are weary and burdened, and I will give you rest. Take my yoke upon you and learn from me, for I am gentle and humble in heart, and you will find rest for your souls. For my yoke is easy and my burden is light."*

At this point, you may be thinking, *spiritual disciplines and practices are starting to sound like more stuff to do that will make me* more *weary and burdened. Didn't Jesus promise rest and freedom from that?*

"My yoke" is, of course, the key phrase to understand what Jesus meant. The Lord did not say, "Come to me and I will remove all yokes." A yoke is what animals wear on their neck and shoulders in order to be lead and enabled to do work. Often younger and older animals are yoked together for the purposes of teaching the younger the way of the yoke. The yoke is the connecting point between the worker and the work, allowing the power in the worker to be transferred efficiently to get the work done.

Jesus promises rest for the deepest part of us, but He requires us to take on His yoke. He offers to exchange the yoke we are already wearing for His yoke. If we won't accept His offer, we will remain yoked to sin, lost dreams, broken relationships, dead religion, or lies. The lie that we are independent is just that, a lie. We always serve somebody or something. The choice for us isn't whether to live unyoked or yoked but to choose the right yoke to wear. When we say 'yes' to Jesus' yoke, which means discipleship, we undertake the lifelong process of learning with Jesus how to live as God requires, which in the end brings us rest.

As R. T. France noted, "We should remember that the 'rest' Jesus offers is not relaxation of the demands of right...It is not the removal of any yoke but a new and 'kind' yoke which makes the burden 'light'. A 'yoke' implies obedience, indeed often slavery! What makes the difference is what sort of master one is serving. So the beneficial effect of Jesus' yoke derives from the character of the one who offers it."[6]

So we can see that the way to be transformed, the way to become a fully devoted follower, the way to be like Jesus is to be yoked to Jesus. And what makes up the yoke? The yoke is in part the very practices we are discussing. But there are great challenges to following Jesus in these practices. My notes from a course on Spiritual Formation at Tyndale Seminary in 2004, taught by Dr. David Sherbino, included the following outline with my thoughts on his points. Here are a few:

- Instant satisfaction. Surrounded and immersed as we are in a world of fast food, sound bites, instant credit, breaking news, push notifications, and the ubiquitous "Like" button, we almost instinctively resist anything that will take time and effort. We've been trained to leap at a chance for great gains with little work. We're attracted to the idea of personal depth but repelled by the idea of time, pain, attention, deprivation, or effort that it might take to reach that depth. We'd rather aim for the accessibility of shallow depth, the contentment and well being of depth without any of the difficulty getting there.

- Skewed perception. Our exposure to authentic disciples leaves us with the wrong impression that these people had some special talent for spiritual discipline. We imagine they don't face the same temptations, weaknesses, or distractions we do, so it's easier for them to give attention to God. In actuality, it's their awareness of their own inadequacy and inability that drives some to undertake the regular practice of spiritual disciplines. They realize that a yoke shared with Christ is far lighter than a yoke shared with anyone or anything else.

- Mechanical legalization. If we reduce the spiritual disciplines to technique and appearance, they quickly devolve into an external facade without underlying reality. The disciplines are never an end in themselves, only a means of placing ourselves where God's Spirit can do His work in us. The temptation is always to set ourselves up as the holy supervisors of others' walk with God when we are not walking with Him ourselves. The psalmists had it right when they said, *"O God, you are my God, earnestly I seek you; my soul thirsts for you, my body longs for you, in a dry and weary land where there is no water"* (Psalm 63:1) and *"My soul yearns, even faints, for the courts of the Lord; my heart and my flesh cry out for the living God"* (Psalm 84:2).

Dallas Willard added this significant observation:

"The elephant in the room: an obvious truth that is either being ignored or going unaddressed. An apparent problem or risk no one wants to discuss. Non-discipleship is the elephant in the church; it is not the many moral failures, financial abuses, or amazing general similarity between Christian and non-Christians. These are only the effects of the underlying problem. The fundamental negative reality among Christian believers today, is the failure to be constantly learning how to live their lives in the kingdom among us. And it is an accepted reality. The divisions of professing Christians and to those for whom it is a matter of whole life devotion to God and those who maintain a consumer or client relationship to the church has now been an accepted reality for the last 1500 years."[7]

A Survey of Spiritual Disciplines

As a way to survey the holy habits we will refer to in this chapter, let's take a brief look at the practices of confession, prayer, simplicity, worship, fasting, biblical secrecy, celibacy, service, solitude, silence, celebration and study. I will try to note how Jesus Himself made use of each of these. This list highlights some of the more common disciplines. Richard Foster's work highlights twelve disciplines in three categories: Inward (practices to do alone), Outward (practices which impact others), and Corporate (practices which include others). In her book *Spiritual Disciplines Handbook* (IV Press, 2005), Adele Calhoun has catalogued 62 spiritual practices divided into seven different categories. It would be fair to conclude that a Christian can never honestly say, "The Christian life is boring because there's nothing to do." Most of the following parallel what Foster calls the "classic" disciplines that have been used by millions of believers across the centuries to place them where God could do his transforming work:

- Confession – This spiritual discipline is rooted in Bible passages like James 5:16, and 1 John 1:9. Some of us were raised in a context where confession was an official religious duty to be dreaded rather than a discipline to be desired. "Authentic confession is sharing our deepest weaknesses and failures with God and trusted others, so that we may enter into God's grace and mercy and experience His ready forgiveness and healing."[8] And we know when we genuinely confess; he will forgive every single time. Easily said, but did you feel this just move closer to home? Our deepest failures need to be confessed to God and others. I'm reminded of Adam's words in Genesis 3, "I will be afraid; I will be naked; I must hide."

  Many of us who are Christians and trust God most of the time will say, "Okay, I will talk to Jesus. I don't need anyone else–I just need me and Jesus!" The practice of confession is directly connected to another practice called fellowship. Time and time again the Bible reminds us, calls us, even commands us to "confess your sins to each other." (James 5:16, and see 1

John 1:9). The confession to God brings forgiveness and the confessing to one another brings assurance of God's forgiveness.

We read in James 5:14, "Is any one of you sick?" I used to read this and think of the physical, from colds to cancer. But I've come to understand that "sick" really means weakness of any kind. It has a broad meaning that includes physical, emotional, mental, spiritual, sexual, and more. Do you have a personal incapacity, a limitation, a character flaw or weakness?

As followers of Jesus we are called to pray personally during trouble. But now James says that we who are weak, the sick among us, are to call on others to minister into our situations. Unfortunately, in the West; no, let me go deeper, much of the time at Sanctus and other Bible-believing churches, we often stop right here. We've been trained to believe weakness, sin, and frailty must be covered, hidden, and cloaked to keep up appearances of being confident, good Christians. And every time we do this, the Holy Spirit is grieved and the work of the kingdom, that is, the reign and rule of God, is thwarted in our own lives, in our families and in the church.

If you find yourself in this situation, you must let go of your pride, take a position of genuine humility, and make the ask. It is not up to the leadership to come to you. Your will is what matters; your willingness to submit to leadership and others is key. It must be volitional. Come to your spiritual shepherds and those you trust in your church community, and ask them to intercede on your behalf. The sick, James says, *"should call the elders of the church to pray over them and anoint them with oil in the name of the Lord"* (James 5:14b). Call upon the leaders to come beside you and perform two actions, to: *"pray over you and anoint you with oil"* (James 5:14c).

If the use of oil isn't familiar to you or practiced in your experience or church, you may wonder what this is about. Let's take a moment to talk about the significance of oil. In ancient times, oil was used as medicine, though this doesn't come close to its purpose here. Oil was and is a spiritual sign with both supernatural and symbolic elements when used for God's purposes. The type of oil doesn't matter. It is *supernatural* in the sense that when an object is thus dedicated, it can become a conduit of spiritual power. As Charles Kraft wrote, "When cultural forms are thus empowered, they *convey* (not *contain*) spiritual power. In the Scriptures we see God empowering such things as the Ark of the Covenant (Josh. 3:14-17), Paul's handkerchiefs and aprons (Acts 19:12), Jesus' gown (Luke 8:42-48) and anointing oil (James 5:15-16)."[9]

Oil dedicated to God can become a conduit for God's *supernatural* power. But it is also *symbolic.* Placing of oil on someone's forehead is an outward, physical sign of the Spirit of God. It was used in the Old Testament to dedicate people or things to God, for example, to set apart priests and consecrate sacred furnishings of the Tabernacle and Temple. Oil was used to anoint kings over Israel as the sign that God's blessing and Spirit was on them. Even in the New Testament, Jesus' close friends did this. But beyond the oil, this next phrase by James is the most important. Anointing with oil is done *"in the name of the Lord"* which means we also call on the Lord to move and appeal to God for His power. Acting in Jesus' name demonstrates that the community belongs to and has gathered under his authority. The point is that oil and people become the vessels God uses to heal, but it is still only about God, His power and His action, not ours.

Next James says, *"And the prayer offered in faith will make the sick person well; the Lord will raise him or her up. If they have sinned, they will be forgiven"* (James 5:15). When a fervent request is offered in faith–trust in His love, strength, and power–some amazing healing can happen! We must remember this also includes an honest acknowledgment of God's sovereignty; we do not have faith in faith, but faith in God.

The next phrase, *"the Lord will raise him up"* is most important for understanding with balance. This promise is for the now *and* the not yet. Many times we should expect people to be healed immediately, set free from physical, emotional or mental bondage. We should come expectantly and in anticipation, not with attitudes like, "Well God, I know You probably won't heal; You never do. But I will ask, sort of, and go through the motions anyway, because it is the right thing to do." It's true, even when we are filled with faith and trust, God sometimes chooses not to heal. This causes some people to become discouraged, and others to defend God by blaming others, saying things like, "You don't have enough faith so you were not healed; your prayers were not fervent or strong enough!"

No, we must remember, "The Lord will raise them up," and that is a promise in part for now and fully in the coming resurrection. God's full and complete healing will happen when we are raised up as Jesus was raised up.

James is not done yet. He continues, *"If they have sinned, they will be forgiven"*. When a person comes forward, when in faith the leadership prays, James then indicates one must also look at sin as a possible root of the problem. Experienced elders in the process of clarifying a need, along with asking questions about the sickness and what has been done to deal with it, will also give the person an opportunity to confess any known sins. The fact is, much of our suffering, though not all can be connected to sin. And so, confession of sin is also significant in the process of healing.

"Therefore confess your sins to each other and pray for each other so that you may be healed. The prayer of a righteous person is powerful and effective" (James 5:16 underline added).

Why confess? We confess because confession is an opportunity to receive healing. While leaders do have a unique spiritual authority, James makes it clear that all believers have the privilege and responsibility to pray for healing. When a person confesses and repents of sin, great power is released. Grace takes on flesh and bones when you share that dark secret or habitual sin, and the person who hears your confession looks back at you and says, "Because of Jesus, you are forgiven." As I already mentioned, this is the assurance we can offer others as we witness their confession.

Confession can fail when it is untruthful or when the truth is spoken with the intent to satisfy God while we fully intend to continue the behaviors we've confessed. This is why confession without repentance is merely going through the motions without the deep awareness of offense toward God that leads to change. Confession isn't about mistakes or slips— it's telling the truth about sin. Confession is telling the truth even when we know it will make us look bad or may change the way others see us. For us, confession really is good for the soul because in it we face our sinfulness and realize how badly we need God and His forgiveness.

Since we previously mentioned Jesus' practice of spiritual disciplines, you might wonder, *if Jesus was sinless, how did he practice the holy habit of confession?*

Jesus never had to confess sin, but He readily confessed truth about Himself to those around Him, even though He knew it would challenge their view of Him and would create offense. This is the sense of the ancient phrase "to confess Christ." The same Greek word for *confess* used in 1 John 1:9 is also used twice in the NIV2011 version of Romans 10:9-10, *"If you declare with your mouth, "Jesus is Lord," and believe in your heart that God raised him from the dead, you will be saved. For it is with your heart that you believe and are justified, and it is with your mouth that you profess your faith and are saved"* (underline added). We practice the discipline of confession when we acknowledge our sins and when we acknowledge our Savior.

- Prayer – This amazingly varied discipline can be simply described as talking to God; it is communicating with our designer and the one who loves us like no other. It's much more than permission to ask God for things. The truth is that for most of us prayer rarely gets beyond the to-do list we present to him. As Dallas Willard has noted, "The 'open secret' of many 'Bible believing' churches is that a vanishing small percentage of those talking about prayer and Bible reading are actually doing what they are talking about."[10]

James was right on target when he wrote, *"You do not have because you do not ask God. When you ask, you do not receive, because you ask with wrong motives, that you may spend what you get on your pleasures"* (James 4:2b-3). Prayer is a practice that connects us with life, guidance, power, healing, and fellowship while it creates a place of love, comfort, and to hear what God wants to say and wants us to do. It's true that the biblical command to *"Pray continuously"* (1 Thessalonians 5:17) sets prayer in a greater category than an optional spiritual discipline. The reason to approach it as a discipline comes from the reality that it's unfamiliar territory for many of us. Making prayer a discipline leads us toward the experience of delight in fellowship with God. I've just used the word *explore* for a reason; there's lots to discover about prayer when we give it the attention it deserves. Richard Foster's book *Prayer* lists twenty-one distinct types of prayer we can use.

Jesus practiced the habit of continual prayer. Once in a while others heard him. The Gospels portray him praying in gratitude and in agony. The disciples were deeply moved by Jesus' habit. *"One day Jesus was praying in a certain place. When he finished, one of his disciples said to him, 'Lord, teach us to pray, just as John taught his disciples'"* (Luke 11:1). Notice that the request wasn't "teach us *how* to pray" but "teach us *to* pray." They wanted more than a technique; they knew they needed a longing to be in communion with God.

If we're going to learn how to pray, if we truly want to encounter the One that is holy love, we must go to the prayer by which Jesus instructed His disciples, a now famous prayer uttered each week by billions around the world, the Lord's Prayer. There are two versions of this small prayer found in the Bible (Matthew 6:9-13 and Luke 11:2-4), and in it the upward, inward, and outward moves of grace can be found. Jesus, under the power of the Holy Spirit, simply invites us broken, sinful, distracted, questioning yet faithful people into the relationship He shares with God the Father Himself.

Most of us learn this prayer without even realizing we're memorizing Scripture. The power in this prayer has nothing to do with mindless repetition of the words, but persistent meditation on all it addresses. Jesus wasn't providing a secret incantation, but a pattern for communicating in prayer. As Martin Luther demonstrated, every word can be seen as a doorway into extended conversations with our heavenly Father.[11]

Every time we pray, because of Jesus, we enter into God's holy presence. Hebrews 10:19 assures us, *"Therefore, brothers and sisters, since we have confidence to enter the Most Holy Place by the blood of Jesus..."* Each time we gather on a Sunday, every time we engage in devotions, any time we as Christians pray personally or together, this space is what we enter into! The *Most Holy Place* is not metaphor or poetic license at its heart. When we pray, we enter right into God's holy presence, with all the angels, with all those who have gone before us and are with Jesus, we enter the place where without Jesus' covering sacrifice we would die. Do you and I believe this; do we realize this is true before we come to pray? If we do, we can expect to experience what the writer of Hebrews also said: *"Let us then approach God's throne of grace with confidence, so that we may receive mercy and find grace to help us in our time of need"* (Hebrews 4:16).

- Simplicity – To adapt a popular catch phrase, it would be true to say that if simplicity was easy, everyone would do it. Richard Foster wrote an amazing chapter on simplicity in *Celebration of Discipline*, and then had enough left over to write an entire book on the subject. As Willard helpfully points out, simplicity is not the opposite of complexity as a spiritual discipline.[12] Nor is simplicity a synonym for poverty. In fact, simplicity isn't really a separate discipline as much as it is the result of the practice of contentment. Because of this, practitioners can live simply in the middle of complex situations. It means there is a significant gap in the time and attention we give to what is most important and then everything else (whether much or little).

The apostle Paul offers us a great description of this practice in Philippians 4:11-13, *"I am not saying this because I am in need, for I have learned to be content whatever the circumstances. I know what it is to be in need, and I know what it is to have plenty. I have learned the secret of being content in any and every situation, whether well fed or hungry, whether living in plenty or in want. I can do all this through him who gives me strength."* The apostle tells us he *"learned to be content"* when he discovered that neither plenty nor poverty were the keys to contentment, but the moment by moment reliance on *"him who gives me strength."*

Foster warns that superficial simplicity, being an outward discipline, carries with it the dangers of Pharisaic hypocrisy. Nothing is more deadly than the thinly veiled claim, "I live more simply than you do," which reveals a pride that must be recognized and destroyed by repentance.

Jesus led His disciples in practicing contentment, which produces simplicity. Whether He was with the twelve, the larger group of His followers, or massive crowds pressing in, the Gospel records present a man who responded to events around Him with grace and dependence on His Father.

- Worship – In an important sense, every spiritual discipline is also a prelude to worship. If we pursue any discipline for a reason other than to place ourselves where God can do His transforming work, we practice for the wrong reason. Worship is giving attention and ascribing worth to God. It involves exploring ways to express to God all that He means to us, not only to supply Him with affirmation but because as creatures we are designed to worship. The purer our worship, the closer we come to fulfilling our purpose for being here.

  Worship is a discipline because we face continual temptation to worship many things other than God, who alone is worthy of worship. Don't miss the crucial significance of the devil's final temptation for Jesus, the offer to give Him the world in exchange for an act of worship. He was offering Jesus what appeared to be a painless shortcut to fulfill the purpose of Jesus' ministry. Jesus responded to that temptation with: *"Away from me, Satan! For it is written: 'Worship the Lord your God, and serve him only'"* (Matthew 4:10). While there are aspects of worship that we can practice as individuals, the best place for worship is in community. Showing up at a synagogue on the Sabbath for worship and study was such a part of Jesus' schedule that Luke called it *"his custom"* (Luke 4:16). In Acts 2:42 we see the early church living out the encouragement of Hebrews 10:25 to not give up meeting together.

- Fasting – This may be an odd concept if the idea of spiritual disciplines is new to you. This practice involves abstaining from food and other integral aspects of our lives that may interfere with our dependence on God. It is a deliberate choice to experience hunger in one area in order to explore our level of hunger for God.[13] What we do in place of eating or consuming other things is crucial. If fasting is simply ceasing to eat while we meditate on the next meal we will have, we've missed the mark badly.

Jesus fasted. We know He did during the forty days He spent in the wilderness at the start of his ministry, but there are other hints that it was a regular practice. For example in John 4, while the disciples were busy getting food in Sychar, Jesus talked to the woman at the well. The disciples returned with take-out and tried to get the Lord to eat. *"My food," said Jesus, "is to do the will of him who sent me and to finish his work"* (John 4:34).

The relative lack of specifics regarding fasting sometimes troubles Bible readers, but Richard Foster rightly points out that fasting was such a part of the culture in which the Bible was originally written that the details of fasting were widely understood.[14] Today people often have to be assured that fasting is a healthy practice. And even if we are assured, we can still miss God's reason for this amazing discipline. I believe Scott McKnight brings home the power of this: "Fasting is a response to a grievous sacred moment."[15] Contact with the sacred ought to transform us. The rule to follow is a simple one: fasting, like all the spiritual disciplines, is designed to develop love of God and love of others. If it is not doing that, something is wrong.

Fasting can be proactive or reactive, and most times in the Bible it is reactive. When mentioned in the Bible, fasting was a spiritual practice engaged in by a person or community in response to huge events, good, godly, or deadly. Almost all fasting came after an event had happened or was already happening. Today we may choose to fast in response to family members who remain far from God, for current troubles, illness, or sin.

Fasting can also be proactive. We may choose to fast and pray when seeking the Lord's guidance in opportunities or decisions that are before us. Either way, one of the key considerations for fasting is motive. I'm sure you can see that the act of fasting, like any godly activity, can look right and be practiced right but be ineffective if you do it with the wrong motives. *"Ask all the people of the land and the priests, 'When you fasted and mourned in the fifth and seventh months for the past seventy years, was it really for me that you fasted?'"* (Zechariah 7:5).

In the Bible, there was one major fast that took place as a yearly regular rhythm of the Jewish religious calendar. It was connected to the Day of Atonement, where the entire nation of Israel was called to go before God and deal with sin. Then, as the act of fasting was carried out year after year, it quietly and slowly began to change. The sacred act of fasting went from a communal act of intercession for repentance to an opportunity for spiritual self-promotion.[16] People would make sure everyone knew that they were fasting by appearing publicly unwashed, unkempt, with their hair lightly sprinkled with ash. Their intent was to seek reaction and admiration from others. Fasting became the ancient religious Instagram "selfie" moment to draw attention to people rather than focus on God.

Jesus addressed this self-righteous attitude directly. *"When you fast, do not look somber as the hypocrites do, for they disfigure their faces to show men they are fasting. I tell you the truth, they have received their reward in full"* (Matthew 6:16). Notice Jesus said "when," not "if." Jesus expects his followers to fast!

The word hypocrite used here is where we get our word "actor". Jesus doesn't want you to play-act so in his religious and cultural situation he gave some helpful instruction: *"But when you fast, put oil on your head and wash your face, so that it will not be obvious to men that you are fasting, but only to your Father, who is unseen; and your Father, who sees what is done in secret, will reward you"* (Matthew 16:17-18). Jesus referred to their preparations for the day–even when fasting–basically saying, "Wash your face, brush your teeth, put on your clothes the way you always put them on, and go about your day like usual!" Why? So you won't be tempted to exchange an eternal reward for momentary satisfaction; so you do not set yourself up to sin.

Let's consider this further. Many believers today have never fasted. Is it possible that our remarkable lack of hunger for God is tied to our unfamiliarity with any kind of hunger? But if we want to be like Jesus and become more fully devoted followers of him, then we are called to the spiritual practice of fasting. This should be part of a normal Christian life. When we do fast, we must be sure our motives and our audiences are clear. Jesus said of those seeking public acknowledgement, *"They have received their reward in full!"* Let that heaven-given statement come close to your heart today. Ask the hard question: "Am I doing this to please the Lord and no one else?"

When you fast, when you serve, when you give money to God, when you pray, when you preach, when you lead worship, when you pray for healing, when you do anything for God, be clear about *why* you do it. Do you practice that discipline to feel better about yourself, or so people will admire you, like you, follow you? When you work to develop that habit in God's name, is it out of duty? In that moment you receive your only reward. You got what you wanted: people's admiration, approval, self-gratification, and elevation in the community. You got what you needed: the look, the praise, the security, the identity boost—but there will be no eternal reward. When we face Jesus, everything we did *not* do for the kingdom will burn before our eyes and whole parts of our ministry life will be like sand slipping through our fingers. The pain will be, that as we see Jesus for all He is our love for Him will overwhelm and consume us, but we will not be able to give back to Him, as gestures of gratitude and obedience, those moments we kept for ourselves. At the end of time all we have done in Jesus name will be tested when we face God. I'm not referring to salvation, but the ability to see the true quality of all we did for Him and what He did for us. As Paul wrote:

"If any man builds on this foundation using gold, silver, costly stones, wood, hay or straw, his work will be shown for what it is, because the Day will bring it to light. It will be revealed with fire, and the fire will test the quality of each man's work. If what he has built survives, he will receive his reward. If it is burned up, he will suffer loss; he himself will be saved, but only as one escaping through the flames" (1 Corinthians 3:12-15).

We will come back to fasting again in a moment.

- Secrecy – This spiritual practice is at the heart of prayer and fasting but also makes a good component of any other discipline. A classic definition of the practice of secrecy is, "conscious refraining from having our good deeds and qualities generally known which in turn rightly disciplines our longing for recognition."[17]

  Secrecy does not involve deceit or lying to keep our activities hidden. It is not evil but actually helps us live for God and not for the praise of other people. But it is so very easy to drop hints about our explorations of spiritual frontiers. Dallas Willard wrote, "The desperate attempts for people to advertise themselves is truly unbelief for it reveals that they need the attention of the others and not the divine. Jesus said a city on a hill cannot be hidden (Matt 5:14) and so we will not be hidden as we do our acts unto God…Secrecy rightly practiced enables us to place our public relations department entirely in the hands of God."[18]

  Secrecy doesn't mean you can never do a public fast. Out of 16 New Testament references to fasting, about half are done in public and in community. Most of the Old Testament fasts where done in community too.

So the goal is again to be clear on why you do this: so spend time communing alone with your Father through prayer or fasting, or to be spiritually recognized by others. We are called to practice fasting *and* we are called to practice biblical secrecy.

So far we have talked about *if* we should fast and *why* we should fast. Now the question is, "When do we fast?" There are at least six circumstances when fasting can be an effective response:

1. **Fast when facing important decisions.** The elders in Antioch were involved in discipline together in Acts 13:2 and God responded to their attentiveness. *"While they were worshiping the Lord and fasting, the Holy Spirit said, 'Set apart for me Barnabas and Saul for the work to which I have called them.'"* Note how Paul and Barnabas continued this pattern of fasting in Acts 14:23.

2. **Fast in response to crisis.** The story of Esther is about a coming holocaust. Thousands were about to be slaughtered, including Esther who was married to the king. She was the only one in a position to try to stop the evil plan. Esther 4:15-16 describes her strategy. *"Then Esther sent this reply to Mordecai: 'Go, gather together all the Jews who are in Susa, and fast for me. Do not eat or drink for three days, night or day. I and my maids will fast as you do. When this is done, I will go to the king, even though it is against the law. And if I perish, I perish.'"*

3. **Fasting as a natural response to the exposure of sin and as evidence of repentance.** Much to his dismay, Jonah saw clear signs of the repentance of the Ninevites when he reluctantly warned them of God's disfavor in Jonah 3:3-10. God saw this too: *"When God saw what they did and how they turned from their evil ways, he relented and did not bring on them the destruction he had threatened"* (v.10).

4. **Fasting and prayer are also tools of spiritual warfare.** Daniel 10:1-13 gives a vivid account of God's servant engaged with the impact of prayer and fasting on earth and in the spiritual realm. And again, Luke 4:1-13 reminds us that Jesus spent his 40 days in the wilderness fasting and praying when he was tempted and the power of evil was first defeated.

5. **Fast as a response to a profound and powerful encounter with Jesus.** As Scott McKnight put it, "Fasting is a person's whole-body natural response to life's sacred moments!"[19] Do you remember when Saul met Jesus for the first time? Acts 9:1-9 describes his response and ends with this note, *"For three days he was blind, and did not eat or drink anything"* (v.9). It is actually quite normal to lose your appetite when God turns your world upside down.

6. **Fast to break through to God's palpable presence.** When we are no longer satisfied with God's omnipresence and hunger for his overwhelming, manifest presence personally known to us in the room, the desire to fast comes naturally. It is a deep longing; it is desperation; it is homesick desire.[20] I love John Piper's simple, raw, and exposing thought on this. "Half of Christian fasting is that our physical appetite is lost because our homesickness for God is so intense, the other half is that our homesickness for God is threatened because our physical appetites are so intense."[21]

- Celibacy/Chastity – Mention this spiritual discipline in public today and you will likely be asked, "Is that even a thing anymore?" In our sex-soaked culture few things sound odder than any statement related to sensual self-control. The word *chastity* is on the endangered vocabulary list, and there are fewer and fewer people willing to admit that chastity is a spiritual discipline we are all invited to practice in order to be more like Jesus. Yes, those who are single, or single again and those who are married–at times–will all be called to engage in this practice.

Here is a great definition of chastity: Purposefully turning away for a time from dwelling upon or engaging in the sexual dimension of our relationship to others—even our husband or wife—and thus learning how not to be governed by this powerful aspect of our life. As 1 Corinthians 7:5 makes clear, chastity within marriage is a temporary practice, while the unmarried are expected to be chaste until marriage. Like other forms of fasting, chastity is not a negative attitude toward sexuality. In fact, it elevates the significance of sexuality while it recognizes the importance of not letting sensuality govern our lives.[22]

Let's go back to the very beginning when God created us as human beings. It is here we find and see the first God-given expression of sexuality. The first two chapters of Genesis make it clear that sexuality was an integral part of God's original design in humanity. There we discover that male and female in complementary roles is God's plan and the full and true expression of sexuality!

We also begin to see that marriage and being single are both reflections of the very nature of the God we worship and love. Marriage is rooted in and best understood as a parallel to God's own self-relationship within the Trinity. Like the Trinity, when one marries and becomes intimate, the Bible says that though we are two individuals, we become one flesh, one essence. The two become one (Genesis 2:24). We are the same and yet we are different. In the same way we know that God is not three gods but one God. He is one; we are monotheists. As Deuteronomy 6:4b declares, *"The Lord our God, the Lord is one."*

Marriage and singleness are both expressions of God's nature and as we read in Scripture are both expressions of His will. They are two equally divine options rooted within the Creator's make up. Neither should be elevated or denigrated.

But at various times in history that is exactly what has happened. The Medieval church thought that singleness was the door to true spirituality, but today it is the reverse. The modern church elevates the nuclear family through strategic programming and church growth as a model for spirituality. Neither reflects the heartbeat of God or the tenor of Scripture. Both are fertile ground, useful to help God's kingdom to come and His will to be done. Male and female is God's ideal and singleness as well as marriage both reflect God and what it means to be made in His image.

When thinking about this spiritual practice we must address the tension created by a high view of sex while living in a very fallen, broken world where as many of us personally know, sex is misunderstood, misused, and broken. Richard Foster says, "Sex is like a great river that is rich and deep and good as long as it stays within its proper channel. The moment a river overflows its banks, it becomes destructive, and the moment sex overflows its God-given banks, it too becomes destructive."[23]

And yet as we keep reading 1 Corinthians 7, Paul moves from chastity as spiritual discipline to chastity as spiritual gift: "I say this as a concession, not as a command. I wish that all men were as I am. But each man has his own gift from God; one has this gift, another has that" (1 Corinthians 7:6). Paul was single and loved it. He viewed it as a holy calling. Without blushing or embarrassment he says "I am single and I think a lot more of you should be single!" But he goes farther; notice he calls his singleness a gift, a supernatural gift. Some, not all will have this gift which God gives. This note is helpful: "The gift of celibacy is the special ability that God gives to certain members of the Body of Christ to remain single and enjoy it; to be unmarried and not suffer undue sexual temptation."[24] Though many of us do not have the gift, we are all called to the discipline of chastity and fasting, either by situation of life (we are not married) or if we are married, by an agreed time of mutually seeking God! Though only some have a spiritual gift in this area, all are called in part or fully to this discipline.

- Service – Whatever we might do for others, we can do as service for Christ. This was Paul's view in Colossians 3:17, *"And whatever you do, whether in word or deed, do it all in the name of the Lord Jesus, giving thanks to God the Father through him."* Jesus defined His own life as the pursuit of service (Mark 10:45), and Hebrews 5:8 indicates that Jesus learned this discipline on the job: *"Son though he was, he learned obedience from what he suffered."* We learn service and we practice service by serving. It's no joke to say that you will never understand what it means to be a servant until someone treats you like one. Genuine service will seldom be recognized. It's wonderful when we take time to note and encourage one another's efforts at serving, but service should never be undertaken because of the positive feedback we will receive from others. In fact, a significant area of service includes intentional anonymous actions to benefit others in which the perpetrator is *never* revealed, combining this discipline with the discipline of secrecy. If we are really practicing our desire to do everything for Christ, only He has to know.

This is why service is a discipline; it's not about the work involved but taming our desire to get credit. Opportunities to practice this discipline far outnumber the moments that we have in any given day. Our practice of this discipline improves as we include in our practice of prayer, making ourselves available for God's use, and asking Him to guide us into places of service that best harmonize with His plans.

- Solitude – In the first chapter of his biography of Jesus, Mark tells us, *"Very early in the morning, while it was still dark, Jesus got up, left the house and went off to a solitary place, where he prayed"* (Mark 1:35). Solitude is not the rejection of human company but recognition of the limits of human company. We need others, but not more than we need God. If we don't willingly put ourselves in places alone with God, we will find it difficult when life puts us in places where others can't join us. It's the same principle summarized in the opening of the 23rd Psalm. Most of us like the idea of having someone in our lives who is a good shepherd, but He won't seem like the Good Shepherd if we've not treated Him first as Lord. If the shepherd isn't first and always also my Lord, when I need a Shepherd He will feel more like a stranger.

Solitude also isn't just time alone; it's time alone with God. The problem is never God's availability, but ours. There is discipline in ordering our lives to create uncluttered moments in God's presence in which we seek to listen as much or more than we speak. And why is this important? If Jesus' whole ministry was a permission-based, only-what-the-Father-tells-Me-to-do reality, then how can we ever listen without these quiet moments? When Jesus was alone with the Father, He was not only being encouraged and refreshed, He was getting specific assignments: "You want Me to cast out that demon, but not that other one? You want Me to find a short man in a Sycamore tree that will become a true Son of Abraham? Next week You want me to give the Sermon on the Mount?" This discipline, along with others, is critical to hearing what God might be asking you or an entire church to do next.

- Silence – Closely associated with solitude is this discipline of quietness, an experience becoming increasingly rare in this world of 24/7 news, live streaming, and ear buds. The ubiquitous presence of noise has generated an industry of headphones that produce "white noise" or just-enough-meaningless-sound to cancel out all the other surrounding sounds. Practicing silence doesn't necessarily mean absolute removal of sound but rather the choice to focus on certain sounds rather than others. For example, we can turn off the stream of human sounds long enough to hear the rest of nature declare the glory of God. The opening of Psalm 19 is an amazing description of what might be heard when we take time to practice silence:

> *The heavens declare the glory of God; the skies proclaim the work of his hands. Day after day they pour forth speech; night after night they reveal knowledge. They have no speech, they use no words; no sound is heard from them. Yet their voice goes out into all the earth, their words to the ends of the world* (Psalm 19:1-4a).

One aspect of Jesus' time alone in the wilderness at the beginning of His ministry was silence. Until the devil showed up with his temptations, Jesus spent days in silence.

- Celebration – The fact that celebration is a discipline reminds us that the world often wonders if Christians actually know how to express joy. Maybe that's why Paul had to repeat himself in Philippians 4:4, *"Rejoice in the Lord always. I will say it again: Rejoice!"* He went on several verses later to offer a list of ideas to jump-start celebration: *"Finally, brothers and sisters, whatever is true, whatever is noble, whatever is right, whatever is pure, whatever is lovely, whatever is admirable—if anything is excellent or praiseworthy—think about such things. Whatever you have learned or received or heard from me, or seen in me—put it into practice. And the God of peace will be with you"* (Philippians 4:8-9). When we stop to realize that a tsunami of bad ideas and negative thinking inundates our lives on a daily basis, it's not surprising that we need to deliberately practice the discipline of thinking what God wants us to think about. The peace that God brings is the atmosphere of real celebration.

It's true that Jesus' parable of the waiting father (Luke 15:11-32) places all of us in the role of the prodigal son who wastes much of his life before he decides to repent and return. But we don't give enough thought to the

Father's insistence on a party at the son's return. Too often Christians act more like the older brother (a living-at-home prodigal in his own right) who resented the younger brother's return and refused to celebrate.

How would our lives be different if we spent more time meditating on Zephaniah 3:17, *"The Lord your God is with you, the Mighty Warrior who saves. He will take great delight in you; in his love he will no longer rebuke you, but will rejoice over you with singing."* God's love for us is a celebrating, singing love that has all the best in mind for us. The discipline of celebration is a deliberate response of joy to how God views us, and the eternal life He has planned for us.

Jesus knew how to celebrate. People found it easy to party in His presence. After Matthew decided to leave his tax-collecting business and follow Jesus, his first act was to throw a party for all his friends (Matthew 9:9-13). Look up the guest list and note how at home Jesus was in that setting.

- Study – At a certain point, our practice of every one of the spiritual disciplines will be shaped by our practice of study. To borrow a helpful definition from the *Spiritual Formation Study Bible*, "Study is the intentional process of engaging the mind with the written and spoken Word of God and the world God has created in such a way that the mind takes on an order conforming to the order upon which it concentrates."[25] At the heart of this is a love and desire to know the written Word of God. In our church, we have expressed this as our first core value: *We value God's Word: We believe in an honest engagement with the biblical text, understanding and applying it in order to find our place in God's unfolding story, becoming more like Jesus in character and conduct.* We simply mirror the orthodox view of Scripture when we say the Bible is God's written Word and the ultimate source for our faith, life, and practice. We of course know God speaks in other ways: through nature, His community, and the use of spiritual gifts, reason, and experience. We can look back through church history to learn what other Christians wrote, wrestled with, and did. Yet the Bible is our ultimate source. And why? This is what the authors of the Bible declare about the very nature of the Bible:

All Scripture is God-breathed and is useful for teaching, rebuking, correcting and training in righteousness, so that the person of God may be thoroughly equipped for every good work (2 Timothy 3:16-17).

For the word of God is alive and active. Sharper than any double-edged sword, it penetrates even to dividing soul and spirit, joints and marrow; it judges the thoughts and attitudes of the heart (Hebrews 4:12).

You cannot divorce the written Word from the living Word's Spirit; you can never understand the Scriptures apart from its author. As Jesus promised in John 16:13, *"But when he, the Spirit of truth, comes, he will guide you into all the truth."*

The more you know the Bible, the more you will know God. The more you know God, the more truth you will encounter and the more you will be taught, rebuked, corrected and trained. The more you know God the more you will know His holy love and will want to walk with Him and be like Him. The Bible not only affects and conforms our thinking, actions, and motives, but it is also calls us, invites us, and commands us to serve.

This is why the spiritual practice of study matters so much to you, to your family, and to your church. Jesus said in John 8:32, *"Then you will know the truth, and the truth will set you free."* As Calvin Miller wrote, "Mystics without study are only spiritual romantics who want relationship without effort!"[26] In other words, if we rely solely on experience and assume we can stay on track we are fooling ourselves. God's Word, studied and applied, keeps us on track. That's why God provided it for us.

This overview of some of the classic spiritual disciplines highlights again the variety and challenge facing us when we choose to engage with life the way Jesus did. Though reading through this list may have raised one other practical question in your mind: How? How do you and I as normal people in everyday life practice these disciplines in order to fully engage in devotion to Christ? We must answer this question or the entire conversation about spiritual disciplines and then spiritual gifts becomes mere musing about holy living without ever taking even a step into the real adventure God has for us. If we wait to figure out the whole journey before we take the first step we will have failed to follow—and following Jesus is ultimately the point (John 21:22).

We must look to our ultimate example of what it looks like to walk with God–Jesus Himself. Not only is Jesus our Savior, not only is He our Lord but also He is our model. He is what it looks like to be a fully devoted follower of God.

To Be Like Jesus

Reading about the spiritual disciplines here it may be easy to wonder, *is it even possible to live like Jesus?* Is it really possible to become like him? After all, He is God; we aren't even close. But remember, we learned that though Jesus was fully God, He chose *not* to use His advantages as God for the very purpose of showing us how to live under the will of God the Father by the power the Holy Spirit. He didn't pretend to be like us—He really was (and is) one of us. He never stopped being God but He didn't use that obvious advantage when He became human. He used the same resources He has made available to all of us. He walked and worked in the Spirit to show us that we could too.

At Jesus' baptism it all became clear. The Holy Spirit was given to lead and empower Jesus to do God the Father's will. Right after the Holy Spirit came upon Jesus, His ministry started and we see how He walked with God. Without the power of the Spirit, Jesus would not have been able to teach or demonstrate the good news. Jesus practiced the spiritual disciplines and He used spiritual gifts! This is how He did not grasp the power or privilege of deity: He did what the Father wanted by the power of Holy Spirit. Jesus did not do ministry out of His deity but under the empowering of the Holy Spirit!

Remember these two crucial verses:

Jesus gave them this answer: "Very truly I tell you, the Son can do nothing by himself; he can do only what he sees his Father doing, because whatever the Father does the Son also does (John 5:19).

I tell you the truth; anyone who has faith in me will do what I have been doing. He will do even greater things than these, because I am going to the Father (John 14:12).

So Jesus said, "Look; I do nothing except what I see the Father doing and what the Father tells me to do I do." How did Jesus hear what He was called to do, since He was not using His own divine awareness? How did He see what God the Father was doing? He did it through the regular practice of spiritual disciplines.

We have the same Holy Spirit that was upon Jesus. And if spiritual gifts were the guaranteed place of power for Jesus and for us, then the spiritual practices, for the believer, are guaranteed places of transformation. Spiritual practices do not make you a Christian, get you relationship with God, or impress God in any way. These are the very things that bring us into His presence so we can be transformed and know what we are being called to do. They bring health to the relationship we are already in, and provide an ongoing dynamic experience in our static positional reality.

There is still one troubling question we must ask. In fact, to be transformed, altered, and changed for this kingdom renovation, this heaven-shaped makeover; for this ongoing remodel to happen we must address one question: Is becoming like Jesus simply an *option* for us as Christians? Does Jesus' example in using these practices function like a buffet of spiritual options from which we can choose depending on taste, time of life, or willingness? In other words, can you really be a follower of Jesus and *not* be a disciple, not be really transformed, not go all in? Are spiritual disciplines optional or essential?

Again listen to the wisdom of Dallas Willard: "Little good results from insisting that Christ is also supposed to be Lord: to present his lordship as an option leaves it squarely in the category of the white-wall tires and stereo equipment for the new car. You can do without it."[27]

To be a Christian *is* to be a follower of Jesus, to be owned by your Master, and to be a disciple. The label *Christian* is only used three times in the Bible, while the word *disciple* is used 269 times! They are synonyms, but many of us separate them – Christian, yes, discipleship, sort of, but not really.

This is the troubling situation facing us today: "For at least several decades the churches of the Western world have not made discipleship a condition of being a Christian. One is not required to be, or to intend to be, a disciple in order to become a Christian, and one may remain a Christian without any signs of progress toward or in discipleship."[28] What were Jesus' last words to the church? *"Then Jesus came to them and said, 'All authority in heaven and on earth has been given to me. Therefore go and make disciples of all nations, baptizing them in the name of the Father and of the Son and of the Holy Spirit, and teaching them to obey everything I have commanded you. And surely I am with you always, to the very end of the age'"* (Matthew 28: 18-20).

Jesus always had all authority but chose to limit Himself until His death on the cross. Now, after the resurrection and the ascension, He sits at the right hand of the Father. He has reversed the "emptying" of the incarnation by taking up again His full authority as God the Son. Now He instructs us to *"Go and make disciples!"* Only disciples can make other disciples. Again Dallas Willard wisely warned us, "Most numbers of converts today thus exercise the options permitted by the message they hear: they choose not to become—or at least do not choose to become—disciples of Jesus Christ. Churches are filled with 'undiscipled disciples,' as Jess Moody has called them. Most problems in contemporary churches can be explained by the fact that members have not yet decided to follow Christ"[29]

But Jesus says, "Discipleship is not an option. Go and make what you are and what you are becoming!" Let me repeat, the spiritual practices, if you are a Christian, are the guaranteed place of ongoing transformation, after you have counted the cost. This is how we thrive, no matter the size of church, no matter the number of believers large or small, no matter the growing hostility from the surrounding world. If you are a church leader, take note of this fact: Lack of discipleship much of the time is the missing component for kingdom momentum.

Out of disciplines and listening comes God-given vision, which for us as a church, has been catalytic in the area of growth. We are all called to what I call common faithfulness, Acts 2:42-47—teaching, community, communion, prayer, the presence of God, giving, loving the poor, large and small gatherings, baptism, and evangelism. Every church is called to this.

For us, common faithfulness and unique congregational calling underpin multiplication, renewal, and growth. At Sanctus we have come to believe that Jesus speaks to congregations uniquely as He did in the book of Revelation. As with the churches in Sardis, Philadelphia, Smyrna, Ephesus, and the others, He is calling us to repentance and endurance.

The Scriptures are full of leaders who were issued God-given assignments. Mission is assigned to all but vision is usually given to leaders: "Moses, I have called you to do this;" "Paul, do that, Philip, go there; when we were fasting and praying the Spirit said..." This implies being open, learning to listen through practice of disciplines such as fasting and praying; and it presumes people who are empowered in their gift mix to discern what is actually from God, what is merely human, from the devil, or the tacos you had last night.

Mission (Acts 2, Matt 28) and common faithfulness never change in any environment. But vision is God-given for a season and will be replaced by new ones. Strategies support vision for a season and can always change during that time. Does this mean God will always speak? No, many times common faithfulness is the only ongoing call from heaven. So we keep in step with the Holy Spirit.

Of course the vision of a leader or local congregation must be in alignment with the biblical narrative and orthodox theology. But visions draw lines of size, emphasis, and calling. They make you say more No's than Yes's. They force your community to join or leave. Vision with plans do not allow vacuums, presumptions or wonderings, they prevent possible civil war. For example, our vision at Sanctus is "To become a regional church of 10,000 meeting the physical, emotional and spiritual needs of people in Jesus' name." I have no time here to get into why *this* vision or why is the number even needed? How was it tested, with whom, and over how long? My question today for you is, "Have you even asked? Have you inquired of the Lord for a vision of His purpose for your church?" As leaders we listen, we get promptings, we test them, and then we plan, in that order. We also, in these critical times, have asked God for promises around our God-given assignment that we could pray back to Him. There has been, since we began to pray back His given promises, massive change. His presence across the church has moved from transcendent to immanent, from never-changing omnipresence to palpable presence. We now have hundreds of documented accounts of supernatural encounters that are similar to those found during the times of Wesley, Whitefield, and Edwards.

My point is, if God starts something, and we are open and our prayer life is focused on understanding our heaven-given assignment, things may not be easy or safe but they will be secure. Why are so many churches dying, so many living powerless Christian lives? I suggest it may be because leaders are not camping in the guaranteed places of encounter to be transformed, to do only what they see their Father doing in this place, in this time, in this moment. The spiritual disciplines offer a standing invitation to convergence.

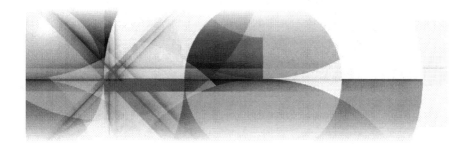

Chapter Four:
What Is a Spiritual Gift?

In the last chapter, we looked at some options God has provided to shape our lives in ways that will allow Him to work in and through us. We encouraged one another with the news that the Spiritual practices, if we are Christians, are the guaranteed place of ongoing transformation after you have counted the cost. The Spiritual practices involve choices we make. Now we will consider some of the choices God made when he entered our lives. When we surrendered to Him, the Holy Spirit sealed us (Ephesians 1:14), entered us (Acts 1:5, 8), and joined us to the body of Christ (1 Corinthians 12:12-14). When He did all this, He also gave us gifts He intends to use as He works through us to accomplish His purposes in the world. Spiritual gifts are for serving others.

Because the Holy Spirit connects us with the Body of Christ, the idea of a Lone Ranger Christian with a self-sufficient, independent spirituality is a foreign concept in Scripture. It fails in the practice of spiritual disciplines since most of them involve a context of community. But it particularly fails in the use of spiritual gifts, since these are intended for use within the Body, often in combination with the gifts of others, and for the benefit of those within as well as outside the Body.

What if you don't know your spiritual gift(s)? Or what if you never have been able to identify them and learn from others with the same gifts? What about the problems we have even in a single local church that result from so many different understandings of the gifts or even what names to use for what we do and experience? Plus, there is often resistance from certain Christians because their previous experiences with spiritual gifts may have been negative. Given the undeniable inclusion of Spiritual gifts in the Bible's description of the Church, is it possible to have a conversation about gifts that is neither a pre-decided effort to explain away their very existence, nor a heavy-handed argument about certain gifts being more significant or even required aspects of our Christian maturity?

We will address these issues head on in this and the chapters to come. The goal for this book reflects the goal of the local church I help lead, which is to have a common script or language in order to develop a common understand of the gifts, so we can begin to use and grow in our gifts and experience the joy that comes from honoring God, serving others, and knowing a part of our purpose in this life that will ripple into eternity!

Let's begin by outlining some of the DNA in our description of the local church. Here at Sanctus we call ourselves Empowered Evangelicals. What do we mean by that? We define it as cross-centered and Bible centered. The message of the cross and the teaching of Scripture shape everything about us. We believe people must choose to trust and follow Jesus, also called conversion. We believe in evangelism, telling the whole world the good news of great joy, that God through Jesus has offered each of us forgiveness and salvation. And not only has He saved us but one day will make all things right in all of creation. We also believe that we need the presence and power of that same Holy Spirit who came on Jesus to be in and on us to do this work. Our doctrine statement at Sanctus reads like this:

We believe in the work of the Holy Spirit in convicting people of sin, the regeneration of those turning to Christ from sin, and his work of sanctification in the believer. As empowered evangelicals we believe in all the gifts and work of the Holy Spirit.

In other words, we believe that all the gifts of the Holy Spirit at work in the church of the first century are available today, are vital for the mission of the church, and are to be earnestly desired and practiced. To be clear, we are not "Cessationists"; Christians who believe that the overt evidence of the Holy Spirit was only for the time of the Apostles and the development of the New Testament and ceased with the writing of the last canonical (Bible) book. We believe that Scripture itself and the abundant evidence of the last twenty centuries of the Church speak powerfully against that position. At the same time, we admit there has been a lot of craziness in Church history, some of it related to identifying the Holy Spirit's work and some of it related to denying the evidence of the Spirit. The Scriptures tell us to "test the spirits" (1 John 4:1), not deny they exist. Before we are finished we will look at the odd and non-normative experiences and discuss ways to determine if we're witnessing an unusual display of the Holy Spirit at work or whether we have encountered a counterfeit or demonic work trying to pass off as God's power. If this only begins to address the questions you have, read on. God has a lot to teach all of us.

With those preliminaries out of the way, let's address some immediate practical questions: What are all the gifts the Bible mentions? What do they look like and what does that mean for me, and what does that mean for our church both privately and publicly?

Let's start with this: What is the difference between natural gifts, acquired gifts and spiritual gifts? Explaining the first category, Robert Clinton wrote, "Natural abilities or talents are given by God through creation; qualities that are 'innate' or 'there from birth' which can be developed over time."[1] Acting, a good memory, athletic prowess, musical talent, creative thinking, and the knack for working with your hands are some examples of natural abilities. These are initial gifts, given by your designer as part of your original make-up. You may never use these, or use them poorly, but they are components of your unique creation.

Another category, based in some ways on your natural abilities and the way you choose to use them, is the category of acquired gifts. Clinton describes acquired skills as abilities developed "through training, education, experience; proficiencies or competencies developed over time through your own effort."[2] If you are originally gifted with natural manual abilities and an interest in music and instruments, you may acquire the tools and develop techniques that make you a master builder of instruments, such as violins or guitars. You might not have musical talent, but you provide for musicians the fine musical tools that allow them to showcase their abilities.

One of the critical issues that can make churches powerless is that many of us confuse those natural or acquired skills with spiritual gifts. God has given us both natural and acquired to come to bear in our lives and in our ministries, but they are not the ongoing, guaranteed places of power. Spiritual gifts are different. Let me give you two different definitions that might help:

"A spiritual gift is a special attribute given by the Holy Spirit to every member of the Body of Christ, according to God's grace, for use within the context of the Body."[3]

Spiritual gifts are "endowments or special skills given by God that enable us to make our unique contribution. They are not natural talents, but divine abilities that enable us to do ministry"[4]

It will become clear as we continue that the working and effects of spiritual gifts are not easily explainable or simple to unpack. There is often a disconnection between the obvious abilities or talents of a person and how God's Spirit uses them in situations.

All the gifts, and there are at least 21 basic gifts in Scripture, can be broken down into three groups: Love Gifts, Word Gifts, and Power Gifts.[5] We will spend time on each group in the following chapters. All Christians have at least one gift, if they're given more than one gift it is usually a unique combination of two or more of the 21 gifts, selected by God's Spirit.

Before we continue with an examination and explanation of spiritual gifts, it would be good to revisit one other group of qualities produced by the Holy Spirit. How do we differentiate the spiritual gifts and spiritual disciplines from the fruit of the Spirit?

The fruit of the Holy Spirit are listed in Galatians 5:22-23, *"But the fruit of the Spirit is love, joy, peace, forbearance, kindness, goodness, faithfulness, gentleness and self-control."* Gifts are primarily related to what we do, while the fruits are about development of our character. We will not all have 21 spiritual gifts, but we are called to have all the fruit of the Holy Spirit. Further, you can never misuse the fruit of the Spirit, but spiritual gifts and spiritual disciplines can be misused or cause discord and conflict through abuse or lack of character connected with their use. The fruit of the Spirit is about being. It is attitudinal. The fruits are a by-product of a relationship with God while the gifts are given to further His work. But notice, both gifts and fruit come from Heaven, not us. We cannot buy, invent, build up, or get training to produce them. They only come from the Holy Spirit. And He only comes into us when we accept the perfect work of Jesus in and over our lives and accept Him as Savior and Lord.

When we accept Jesus as our Savior and Lord, life becomes an ongoing process of becoming like Him. We must be filled with the same Spirit that was in Him and we must incorporate the disciplines He used to connect with the

Father. Again, spiritual practices primarily strengthen individuals while the gifts are needed to serve or strengthen others. Yet all three; the gifts of the Spirit, the fruit of the Spirit and the spiritual disciplines form a nexus of godly power that are needed and necessary for effective ministry.

The Apostle Paul writes about gifts in many places, but let's begin in Romans 12 to provide a biblical context for our extended conversation about spiritual gifts. The chapter opens with a memorable description of discipleship: presenting ourselves to God as living sacrifices:

> *Therefore, I urge you, brothers and sisters, in view of God's mercy, to offer your bodies as a living sacrifice, holy and pleasing to God—this is your true and proper worship. Do not conform to the pattern of this world, but be transformed by the renewing of your mind. Then you will be able to test and approve what God's will is—his good, pleasing and perfect will* (Romans 12:1-2).

As we look at what can be viewed as the rarified atmosphere of spiritual living, let's also remember the old graffiti wisdom, "The only problem with a living sacrifice is it keeps crawling off the altar." Which is exactly the awareness we see in Paul as he continues:

> *For by the grace given to me I say to every one of you: Do not think of yourself more highly than you ought, but rather think of yourself with sober judgment, in accordance with the faith God has distributed to each of you* (Romans 12:3).

The last phrase in that verse can be translated *"according to the measure of faith God has given you."* This means several things. First, we should be sober because of how we all received peace with God. The ground is level at the foot of the cross. We are to see ourselves as God sees us, and no one else. This is best informed by our experience of salvation. All believers are chosen by the sovereign will of God; the choice is the result of unmerited favor; and this grace is received through faith in Jesus Christ. So for every one of us it's salvation by grace alone, faith alone, through Jesus alone. How could we ever think we are better than another Christian because of money, clothing, spiritual gifts, experience, natural or acquired skills, maturity, race, education, or anything else? If salvation is truly 100% the result of God's action, then humility is our only response.

In Romans 12, Paul is about to talk about spiritual gifts. The Greek word he uses is *charisma* from which we get our term *charismatic*. Each one of us has been given at least one gift. We should see ourselves through the gifts we've been given and the differing strengths or authority of those gifts. Let me offer this warning right up front: Do not spend your life trying to be something God did not make you to be. Do not wish for other gifts not given to you by the Spirit. Do not waste your time trying to work in ministry areas that you are not gifted in. The reverse is also so true—do not expect others to be or become something God has not gifted them to be. To put it in Paul's words, don't think of yourself too highly or lowly; but with sober judgment, and perhaps the helpful perspective of others.

Paul was laying an important foundation in the next two verses:

For just as each of us has one body with many members, and these members do not all have the same function, so in Christ we, though many, form one body, and each member belongs to all the others (Romans 12:4-5).

When you are in Christ, you are not just a member in an organization but a part of a living organism. We are the actual body of Jesus Christ on earth; none of us is the head, but we all form one community, bound together by the Spirit of Christ, the same Spirit that raised Jesus from the dead. The power of God, the reign and rule of God is most strongly expressed when we know we are bound together by Jesus, for Jesus, and under Jesus. Out of this unity in Jesus there is diversity in the gifts sovereignly given by the Holy Spirit. The expectation here is not for independence, nor dependence, but interdependence.

Let me add a side note here. In our worship service each week we pray for another local church by name. We long to express unity with them. Is this not a good way to remind ourselves that we are not the only or best church in town? We are just one small part of God's vast kingdom. Clement of Rome wrote, "Why do we divide and tear to pieces the members of Christ and raise up strife against our own body, and why have we reached such a height of madness as to forget that *we are members one of another?*"[6]

Missionary and world-class surgeon Paul Brand brilliantly suggested that today we ought to think of Paul's words about our roles in the Body of Christ not so much as "members" but as individual cells in the body. He and Phil Yancey wrote two books on the amazing spiritual lessons present in the wonders of the human body.[7] Every cell in our bodies has a specific design and function. Likewise, each of us has a unique function under the direction and power of the Holy Spirit to accomplish His purposes. As the Scriptures say:

We have different gifts, according to the grace given to each of us. If your gift is prophesying, then prophesy in accordance with your faith; if it is serving, then serve; if it is teaching, then teach; if it is to encourage, then give encouragement; if it is giving, then give generously; if it is to lead, do it diligently; if it is to show mercy, do it cheerfully (Romans 12:6-8).

Prophesying, serving, teaching, encouraging, giving, leadership, and mercy make up Paul's overview of spiritual giftedness. This is not an exhaustive list at all. You can read 1 Corinthians 12, Ephesians 4, and 1 Peter 4 to see these and other gifts all in operation. Paul's point here is that when the Spirit of God is working, there is great diversity. But the diversity is designed to work together.

Before we walk through all the gifts one by one, we need to build the right foundation. We will be held accountable for all we've been given— natural gifts, learned abilities, and spiritual gifts. As Christians we will all face Jesus at the end of our life and give an account. Much of Jesus' teaching was to prepare people for his return even though he had not left yet. One of the most powerful teachings on accountability and what we have been given comes from Matthew 25:

Again, it will be like a man going on a journey, who called his servants and entrusted his property to them. To one he gave five talents of money, to another two talents, and to another one talent, each according to his ability. Then he went on his journey (Matthew 25:14- 15 underline added).

Our English word "talent" actually comes from the use of the Greek term *talanton* in this passage. In the first-century Roman world, a talent was the largest unit of currency, equivalent to twenty years of income at minimum wage. But Jesus is not teaching accounting here. As Craig Blomberg wrote, "Rather, as in all his parables, Jesus is using familiar imagery to symbolize spiritual truth. Everything God grants us—our possessions, abilities, opportunities, time, and circumstances—he commands us to steward well. If it were Paul speaking, he would probably talk about our various spiritual gifts. Whether talents or gifts, the principle remains the same; what may not always be true in the economic realm is clearly true in the spiritual realm: 'Use it or lose it!'"[8]

The Holy Spirit doesn't pass out gifts haphazardly. There's wisdom and intention behind the gift each of us has been given. The call for us is to discern just what the gifts and opportunities are and how we are to use them. Jesus continues His story this way:

The man who had received the five talents went at once and put his money to work and gained five more. So also, the one with the two talents gained two more. But the man who had received the one talent went off, dug a hole in the ground and hid his master's money. After a long time the master of those servants returned and settled accounts with them. The man who had received the five talents brought the other five. "Master," he said, "you entrusted me with five talents. See, I have gained five more." His master replied, "Well done, good and faithful servant! You have been faithful with a few things; I will put you in charge of many things. Come and share your master's happiness!" The man with the two talents also came. "Master," he said, "you entrusted me with two talents; see, I have gained two more." His master replied, "Well done, good and faithful servant! You have been faithful with a few things; I will put you in charge of many things. Come and share your master's happiness!" (Matthew 25:16-23 underline added).

I like the Amplified version better for the closing thought: *"Enter into and share the joy (the delight, the blessedness) which your master enjoys."*[9]

Notice two things. First, the characters in the story are called servants, but the term used is actually *slave* in Greek. As Christians we know we are "not our own; we were bought at a price" (see 1 Corinthians 6:19-20). We have chosen Jesus to be our Master and we want to be owned by Him because He will do so much more with our lives than we could, or money, sex, power, politics or any alternative "master" we might choose. The point is we are no longer in charge; Jesus owns us and gives us delegated responsibility. There cannot be two wills, only one; and the more His will is in us the less our will can be present. As John the Baptist cried out, *"I must decrease and he must increase!"* (John 3:30).

Second, there is joy not only in serving now but there will be a joy that comes later. Joy has been given; joy is being given, and will continue to be given. But (and this is really big), future joy or sorrow is connected to accountability.

Then the man who had received the one talent came. "Master," he said, "I knew that you are a hard man, harvesting where you have not sown and gathering where you have not scattered seed. So I was afraid and went out and hid your talent in the ground. See, here is what belongs to you." His master replied, "You wicked, lazy servant! So you knew that I harvest where I have not sown and gather where I have not scattered seed? Well then, you should have put my money on deposit with the bankers, so that when I returned I would have received it back with interest" (Matthew 25:24-27).

I love what a friend of mine, Brian Stiller, wrote:

Before we run off and start a new church that teaches that we get into heaven by our good works, let's carefully examine the text to see what Jesus is saying. Throughout the Bible there is an underlying understanding that God sees what we do. After Jesus' resurrection, He ascends back to the Father with the promise that He will return. Though we have been given much, we are warned not to take it for granted. Just as at work we are evaluated, so God *evaluates us* today and every day and His final assessment will be delivered on the judgment day. This idea of accountability that Jesus presents to His disciples is not new. Note that this story is not for the religious leaders or crowds but for His disciples--those who live with Him every day. Jesus wants them to hear how tough and demanding God really is.

If you are a Christian, one who believes that Jesus is the Son of God, and if you trust in His death and resurrection as the payment for your sin, then this story is for you. For when we come to Christ in faith, a new life is born in us. One of the results of that new life is that someday we will live forever with Jesus.

But there is another, more immediate aspect to being a follower of Jesus: We now understand that our Creator invests in us God's life, by the gift of the Father's Son and by God's Spirit who lives in us. He entrusts us with certain potential from which He expects a good return. We now have a responsibility to live out God's life in the world.[10]

You may not see yourself as a "super-Christian" along the lines of Billy Graham, Mother Teresa, or Carl Lentz, but God values you deeply. It's not about gifts or talents you are given, or how large or small the authority behind them is, God still gives you something of great value to use for His glory.

We all have gifts: natural, learned, and Holy Spirit-given. The spiritual gifts are not based on personality, prosperity, or patronage but on God's sovereign choice. As we will unpack further in the next chapter, Paul made the role of the Holy Spirit clear when he wrote in 1 Corinthians 12:11, *"All these gifts are the work of one and the same Spirit, and he distributes them to each one, just as he determines."* Desiring certain gifts or even longing for certain results to flow from our gifts may be either a genuine expression of commitment to service or, unfortunately, a case of jealousy or selfishness. The distribution of gifts is entirely up to God.

The gifts will also have different strengths, or effectiveness, and that is not up to us but the One that gives them. We will only find joy when we are okay with what He has chosen to do in us. He knows us better than ourselves. Don't waste your life second-guessing God; put yourself completely at His disposal. No matter who we are, all of us are called to be faithful to Jesus even as we seek to know the gifts we have been given and how to use them.

We should not compare ourselves with others. In the parable of the talents, the master didn't compare the amount entrusted to or even the results of his servants. He declared goodness and faithfulness based entirely on what each servant had accomplished with what he entrusted to them. Comparisons are not on God's agenda and it is a waste of valuable kingdom resources to pursue achievements that will ultimately burn away in the end.

We will be held accountable by Jesus Himself for everything we do. Don't miss the fact that the guy who did nothing with his gift chose not to use it because of misplaced fear. His fear of failure was greater than his fear of the Lord. How foolish if we did the same, never to discover what God has given or what might happen if we put it to use. We have to move from distracted and domesticated faith to a powerful, real, all-consuming trust relationship with Jesus, a get-out-of-the-boat type of trust in Jesus that doesn't let conditions dictate our obedience. Stepping into the storm-tossed seas of the world will require that kind of faith. Faith, not fear, must drive us!

Brian Stiller continued:

We also begin to operate out of fear and not faith. There is always the danger of failure. Investing in a project, a stock, an invention, or service does not mean one is guaranteed success. However, the nature of faith is to risk, not to be cautious. In God's upside- down economy, failure is due not to one's being prudent but to an unwillingness to take a risk. The Scriptures tell of those who risked in faith. What if Abraham had been careful to leave the lands of his parents in response to God's call or if Moses had been reluctant to lead the people of God into the Promised Land? Remember Peter, "If it is you, Lord, ask me to come on the water." Jesus replies, "Come," and Peter steps out of the boat. When we hide a talent in the ground, it's like putting faith in a drawer for safekeeping. We take it out Sunday morning and display our symbol of faith in sacramental liturgy for an hour or so, maybe even adding some polish. Then, before afternoon football or golf, we put it back in the drawer as if it has nothing to do with how we live the rest of the week. To such behavior Jesus says, "Get out of my sight!" and gives the buried talent to the risk taker.[11]

As a way of dealing regularly with the call to gift-wielding discipleship, our church developed a prayer rooted in the Lord's Prayer to encourage and challenge one another away from fear and toward faithfulness:

"Do whatever You must in my life, in Sanctus, for Your glory and my freedom, so the world can see Jesus clearly!"

What we are saying is:

- Yes, I am a slave of an unhealthy fear of You. I fear what You might do in me, and in this church. I fear being called out in failure. I fear that You might not be all I thought. And every one of these fears points to an area in which I need to know and trust You better. Lord I believe; forgive my lingering fears and lead me with Your power.
- Yes, I want to know my gifts and I am ready to use them and be used by You.
- Yes, I acknowledge that I will be held accountable for my actions in every area of life, anticipating Your good purposes for my living.
- Fear will not be my god; You, God, will be my God.

As a church we are seeing an increased desire to welcome God's work in us and in the world. We are no longer willing to accept in ourselves or in one another the condition of being overly informed without appropriate action, or conformed to something worldly that will not accomplish God's purposes. I want for myself and for you to be transformed by the holiness and love of God as evidenced in joy and expressed in the work of His Spirit through us.

This is why we must stop and talk about character before we delve into the gifts themselves. The desire to be Spirit empowered must be tempered by a sober understanding of our selves, an understanding best seen modeled by Jesus.

Chapter Five:
Spiritual Gifts and Character

The content of this book is based on the unfolding experience of a local church in a very real setting, with much to be celebrated alongside plenty that can be improved. It's easier to see the mistakes we have made along the way than to describe what we have intentionally done right. Often great things have happened in spite of us. But now and always, God continues to demonstrate Himself faithful and able to work in His church for His glory. And we are more and more convinced that the work God does, He does through His Holy Spirit.

As a church we have expressed this conviction as one of our core values:

We believe every Christ-follower is called to impact those around them through loving, joyful, gift-based service.

This core value is focused on spiritual gifts and their essential role in directing the way we serve one another. In other words, as a church we are working hard to move from a program based, service slot mentality asking volunteers to fill them in a first-come, first-served basis. Because the local church is an organism, God has designed it with specific roles and functions that he fulfills through the gifts He's placed in His people so these roles can be filled and needs are met.

In the last chapters I made an effort to show the difference between natural, acquired, and spiritual gifts as well as to differentiate between those gifts and spiritual disciplines and the fruit of the Holy Spirit. We will now continue to build a needed foundation so that when we deal with each gift we will be able to approach it with right motive, attitude, and understanding. Again, my purpose in laying this groundwork is so the following chapters build on one another like Lego blocks.

In 1 Corinthians 12–14 we find an extended treatment of the spiritual gifts to which we will return again and again. They are highly instructional for us, because they were also corrective in nature. Things were getting off track in this local church at Corinth, and Paul provided them with needed instruction. Their obvious abundance of spiritual gifts did not prevent horrendous interpersonal and spiritual problems. In these passages we will see that Paul shows us time and time again that the goal of a pastor or leader is not to dismiss or stop spiritual experience in private or public but to understand its source–human, demonic, or godly. If the experience is from God Himself, no matter how uncomfortable we may be with its expression, Paul wants us to deal with motives behind the gift. That is why between chapters 12 and 14 we find a chapter devoted to the centrality of love. Though usually read at weddings, it is actually all about the community of believers and using God's gifts correctly.

The gifts of the Spirit are undergirded by the fruit of the Holy Spirit, and must access a place of developing character, a deep reservoir of love, joy, peace, patience, kindness, goodness, faithfulness, gentleness and self- control. In fact, unless the gifts proceed from and produce this fruit, their authenticity and use should be considered suspect.

Think about Moses for a moment. God gave him the gift of a staff, a powerful gift of God given for God's work. Time and time again Moses used it correctly, but he also sinned with this gift by wielding the staff in anger. Even though it was the gift of God, the staff could still be used for wrong purposes and with damaging results. I find it interesting that Christians are quick to say a gift is not of God if character is lacking, when the Bible illustrates repeatedly that the people God used also had major character flaws. Don't dismiss God's gifts quickly. Real gifts often reside in poor containers. This reminds us, as Paul says Paul in 2 Corinthians 4, that neither the gift nor the power is from us but from God. But this is why growing character matters–it allows further trust and dialogue about the gifts. God wants to use His gifts *through* us while he continues to work *on* us.

With these necessary cautions in mind, we come to one of the most explicit outlines or criterion for what a genuine work of God will look and feel like. Paul starts by saying: *"Now about the gifts of the Spirit, brothers and sisters, I do not want you to be uninformed"* (1 Corinthians 12:1).

This statement is the biblical foundation for our goal to have a common script so we have a common understanding of the gifts, in order to use and grow in our gifts. Then we will experience the joy that comes when we honor God, serve others, and know our part and purpose in this life ordained by God. We want to be rightly informed, and then follow through on God's directions when it comes to the use of the gifts of the Spirit.

Also notice Paul's statement is addressed to the whole church. God gives all his gifts to both men and women; gender has nothing to do with God's work through the gifts. Though when we consider offices in the church, other teachings about gender and gifts must also be considered.

Paul continues, *"You know that when you were pagans, somehow or other you were influenced and led astray to mute idols"* (v.2). The designation of *pagans* at one point simply meant non-Jewish people but later became the term used among Christians to talk about a life before knowing Jesus. In the church at Corinth, almost all of the believers came from various pagan religious systems practiced in the Roman Empire. Paul can say that in their previous situation they were *"influenced,"* a word that is a reminder that all of us enter life in Christ with baggage from the past. Many of these believers were also *"led astray."* This is the term used for condemned prisoners, as they were led to prison or execution! What a powerful and important image. When we worship anyone else or any other so-called god, we are placed in bondage and condemned to a walk that leads to death. That is why we cherish being led to Jesus, to be a slave to Him for He alone allows us to live as we are called to live.

Paul also offers an interesting description about the *"mute idols"*. We all know that idols are mute. They are made of inanimate materials that don't have life; fashioned out of wood, stone, jewels, money, education etc. But the obvious is never the whole story. Paul knew and already taught this community that behind the idols themselves and the competing systems of worship there are actually fallen angels, demons that love to promote and glory in false worship. Just because idols can't think or speak doesn't mean they are not used by very active and thinking beings with destructive plans for those they can deceive and control. Paul had warned, *"Do I mean then that food sacrificed to an idol is anything, or that an idol is anything? No, but the sacrifices of pagans are offered to demons, not to God, and I do not want you to be participants with demons"* (1 Corinthians 10: 19-20). He's pointing beyond the physical realities to the spiritual realities that confront the Corinthians.

The relevance for us today is Paul's teaching about how to discern among the spirits. Paul was reminding the Corinthians that in their pagan worship services supernatural activity would happen, and now things were happening in the church that looked and felt very similar. As Paul is dealing with Spiritual gifts, he also teaches this church and all of us to discern the difference between which spirit is actually at work. Much of the time manifestations of the supernatural will look almost, if not exactly, the same. Many of us that grew up in church instinctively react by saying if it looks weird or doesn't seem in "order" according to our cultural tradition, then it must be demonic, physiological, or mental illness. I now say, "Stop and evaluate. Weird or uncomfortable does not automatically mean *not of God.* There's the real thing and a lot of counterfeits designed to look like the real thing." Second Corinthians 11:14 tells us, *"And no wonder, for Satan himself masquerades as an angel of light."*

In many cases the question is not about what spiritual activity looks like, but what source it is coming from and the fruit it produces. Think about a plug in a wall socket. The question for Paul isn't whether the experience of sparks or lights should happen, but what source of power is at work. There's a lot of attention being drawn to the reality of spiritual warfare today without enough attention given to the reality of the spiritual realm intersecting and impacting all of life in the earthly realm. In Western cultures, our current materialistic/scientific worldview has convinced us that everything real can be explained and controlled by us. We therefore are set up to be unsettled and confused when evil spins out of (our) control or we see evidence of power that violates our scientific assumptions. Even as Christians, we can tend to isolate God's power to a small area of spiritually acceptable actions (like sometimes identifying our inner response to worship as proof God was present and at work) while not expecting or even resisting the idea that God's presence might cause repentance to break out, the demonic to be unmasked, or a message from God's Spirit to be uttered.

As elders and pastors in the church, we are not empowered to dismiss experience but to discern where it comes from: God, the individual, a medical condition, or the demonic. That's why Paul says, *"Therefore I want you to know that no one who is speaking by the Spirit of God says, 'Jesus be cursed,' and no one can say, 'Jesus is Lord,' except by the Holy Spirit"* (v.3). Three things here are really important about the phrases, "Jesus be cursed" and "Jesus is Lord".

First, Paul wants to help them understand that both evil and Godly supernatural experience will look (and sound) exactly the same much of the time, but the source and the fruit are what matters. As Gordon Fee wrote:

> In keeping with his Jewish heritage, Paul scorns the idols as mute because they cannot hear and answer prayer; nor can they speak—in contrast to the Spirit of God who can. But he has also argued earlier that the mute idols represent demons (10:20-21)—which can and do speak through their devotees. Most likely, therefore, he is reminding them of what they well know, that in some of the cults 'inspired utterances' were part of the worship, despite the 'mute' idols." If so, then his concern is to establish early on... that it is not 'inspired speech' as such that is evidence of the Spirit. They had already known that phenomenon as pagans. Rather, what counts is the *intelligible and Christian content* of such utterances.[1]

Second, Paul is saying that salvation comes 100% from God, not from us. Anyone can say Jesus is Lord, but saying it and meaning it are different. Salvation, really knowing Jesus, is a God act. Salvation is His gift to us and comes to us in no other way (Ephesians 2:8-9). Because salvation is 100% God and His mercy, graciously given to us, then humility is the very place Paul must focus as he deals with this broken church.

Third, "Jesus is Lord!" became our earliest Christian confession of faith, which stood up against three things. It negated pagan affirmations of any other deity, rejected political affirmations of the emperor as god and master, and overcame Jewish insistence the Yahweh alone merited the title."[2]

Consider how politically incorrect it still is today to say, "Jesus is Lord!" That is why Paul included in the book of Romans 10:9-10, this phrase as a statement we must believe with all our hearts and speak with our mouths: *"If you declare with your mouth, 'Jesus is Lord,' and believe in your heart that God raised him from the dead, you will be saved. For it is with your heart that you believe and are justified, and it is with your mouth that you profess your faith and are saved."* "Jesus is Lord" isn't a secret password that gets us in the door of a club; it's a public declaration and personal conviction that affirms our complete dependence on God. Jesus of Nazareth, the crucified One, is, by His resurrection and ascension, the Lord of the universe. There is no other God, no other way of forgiveness, no other path to heaven or eternal life— Jesus is Lord!

Paul moves from the past to the new present and begins to work through what the gifts of God look like personally and corporately. *"There are different kinds of gifts, but the same Spirit distributes them"* (1 Corinthians 12:4a). The Holy Spirit is the one that gives his *"different kinds of gifts"* to the church. Notice again and again, God gives the gifts to whomever he chooses, we do not have a say in this at all. This should lead us to a deep place of humility to see God at work so that we could never use our gifts as a matter of pride or use them against one another.

Paul continues, *"There are different kinds of service, but the same Lord. There are different kinds of working, but in all of them and in everyone it is the same God at work"* (vv.5-6). Gifts, service, working; three words with the same meaning, all are the manifestations of the Holy Spirit. This is God being expressed in his fullness; the works of God are grounded in the Trinitarian relationship. It is no mistake that Jesus is included between God the Father and the Holy Spirit, always the revealer and mediator. And notice with Jesus, the word used is *service*. Does this not give us the needed grounding to use our spiritual gifts? Humility, meekness and weakness are never to be despised or resisted but welcomed. As Jesus showed us, even in weakness there is massive and heaven-given power.

Lastly, we are warned as well as encouraged. We are warned never to make gifts about our own identity, pride, PR, or status. The reverse is so also true; what a relief to realize we don't need to bribe God or spend our lives trying to be something God does not want us to be. We can give ourselves to what God has gifted us to do without grasping for more.

Paul drives this point home with this declaration: *"Now to each one the manifestation of the Spirit is given for the common good"* (v.7). This verse is the best summary for the entire purpose of gifts! As Christians we all get at least one gift and the gifts are given for one thing and one thing only: the common good. They are to build up, rebuke, encourage, challenge, and bring life to the community. They are not given for rivalry or jealousy; they are to be used and not hidden in fear or suppressed for any reason.

To emphasize the common source for the gifts, Paul quickly reviews a few of them:

> *To one there is given through the Spirit a message of wisdom, to another a message of knowledge by means of the same Spirit, to another faith by the same Spirit, to another gifts of healing by that one Spirit, to another miraculous powers, to another prophecy, to another distinguishing between spirits, to another speaking in different kinds of tongues, and to still another the interpretation of tongues* (1 Corinthians 12:8-10).

I won't go through these gifts in detail here; like Paul, we're focused on recognizing the Holy Spirit as the generator and giver of gifts. But as you look over his list it's possible the entries tell us we are about to be pushed far beyond the comfort of our traditional evangelical views. But before we can start editing the list to what's "acceptable," Paul adds, *"All these are the work of one and the same Spirit, and he distributes them to each one, just as he determines"* (v.11).

We are moved to see that God is at work and that spiritual gifts are His will. This also serves as a needed caution for any of us to want or even demand that everyone else have our gift or be gifted in the ways we think best. We must neither impede nor imitate someone else's gift; we have our own to manage. Our unity comes from the divine purpose expressed through the one Spirit by whom we are all possessed. Only He can coordinate and harmonize everything He has given and all He wants to accomplish. The word *distributes* in Greek combines *always* and *containing*. So as a general rule, the gifts are given and are part of you for a lifetime. You get gifts, you grow in your gifts, and you need others to work alongside you; interdependence is God's heart. We see it worked out in the Trinity, in marriage (Ephesians 4:21) and in the call for the people of God to reach the world.

From gifts and the source of the gifts we now get Paul's important summary of what the church is and must continually become. *"Just as a body, though one, has many parts, but all its many parts form one body, so it is with Christ"* (v. 12). Notice that the church is not seen or expressed as a democracy, a dictatorship, nor some form of lesser anarchy. It is seen as a body that is made up of different people and gifts in mutual submission! It's a clear picture of interdependence. Physically, each of us is a walking, talking, breathing example of the corporate reality that God in Christ and by His Spirit wants to create with all of us. Though we are all different people and even have different gifts, this does not affect our fundamental unity at all. Why? Because Jesus Christ is our head. And to be with Jesus, you must be with others. Church is community, period.

Some of us might be tempted to consider how best to create this unity Paul describes. But the origin of unity isn't up to us. God Himself, by his Spirit, brings about the unity that is the Body of Christ. Our role is discovery and participation, not creation. As Paul says, *"For we were all baptized by one Spirit so as to form one body—whether Jews or Gentiles, slave or free—and we were all given the one Spirit to drink. Even so the body is not made up of one part but of many"* (vv. 13-14).

These verses were like an earthquake shaking the very foundation of the Roman and Jewish worldview of the day and even ours today. Every single ethnic and socioeconomic bracket of the ancient world was swept aside by the Spirit baptizing all believers into one Body. See the power of this; all the religious, gender, economic, and racial barriers that governments, education, war, and writing have never been able to root out, God's Spirit does in power! All human distinctions are broken. Flesh gives birth to flesh but Spirit gives birth to spirit.

Think about this: as a Christian, the Holy Spirit living in you is the only thing that really distinguishes you from those that do not know Jesus. He marks the beginning of our walk, He makes us a child of God, He binds us together, He convicts us and empowers us both to live like Jesus and serve with the same power Jesus had.

But this passage also shows us that the baptism of the Holy Spirit is not a "part-two" or separate spiritual experience. It is what happens at conversion. When you become a Christian you receive the Spirit of Christ, He comes into you (Paul's picture of drinking the Spirit), and you are baptized in the Spirit.

The Spirit can fill us time and time again over our lifetime, which can take many forms, but accepting Jesus and receiving the Holy Spirit is the same thing. I love that Paul also uses the image of drinking the Spirit or being watered by the Spirit. It comes from the idea of irrigation. You can translate this "we have all been saturated with one Spirit." This ties both baptisms together so well. Water baptism represents and affirms the Spirit's baptism. Spirit baptism happens first and then water baptism, like a wedding ring given with the vows that publicly says to everyone who sees it, "I belong completely to another and am no longer my own."

Still holding back on addressing the individual gifts, Paul wants to make sure we have the right attitude about being in the Body—as any part of the Body. *"Now if the foot should say, 'Because I am not a hand, I do not belong to the body,' it would not for that reason stop being part of the body. And if the ear should say, 'Because I am not an eye, I do not belong to the body,' it would not for that reason stop being part of the body"* (vv. 15-16). Notice Paul's description starts at the bottom and works its way up, lower to higher. Some of the humbler members of the church who did not have spectacular gifts or wealth or position thought they might be disqualified from being a useful or powerful Christian. Not so! Interestingly, this is not a problem with inflated importance but a failure to see that God has a purpose for *everyone* who makes up the Body of Christ.

To those prone to devalue their place or role, Paul says, *"If the whole body were an eye, where would the sense of hearing be? If the whole body were an ear, where would the sense of smell be? But in fact God has placed the parts in the body, every one of them, just as he wanted them to be. If they were all one part, where would the body be? As it is, there are many parts, but one body"* (vv.17-20). God's care is not just extended or given to those parts that are more prominent; God has simply ordained them all. Their interdependence becomes obvious if you exalt one to sole importance. It is ludicrous to imagine an eye, nose, or ear functioning without the assistance of the rest of the body. And God wills it this way. Unity and diversity founded on God's choosing is the heart of the church. No one effectively serves the Body without at the same time being served by the rest of the Body. It may appear at first that we can dispense with certain roles or gifts in the Church, but eventually their absence will be felt. I think it may be an accurate statement to say that the Church today often acts like a severely impaired body trying to function without significant capacities.

This gets to the problems that were facing the Corinthian church. Some thought because of money and gifts that they were better than others. That is the sin I have committed so many times as a pastor and Christian: pride, vanity, and self-sufficiency. Just look at what was happening during communion in this church back in chapter 11–arrogance and non-unity. Their behavior had become so offensive that God was allowing sickness and even death in order to get their attention about their dysfunction.

Next, see how Paul reverses the conversation. He moves from the more humble members to those that have the so-called greater gifts or socio-economic status, who in this church are looking down on the less gifted brothers and sisters.

The eye cannot say to the hand, "I don't need you!" And the head cannot say to the feet, "I don't need you!" On the contrary, those parts of the body that seem to be weaker are indispensable, and the parts that we think are less honorable we treat with special honor. And the parts that are unpresentable are treated with special modesty, while our presentable parts need no special treatment. But God has put the body together, giving greater honor to the parts that lacked it, so that there should be no division in the body, but that its parts should have equal concern for each other (vv. 21-25).

Notice that the so-called "lesser" people are not just a nice thing to have or even a welcome addition, but they are *"indispensable"* for the proper functioning of the Body.

The point is that those with what we might consider less "flashy" gifts or less privileged lives are also given to us by God, and are loved by God. Their value is such that the body cannot work without them. Heaven cries out, "Appearances deceive, all are necessary for I am the Lord and I will build my church." If you're reading this and have felt less than or insignificant around other Christians, God comes to you and says, "You are mine. You are not less and you are right where I want you to be. Do not live in the shadow of others! Do not be given to jealousy or anger. And don't allow others' looks or comments or opinions to form you or your identity. I have formed you, I love you, and I am pleased with your service."

And for those who don't identify with God's statements above, He adds, "You that have stronger expressions of gifts or more "spectacular" ones, do not be prideful, do not look down on others, and do not think you are more important or better. I give and I take away, I raise up and I bring down. Look to Me and see if I am pleased with how you are using your gifts. With greater gifts and great wealth comes greater responsibility. It is my will that you love and uplift what heaven has called indispensable. I build and sustain my church. Do not be divided. All of you show equal concern for each other.

What our physical bodies demonstrate is also true in the Body of Christ: *"If one part suffers, every part suffers with it; if one part is honored, every part rejoices with it"* (v. 26). You know this is so true if you have ever had a bad toothache. You understand how your whole body was affected. So our personal walk affects the whole Body of Christ.

Back to the big picture: *"Now you are the body of Christ, and each one of you is a part of it. And God has placed in the church first of all apostles, second prophets, third teachers, then miracles, then gifts of healing, of helping, of guidance, and of different kinds of tongues"* (vv. 27-28). This is about influence, purpose, and even authority, not importance. Apostles, prophets, teachers are not offices like elder or deacon; they are listed as gifts.

I love what Craig Blomberg said about the way this sequence of God's gifts highlights timing, not importance. He wrote, "To establish a local congregation requires a church-planter. Then the regular proclamation of God's Word must ensue. Next teachers must supplement evangelism with discipleship and the passing on of the cardinal truths of the faith. Only at this point does a viable Christian fellowship exist to enable all the other gifts to come into play. Tongues may be last on the list because the Corinthians were overestimating their value, but it cannot be demonstrated that Paul assigned them any inherent inferiority."[3]

Once Paul has given a quick overview of the way God assigns His gifts, he immediately emphasizes the theme of interdependence by making sure there is no justification for raising one gift over others. *"Are all apostles? Are all prophets? Are all teachers? Do all work miracles? Do all have gifts of healing? Do all speak in tongues? Do all interpret? Now eagerly desire the greater gifts. And yet I will show you the most excellent way"* (vv.29-31 and 13:1).

First, the rhetorical questions presume a "no" answer because a church of all apostles or all prophets would be as silly and ineffective as a body made up of all eyes or ears. Second, while Paul's questions are often interpreted to be a list denoting importance and therefore a hierarchy as we *"eagerly desire the greater gifts,"* this approach, along with others, doesn't fit with the rest of the chapter, nor does it fit with what Paul is about to tell us.

To eagerly desire or seek the "greater" gifts means simply that we may ask God for His gifts without making demands, allowing Him to say "yes" or "no". We must also understand that the nature of every gift as essential for the right functioning of the Body means that at the right time and place each gift can have the designation of "greatest." This allows us to pray in gratitude for the gift(s) God has given us while asking for wisdom to put them to use where they will have the greatest (most effective) results.

Once Paul has laid out the rationale for every gift as a significant part of the healthy functioning of the Body, he shifts to calling the Corinthians and us to *"the most excellent way"* described in chapter 13. Here Paul will stress that without love the gifts are worthless. Love has to be the motivation, purpose, and objective of any and every gift. The fact that we're thinking about the intimate life within the Body of Christ puts a new spotlight on Jesus' answer to the question about what's the most important thing in all of life. The Great Commandment doesn't change; it becomes more insistent and crucial among those who follow Christ and are members of his Body. Mark 12:29-31 captures what Jesus saw as the bottom line of everything we do and are:

> *"'The most important one,' answered Jesus, 'is this: "Hear, O Israel: The Lord our God, the Lord is one. Love the Lord your God with all your heart and with all your soul and with all your mind and with all your strength." The second is this: "Love your neighbor as yourself." There is no commandment greater than these."'*

Paul and Jesus were of one mind in calling us to humility as they called us to love. All the resources God makes available to us to live as believers and function as His Church must be viewed and used in the context of love. Whether there is a proliferation of Spiritual gifts, as there was in Corinth, or a scarcity of acknowledgment, as there seems to be in many churches today, the centrality of love cannot be denied. Without love, as Paul says, the church becomes nothing but a noisy and useless place, even if the gifts are on display. The problem is never the gifts themselves, rather the character of those who have been gifted and how they see and use what God has given them.

Let me help you reflect on the part your own character plays in your role within the Body of Christ:

- Do you currently think right now that because of your gifts, age, race, gender, education, or experience you are somehow better than other Christians in your church or elsewhere? This is a motive question. Repent because your attitude is a violation of God's grace, mercy, and sovereignty. A real move of God in a life and in a church happens when our real motives are brought up and dealt with. Are you willing for God to really set you free so you can have joy and can be a place of joy for others?
- Are you a person that thinks you are lesser in the Body of Christ? Or are you someone full of anger, envy, jealousy, and resentment towards God

Himself or to others in the church that have stronger versions of your gifts, or a different gift you would prefer? Do you experience self-hatred because you want to be something God has not created you to be, and so you have no joy? Maybe you have allowed others to form you and not let God say over you what you are. God says to you, "Fully surrender and let Me show you how indispensable you are." Then, and only then, will you find joy.

- Are you willing to pray right now, "Yes I want to know my gifts and I am eager, but I acknowledge they are Yours to give, so I ask for the gifts You want me to have and will depend on You to lead me in using them for Your glory and not my own"? You can expect God to answer a prayer like that.

- Have you put God in a box because your fear or your theology says "God cannot do that" or "I don't want to be in a church where all that will happen"? Repent; never say, "Do not!" to God. He will trample your sensibilities for your own good and His glory.

- Last and most important, would you ask God to actually give you the character of humility and love so the gifts He has already given you are made right and used rightly?

For any or all the cases above, use the following passage as a prayer:

Love is patient, love is kind. It does not envy, it does not boast, it is not proud. It does not dishonor others, it is not self-seeking, it is not easily angered, it keeps no record of wrongs. Love does not delight in evil but rejoices with the truth. It always protects, always trusts, always hopes, always perseveres (1 Corinthians 13: 4-7).

Chapter Six:
Spiritual Gifts– The Love Category

Over the last couple of chapters we have been building a needed foundation for understanding the various Spiritual gifts. Part of that foundation will always be the awareness that Jesus is our model for every aspect of life, including the empowerment that comes to us from the Holy Spirit, whom Jesus depended on fully as He lived on this earth. If Jesus needed and depended on the Holy Spirit, how much more should that be true of us!

We have come to understand that not all the gifts we have are spiritual gifts, that God is the one that chooses our gifts, and that we will be held accountable by Jesus for using or not using our gifts. In the last chapter we focused on our deep need for humility and the importance of character to back up and support the gifts. We are now going to dive in the gifts and begin with the Love gifts.

At Sanctus we divided all 21+ gifts into three groups: Love Gifts, Power Gifts, and Word Gifts. I appreciate how J. Robert Clinton simply outlined these three groups. Love Gifts manifest the love of God in practical ways. Power Gifts demonstrate the power, presence, and reality of God. Word Gifts clarify the nature, action, and purposes of God. Together the three categories of gifts create amazing harmony, unity, and clarity in our Church.[1]

Every church needs all three types of gifts. If we do not have and use all three, we will be lopsided; our churches will tend to over-emphasize one aspect of ministry or only focus on part of what each local church is called to do.

Let's discuss two questions right up front that impact our very willingness to think seriously about the place and importance of spiritual gifts in the Church:

Question 1 – Why do some gifts seem more supernatural than others? Would it be better to say that some spiritual gifts are natural and others supernatural?

Answer – No, this is not our worldview as Bible-centered Christians at all. Our faith has never bought into the idea of a division between natural and supernatural, or spiritual and un-spiritual. For us the sacred and secular do not exist as separate entities. We have an integrated worldview. Remember Jesus was both fully God and fully human. The Bible is the Word of God, fully divine yet written by humans with their own unique personalities, history, ethnicity, and education under the Holy Spirit's direction. Natural and supernatural are not separate categories but together make up reality. Spiritual gifts are all from God, all are spiritually powerful, but will take on different emphases. As Wayne Grudem explained, "The worldview of Scripture is one of continuity and continual interaction between the *visible world* that we can see and touch and the *invisible world* that Scripture tells us is there and is real. God works in both, and we do ourselves and the church a great disservice by separating these aspects of creation into 'supernatural' and 'natural'."[2] Pretending these two aspects of reality are separate or that they don't affect each other puts us in danger of making serious mistakes and becoming victims who fail to see the source of danger.

Believers with gifts that do not look supernatural may feel like they must be lesser Christians, or don't know Jesus as well as those Christians with the "weird" gifts. Many could start to assume that those "weird power" people think they are much more spiritual than us. Many feel pressure as they use their gifts because they feel judged for attitudes they do not have.

As a church, unity will be achieved when we all learn to accept a wide range of gifts that look and are utilized differently, and stop presuming we know what others think. If you have participated in church for a long time you will notice that churches tend to emphasize one or two of the three groups of gifts, so that those with the other gifts feel they must go find churches open to what God calls them to do. At Sanctus we realize it has not always been easy to acknowledge and welcome all three of the gift categories. But we know it is God's plan so we work to be open to it.

Question 2 – It seems like many of the spiritual gifts are actually things we are all called to do. What's up with that?

Answer – We are all called as Christians to do many of the actions covered by the gifts but the gifts themselves are present in certain persons when they have a passion and unnatural ability or stronger ability than the normal Christian call. Think about some of these gift functions, like pastoring, evangelism, or discerning of spirits. We are all called to care for others, as shepherds do. We've all been called to be witnesses about Jesus and our faith in him, following the example of those with the gift of evangelism. The gift of faith sets the standard for all of us, encouraging greater trust in God. Every one of us should continually ask for greater sensitivity to discerning of spirits. None of us should be strangers to the habit of praying for all kinds of healing for others. We're all expected to give not only of our material resources but also of our mercy. These are all examples of universal spiritual practices for believers, which in some cases are given as particular spiritual abilities to some among us. When you have a gift, it is more than a common shared duty; it is what God has empowered you to do with greater frequency and power. You know it's a gift when you can do it over the long haul with joy, without duty and with heaven-given results in many forms.

Here is one way I have used to differentiate spiritual gifts from spiritual practices: The Rule of Dots. We've all walked into an environment like a bookstore or bar and felt spiritually uncomfortable. Does that mean I have the gift of discernment? Not necessarily. We all have the Holy Spirit and the Scriptures and are very well able to discern at times when something is not right. This is the rule: When an experience of discernment is noticed, think of it as one dot. If that experience is repeated, it's two dots and worth evaluating. If the experience is regular and repeated, three or more dots might indicate this to be a spiritual gift. As a Christian, watch for those moments when you think, *this always happens to me.*

After years of talking through and exploring The Rule of Dots, I've discovered that finding your spiritual gift can also be worked out this way: where you tend to be angry in church is where you tend to be spiritually gifted. What bothers you and makes you a little crazy about your church is usually a pointer to where you are gifted. As an example, if you think, *this church can do so much more to help those in need*, you may have the gift of mercy.

The other lesson here is that in the areas where you are not spiritually gifted, you must exercise a spiritual discipline. We all don't have mercy, but we are called to be merciful. We all don't have the expression of helps called hospitality, but we are called to be hospitable. For the sake of church unity, this is why having character and mutually submitting to one another matter so much in this spiritual gifts conversation.

LOVE GIFTS

We begin our survey of spiritual gifts with a look at four gifts that can be classified as primarily Love Gifts. These gifts are keys to the right working of the church. Love gifts are supportive in the sense that they build up what God has accomplished and is establishing through the leadership of a local church. The Love Gifts we will examine are administration, helps, mercy, and giving. These are referred to in 1 Corinthians 12:27-28 and elsewhere. *"Now you are the body of Christ, and each one of you is a part of it. And God has placed in the church first of all apostles, second prophets, third teachers, then miracles, then gifts of healing, of helping, of guidance and of different kinds of tongues"* (underline added).

Administration

The *gift of administration* is also called the *gift of guidance.* It is important to understand that administration is not always a leadership gift. Notice in the passage above it is placed alongside the supportive gifts, not the word/ruling gifts. The ruling gifts are about leadership, vision, and inspiration while administration/guidance is about supporting that vision. The key is that this gift must come under the global mission of every church and must submit and support the local church's Jesus-given vision. If you have this gift but do not support what God has given through the gift of leadership, you will be perpetually frustrated. The "where" is not your call, you must be about the "how"! In other translations this gift is also the gift of guidance or wise counsel to the community as a whole, helping to unpack and apply the vision of leadership.

More importantly, the word used here for this gift is *helmsman,* a nautical term. Helmsmen are the persons guiding a ship to its destination. The person at the helm carries out the instructions of the captain without deviating by his own interests or concerns. The owner and the captain of the ship make the basic decisions as to the purpose of the voyage, the ship's destination, and what will happen when it arrives, but a helmsman makes sure it gets from points A to B.

Here is one definition of this gift, adapted from J. Robert Clinton: "The *gift of administration* involves a capacity to manage details of service functions so as to support and free those in leadership to prioritize their efforts."[3] Bruce Bugbee describes this gift as the "divine enablement to understand what makes an organization function, and the special ability to plan and execute procedures that accomplish the goals of the ministry."[4]

Here are a few telltale signs of this gift that others may notice: You have an effortless skill for organizing tasks and people. You like to streamline and clarify the steps required to accomplish more complex tasks. You think about more than work; you imagine ways to help others reach their goals. You have a concern for the good of the whole group when you are in charge of that group, though you don't gravitate to that top leadership role. You're at your best meeting not only the needs of the group but also the needs of the leaders. You like to do things that help other people, and don't mind managing things or carrying out the details involved.[5]

One of the best pictures of this is when the young church in Acts chose deacons for the first time. Like an elder, Deacon is not a gift but an office; yet one key gift we see in some Deacons is this ability for administration.

In those days when the number of disciples was increasing, the Hellenistic Jews among them complained against the Hebraic Jews because their widows were being overlooked in the daily distribution of food. So the Twelve gathered all the disciples together and said, "It would not be right for us to neglect the ministry of the word of God in order to wait on tables. Brothers and sisters, choose seven men from among you who are known to be full of the Spirit and wisdom. We will turn this responsibility over to them

and will give our attention to prayer and the ministry of the word"
(Acts 6:1-4).

Again, notice the Apostles instructed the disciples to identify those of wisdom and full of the Spirit to coordinate the waiting on tables. They recognized certain needs were not being met, but they themselves already had their hands full with *"prayer and the ministry of the word."* People with the gift of administration allow others to pray, to preach, and to give vision and they celebrate this at their core. You find heaven-given joy when others are set free to do their jobs. Is this you? Remember, if you have a passion for this work done in the name of Jesus and for his glory, there is a good chance this could be a spiritual gift.

If you are reading this as a pastor or church leader, in all likelihood you function under a job description that was not developed with your gift orientation in mind. It is probably primarily a combination of what your church has traditionally expected of those in your role combined with the current and often unrealistic expectations of those overseeing your work. You may be working in a framework that frustrates your spiritual gifting as often as it facilitates your use of it. But what if your title, and even more important, your job description really reflected your gift orientation?

We haven't entirely solved this tension at Sanctus. After all, we are still operating in a fallen world and ministry will always, no matter the field, still include some hard work. But our still-unfolding story may be helpful for you. In 2005 I became the Senior Pastor of our church whose current congregation numbered around 1,000, as I shared in the introduction to this book. I always knew I couldn't do it all alone. Through trials and a lot of errors, I came to realize I was primarily a visionary preacher and cultural architect.

I eventually hired Dave as an Executive Pastor and we have served as the primary leaders in our church for the last eight years. He came to us from a position as a senior pastor, and previous to that had been a senior manager in a large, multi-million dollar corporation. In our earliest conversations, Dave said, "Jon, I don't want your job," (which was reassuring). He also said he wanted to spend much of the second part of his life using his gifts of encouragement and building up.

As we moved forward and added staff, clarified vision, and began to work out the implications of convergence in our church structure, Dave and I maintained the same titles but worked closely with each other. Eventually we realized if our church culture was going to follow the pattern of convergence, our titles ought to actually reflect the language and values we were trying to live out. As a result, for the last several years, I have worked under the title of Vision and Preaching Pastor; Dave is the Lead Pastor. Together, we represent the senior pastor role.

Here's how we worked this out. The biblical leadership model we use is Moses and Aaron. I'm Moses; Dave is Aaron. Like Moses, I walk in front of the people. As a side note, I often point out that Jesus started a movement; He never led one. Moses led a movement. This is not to say Jesus wasn't a profound leader—He was the best leader. But for help in understanding the dynamics of leading a movement, Moses offers a better model. In our framework I'm charged to go before God as Moses did, going up the mountain to inquire what our next steps should be, seeking the Lord's guidance for direction, sermon series, and long-term decisions. When I "come down from the mountain," I confirm what I've heard with Dave and only when we are of one mind will we move forward. Our commitment as a church to the convergence model continues to be worked out in all details, including defining our roles based on gift orientation. This has allowed Dave and myself to exercise our gifts without some of the unrealistic expectations that go with traditional church leadership models. The emphasis on gifts at the staff and elder level has not only affirmed the importance of gifts but has also acknowledged significant limitations. None of us function effectively apart from the rest of us. The body of Christ is healthiest when every member is carrying out his or her unique role within the body.

A biblical term that describes our goal is "mutual submission." It begins with Dave and myself and extends throughout the church. Just before Paul describes the unique relationship of marriage as the primary picture of the relationship between Christ and his church (Ephesians 5), he pauses to say, "Submit to one another out of reverence for Christ" (Ephesians 5:21). Though we have complementary roles as senior leaders in the church, Dave and I have found our persistent practice of mutual submission in leadership to be freeing, significant, and healthy not only for our relationship, but in how it impacts relationships all through the church.

This works out very obviously in our hiring practices. One of the first questions we ask people is "What are your spiritual gifts?" We often find that people have little understanding of their personal gifts and a poor gift theology, which tells us we have a lot of work to do before we can engage this person in ministry. We've actually helped a lot of people in our interviews because when they do discover their gift-orientation, they realize they would never have wanted the job they applied for. And we were able to send them joyfully on their way.

By the way, one way to respond to complaints or cases where injustice is uncovered is to ask, "What gifts are not being engaged that have created this situation?" The squeaky wheel may call for the application of gift grease we have overlooked.

Helps/Serving

Paul mentions these gifts in 1 Corinthians 12:28, but they are also highlighted in 1 Peter 4:10-11.

Each of you should use whatever gift you have received to serve others, as faithful stewards of God's grace in its various forms. If anyone speaks, they should do so as one who speaks the very words of God. <u>If anyone serves, they should do so with the strength God provides</u>, so that in all things God may be praised through Jesus Christ. To him be the glory and the power forever and ever. Amen" (underline added).

Note the universal application of *"whatever gift you have received"* to the call to *"serve others,"* followed almost immediately by a specific indication that some are called to serve in a primary way, depending on *"the strength God provides."*

Paul also includes this gift of helps or service in Romans 12:6-8:

We have different gifts, according to the grace given to each of us. If your gift is prophesying, then prophesy in accordance with your faith; <u>if it is serving, then serve;</u> if it is teaching, then teach; if it is to encourage, then give encouragement; if it is giving, then give generously; if it is to lead, do it diligently; if it is to show mercy, do it cheerfully (underline added).

This gift is given mainly to aid others in practical ways; it offers effective service to people in need. It takes on commonplace tasks cheerfully, regularly, and even worshipfully. Much of the time the gift of helps is one-on-one ministry and a large percentage of people will have this gift in any local church.

Here is a great definition: "The gift of helps refers to the capacity to unselfishly meet the needs of others through very practical service."[6] People with this gift render practical service in the church to people in need. They find joy in doing the simple and messy tasks others will avoid. They are the "foot washers" after the model of Jesus. The actual work done by the gift of helps is very often overlooked precisely because it allows others to accomplish with their gifts much more obvious tasks. The gift of helps is instrumental in liberating and encouraging others to fully engage their gifts. But most importantly, it demonstrates the love of God in the most practical way!

Here are some clues offered by J. Robert Clinton that help identify this significant yet undervalued gift. If you realize you have an urge to help others and you seem to notice without being told ways others can be assisted, you may have this gift. If you don't mind taking on behind-the-scenes work outside the spotlight and actually enjoy doing what others have been avoiding, you are demonstrating the gift of helps. This gift does small things without expecting any credit. The work is done for the simple joy of using a talent, ability, or skill to help others within the church. A deeper enjoyment comes from seeing how your effort on behalf of others enables and encourages them to better use their own gifts. Leaders will be severely hampered without the support of a significant number of those with help gifts.

Again, Scripture calls all of us to help others in the power of God. Spending yourself helping and serving outside of God's empowerment can leave you feeling used, and even bitter because you will end up not doing it for God. Don't forget, God has called you to serve so others can be set free to use their gifts. Allow him to provide the reward for your obedience. When you exercise this gift in the power of the Holy Spirit and you serve in small or large and hidden or public ways, joy will come to you! Do you find yourself resonating with this gift?

Mercy

A close companion of the gifts of administration and helps is a reclusive but powerful gift of mercy. Paul mentions this gift in Romans 12:8d, *"if it is to show mercy, do it cheerfully."* This gift is about pity, compassion, and showing gracious favor. Mercy sees what someone needs even when they may not see it themselves. The gift of mercy is not an emotion but a deep calling; it is divine love under the power of the Holy Spirit, practicing compassion in Jesus' name and bringing glory to God the Father. Genuine mercy is never applied with a sense of duty or out of anger or with a scowl. It is cheerful service to those in great need.

Here is how Bruce Bugbee describes this particular gift: "The divine enablement to cheerfully and practically help those who are suffering or are in need."[7] To which C. Peter Wagner adds:

Mercy is a special ability that God gives to certain members of the body of Christ to feel genuine empathy and compassion for individuals (both Christian and non-Christian) who suffer distress, physical, mental or emotional problems, and translates that compassion into cheerfully done deeds which reflect Christ's love and alleviating of suffering.[8]

Every disciple of Jesus hears the call from him to practice mercy: *"Be merciful, just as your Father is merciful"* (Luke 6:36). But according to Romans 12, some of us are particularly gifted with this capacity, though Paul adds an interesting challenge that ought to bring pause to all who claim this gift: *"If it is to show mercy, do it cheerfully"* (Romans 12:8d). Spirit-sparked mercy is given without a hint of attention to itself. There is a recognizable impulse towards mercy in humans, particularly if we have been the recipients of the mercy of others, but the Spiritual Gift of mercy is, by its nature, deeper and unexpected.

Mercy is not common courtesy or tears over an emotional story. Mercy can be illustrated in the way we are moved emotionally and volitionally by the needs of another. The impulse to embrace a sinner is often an expression of mercy; so is the willingness to weep with those who weep. When the circumstantial and demonstrable evidence goes against someone, it is mercy that stands next to the accused and says, "Let those without sin be the first to carry out judgment." You may have an inborn tenderheartedness toward the pain or sadness of others, but the spiritual gift of mercy goes beyond this. The gift is particularly noticeable in those who have been unmerciful before they surrendered to Christ. As evidence of the indwelling Holy Spirit, the evidence of the gift of mercy is sometimes surprising even to those who have been given that gift. They report that the gift has over-ridden past and even current tendencies to be resistant to the flaws and failures of others. It's one thing to be amazed by God's mercy toward us; it's another to be amazed that we have been moved to unexpected mercy toward others on an ongoing basis. Once you identify that this gift has been given to you, you will continually seek out those who know they are not worthy of what you give them.

There is a great example of this in the book of Acts 9:36, *"In Joppa there was a disciple named Tabitha (in Greek her name is Dorcas); she was always doing good and helping the poor."* Other translations say that she was full of charity or was always doing alms deeds. At its heart, her actions can be translated mercy-deeds. She is an amazing example of a person with the gift of mercy. Her sickness and death created such a vacuum that those she had helped immediately sent for Peter. The evidence of her mercy provoked Peter to pray for her resurrection, a prayer God answered. Mercy that finds its motivation in the needs of others can easily trigger the exercise of many other gifts.

There is one key question that will be helpful to talk about before we move on: How is the gift of mercy different than the gifts of helps? The difference can be seen in the primary recipients of these two gifts. The gift of helps is directed toward Christian leaders in order to release them from different services so they can concentrate on their primary ministry. It is about doing the many small tasks and taking care of details so the church and many individual ministries can function smoothly. The gift of mercy is directed toward helping those in immediate distress.

Giving

Another fascinating gift in the love gifts category is the spiritual gift of giving. We saw this gift mentioned in Romans 12: 8 where Paul wrote, "*if your gift is giving, then give generously.*" People with this gift have a deep sensitivity to God and a desire to channel resources to others, and they do it with joy, with right motive, and with great generosity. These are often, but not necessarily, people with supporting capabilities for generating resources.

It's not unusual for people to learn about this gift and immediately think, *Great! That's definitely not my gift, so I don't need to give!*

But stop and understand that God is clear about this—all Christians are called to give. Rich and poor, children, teens, young adults, adults, the less and more mature, all must give back to the God who has given so much to us. As I read the whole of the Bible, it is clear that we are all called to give 10% of what we earn or receive to the Lord and His work. The tithe is really the minimum for each one of us. And the truth is that many among us are not willing to make lifestyle changes or work to get our fiscal house in order so we're able to obey God in these clear matters. One Old Testament and one New Testament verse best summarize the common Christian call for radical other-centered giving:

"Bring the whole tithe into the storehouse, that there may be food in my house. Test me in this," says the Lord Almighty, *"and see if I will not throw open the floodgates of heaven and pour out so much blessing that there will not be room enough to store it"* (Malachi 3:10).

"Each of you should give what you have decided in your heart to give, not reluctantly or under compulsion, for God loves a cheerful giver" (2 Corinthians 9:7).

This generosity is not the spiritual gift of giving. Those with the gift of giving give more and regularly to God's work. They are always thinking about ways to give and are sad when they cannot. They discover that being presented with a need not only inspires them to give but also makes them more aware of resources to use in the giving. Most people do not go around thinking or saying, "How much more can I give away?" with joy in Jesus' name.

Notice again in the Romans 12 description that the call is to give generously. The word *generously* literally means "without folds in a cloth." The significance of this is that folds could hide any defects in a cloth. The expression goes to motive. Those with the gift of giving have a way of giving what is needed, neither a shortfall nor a wasteful indulgence, but resources equal to the task— evidence that the knowing Holy Spirit is motivating the giving. If you have the gift of giving, your motive is not political, it is not about tax receipts, it is not about what you can accomplish, it is God-given stewardship.

Here's a great definition: "The gift of Giving refers to the capacity to give liberally to meet the needs of others and yet to do so with a purity of motive which senses that the giving is a simple sharing of what God has given."[9] Here are some identifying traits of this spiritual gift: Do you find yourself earmarking certain amounts because you have a strong sense that an opportunity to give will be presented? Are you tuned in to settings and lives in a way that makes you aware that a material gift would significantly impact what God is doing through a group or in a person's life? Do you get great joy out of helping someone without them ever knowing who delivered the assistance? Do you find yourself holding possessions and resources lightly, always on the lookout for someone who might have a greater need for what you have? Have you discovered that following the Holy Spirit's prompts about giving is part of an amazing process in which your own needs continue to be met? These are indicators of someone with the gift of giving. Such a person is frequently prone to carefulness in handling finances with a bent toward living a simple lifestyle, a conviction that all of what they have belongs to God and they are simply stewards of his resources. You may not connect with all of these, not all with the gift of giving make tons of money. The gift is not measured by amounts given but by whether or not you find great joy in giving.

One very powerful example of the gift of Giving comes from Acts 4:34b-37: *For from time to time those who owned land or houses sold them, brought the money from the sales and put it at the apostles' feet, and it was distributed to anyone who had need. Joseph, a Levite from Cyprus, whom the apostles called Barnabas (which means "son of encouragement"), sold a field he owned and brought the money and put it at the apostles' feet.*

Again notice that this is a supportive gift, which works with and under the leadership of a community. Every week in a typical church, particularly one that is spiritually alive and actively seeking to be used by God in the world, people in the mold of Barnabas show up and support the church financially in ways only a few others know. The gift of giving is unexpected, powerful, faith filled, and is an amazing public testimony that had a huge impact on the early church (in Barnabas' case) and is true among disciples today. And did you catch that he gave in public?

Yes, Jesus said in Matthew 6:3-4 "But when you give to the needy, do not let your left hand know what your right hand is doing, so that your giving may be in secret." His point is not to forbid testimony, but that our motives must be clear. "Be careful not to practice your righteousness in front of others to be seen by them. If you do, you will have no reward from your Father in heaven (Matthew 6:1). That's the context. Actually, as God moves, more and more giving needs to be out in the open so we can give praise and build faith together within our community. I love the Barnabas story. We see the man's name, we see how much was given, and it still is being talked about 2000 years later! We need more stories, more testimonies of every kind, to build faith and inspire others to do the same. How can people grow in the practice of giving and develop into mentors if every Barnabas is hidden?

Jesus' point is simply that when you do give quietly or publicly, you do it for God and His kingdom, not you and your kingdom. There's no saying, "Attention everyone, I am giving!" God tells us to do it, follow through and walk away. *"Then your Father, who sees what is done in secret, will reward you"* (Matthew 6:4).

Let me emphasize again that a large portfolio and bank account are not necessarily the signs of the gift of giving. This gift is often effective in the way a little boy's gift of five loaves and two fishes was used by Jesus to feed a multitude. And Paul complimented the Macedonian Christians who managed to display a generous spirit toward the believers in Jerusalem who were suffering:

And now, brothers and sisters, we want you to know about the grace that God has given the Macedonian churches. In the midst of a very severe trial, their overflowing joy and their extreme poverty welled up in rich generosity. For I testify that they gave as much as they were able, and even beyond their ability. Entirely on their own, they urgently pleaded with us for the privilege of sharing in this service to the Lord's people. And they exceeded our expectations: They gave themselves first of all to the Lord, and then by the will of God also to us (2 Corinthians 8:1-5).

These were not Christians being generous with their excess; they were suffering hardship themselves, but they still made what they had available for the Lord to use. The early Methodists were for the most part believers who came to Christ from the lower classes in Britain, and yet their faithful giving out of poverty funded a movement that rocked the Empire and spread across the New World. All of us need to remember the reality that until God has access to our treasure He doesn't have access to us. The gifts remind us that some among us have been designated by God's Spirit as givers, and we should appreciate their role, even when we don't know who they are.

We've now looked at four spiritual gifts that fall in the broader category of Love Gifts: administration, helps, mercy, and giving. They are all powerful spiritual gifts that allow believers to express their love for God and for others in practical and sometimes overlooked ways. They are special ways God's Spirit equips some among us for special service to all of us.

Did you find yourself connecting with one or more of these gifts?

Chapter Seven:
Spiritual Gifts– The Word Category, Part One

I trust the last chapter was an encouraging introduction to the gifts of the Spirit as a starting point for discovering your own gift(s). I also hope it gave you a new appreciation for other disciples of Jesus you know who are different in ways you now realize have to do with their spiritual gifts. In this chapter we examine the Word Gifts. Here again is a brief description of each of the categories:

Love Gifts manifest the love of God in practical ways.
Power Gifts demonstrate the power, presence, and reality of God.
Word Gifts clarify the nature, action, and purposes of God.[1]

The Word Gifts we will examine in the next few pages are teaching, exhortation, and apostleship. But before we review those specific gifts, let me answer several other questions that many think about when considering spiritual gifts. Once disciples of Jesus realize that everyone has a gift from the Holy Spirit and that what He gives to each of us is unique, a question that always arises is: *Can I have more than one gift?* Yes you can. Our frontline experience has been that many believers are given one dominant gift that may be slightly shaped by secondary gifts, and many believers report a kind of gift matrix in which several gifts work together in them as they go about serving the Body of Christ. This service goes in two directions. First, the spiritual gifts are used primarily as ways to serve the Body of Christ from within the Body of Christ. And second, there are some gifts specifically designed to serve the Body in a representative way to the world. As an example, an apologist helps other believers develop clear ways to give a reason for their hope while at the same time inviting non-believers to the veracity and authority of the message. Never forget that spiritual gifts are not about ego, duty, or identity. They are given for the good of the community and produce joy in us.

A second question is also almost universal: *What should I do if I'm unsure about the gifts I think I have?* Well, first ask God. He will affirm truth to you. There's no reason He would give you a gift only to keep it hidden from you. Then surrender all your dreams, ideas of what it might look like or feel like and any agendas for a gift you think you may have as a way to clarify your motives. Learning about these gifts will sometimes connect with you because a certain gift may appeal to your pride, but it may also engage you because it is, in fact your gift. As you serve in your church, also make it a point to ask the community of faith to affirm the gifts you have. What you can't see in yourself is often obvious to others. Those who serve with you will tend to see gifts before you do and can speak into your life. God will affirm your gift; the community will confirm it and you can put it to work.

Once believers discover and begin to use their gifts, a third question often emerges: *Why do I tend to have difficulties with some people with gifts different than mine?* We're going to talk at length about this later, but here are some preliminary thoughts. It's not about personality; this might better be acknowledged as "gift tension," and it isn't necessarily a negative thing.

Unfortunately, the tension can often be caused by pride and sin, even and perhaps especially when we are exercising spiritual gifts. The enemy seeks to nullify what God can do through our gifts by creating sinful distractions and detours. At other times, gift tension arises out of wrong expectations and assumptions that all people should have the same passion we do, even though each of us has a different calling. But there is another important reality that must be understood. Certain gifts tend to be person-oriented and others tend to be community-oriented, and that difference causes much of the tension we have found as we have explored and employed spiritual gifts at Sanctus.

As we realized there can always be tension between the gifts in your own life and the audience your gift is designed to serve, we made it our goal to encourage everyone never to serve in areas that force someone into a role or setting in which they are not gifted to serve. In other words, you should not be in a key leadership area if your primary gifts are person to person, because you will tend to sacrifice the whole group for one person. Yet if your strongest gifts or your only gifts are community based, be careful too; don't serve in a one-on-one setting or you may easily wound the person or small group you are trying to help. Notice again that in 1 Corinthians 12:27- 28 Paul said, *"Now you are the body of Christ, and each one of you is a part of it. And God has placed in the church first of all apostles, second prophets, third teachers. "* He starts with all community gifts rather than person-based gifts because he is talking about leadership gifts required in the founding and building of a community. The "first" is not about order of importance, but order of impact. None of these gifts are more valuable than the others but the roles are different and sometimes appear to have broader influence than others.

Teaching

The spiritual gift of teaching is Bible centered and clarifies God's truth. Teachers don't proclaim as much as they unpack. They help groups of disciples understand the themes and principles of Scripture. What 1 Corinthians 12:27-28 shows us is that teachers are third in the line of responsibility after the apostolic and prophetic gifts have done their work of establishing the church. *"Now you are the body of Christ, and each one of you is a part of it. And God has placed in the church first of all apostles, second prophets, third teachers."*

Paul talks about this gift also in Romans and in Ephesians. In Romans 12:7 he wrote, *"if it is serving, then serve; if it is teaching, then teach,"* emphasizing the idea that we should do what we are gifted to do. Ephesians 4:11-12 provides a more comprehensive list of the community word gifts: *"So Christ himself gave the apostles, the prophets, the evangelists, the pastors and teachers, to equip his people for works of service, so that the body of Christ may be built up."*

Teaching, like other community gifts, equips us to know God, to obey Him, and to be encouraged as we pursue discipleship. Teaching helps sustain us personally and corporately. As one author defined this gift, "A person who has the gift of teaching is one who has the ability to instruct, explain, or expose biblical truth in such a way as to cause believers to understand the Biblical truth."[2] While this is a clear explanation, it seems to be missing some needed punch to account for the spiritual aspects of this gift. The definition needs to include the idea that this particular kind of teaching is the supernatural ability to explain and apply the Scriptures. Many people in a typical church may be professional teachers or instructors in a secular setting, and their skills and abilities can be useful in teaching in a spiritual setting. But the way in which the spiritual gift of teaching differs is in the anointed impact of the communication; people get it when someone with that gift teaches. It can't be explained by technique or personal charisma alone. This gift communicates biblical truth that leads to obedience, it supports the Lordship of Jesus, it deals with the roots of worldview and motive, and it is one key vehicle to encourage spiritual living. Spiritual life is not given when you teach math or hear a politician give an amazing oration. This is God-empowered communication for kingdom purposes.

Teaching is the Living Word, Jesus, using His written word, the Bible, by the Spirit of Christ to bring attention to the will of the Father. The teaching gift of the Holy Spirit is both deeply intellectual and highly powerful. It is Bible centered. It helps bring and establish the reign and rule of God on earth, in hearts, in people groups, and in society.

In my connect group there are several public school teachers. When we were doing an extended study on the gifts, I asked the teachers in my group what they thought the difference might be for someone who worked in the teaching field and someone gifted by the Spirit for teaching.

They said, "Oh, we enjoy teaching and we use natural talents and learned skills in the classroom, but we don't really experience spiritual joy and we don't see any kingdom outcomes from the work that we do. We know what we're doing is valuable, but it doesn't have to do with clarifying God and His kingdom."

Their response clarified a number of things about the unique effectiveness and use of spiritual gifts. It did not devalue what they were doing in the context where they were working, but it also made the point that their work didn't directly bring God glory or bring people to Christ.

That is why the very first description in the New Testament of established life in a church starts with teaching. Think about the new believers gathering in Jerusalem in the weeks following the resurrection and ascension of Jesus. This was church from scratch with the Holy Spirit leading every step of the way. *"They devoted themselves to the apostles' teaching and to fellowship, to the breaking of bread and to prayer"* (Acts 2: 42). The apostolic proclamation of the Gospel launched the church at Pentecost, but the daily living and growth of the believers depended on apostolic teaching. It's worth noting in passing that none of the original apostles, or Jesus Himself, was a schooled academic. Acts 4:13 says, *"When they saw the courage of Peter and John and realized that they were unschooled, ordinary men, they were astonished and they took note that these men had been with Jesus."* Seminary training and advanced degrees do not insure that you have the spiritual gift of teaching, though scholarship broadens the content you can use if you have the gift. Note that Paul was formally trained, but it wasn't until after his conversion that the Holy Spirit used his learning in service of the gospel.

I have offered some descriptions of the gift of teaching, but let me suggest some of the clues you might look for in discerning whether this is part of your gift from the Holy Spirit.[3] An effective spiritual teacher not only has people verbally confirm that they can understand Scripture better as a result of the teaching but also sees people put into practice the applications drawn from the Bible. Those with this gift are also enthusiastic learners, seeking mentors with the same gift who have greater experience and knowledge. All believers should develop a hunger for God's Word, but someone with the gift of teaching knows they need to fill themselves with Scripture in order to deliver to others what they are learning themselves. Alarm bells go off when the Scripture is misused, misunderstood, misapplied. And always, the gift of teaching results in a setting where God's Spirit is working on the audience in ways that cannot be directly explained by the content of the teaching alone. To put it another way, there would be a marked difference in the response if someone with the gift of teaching taught from the same outline as someone without that gift. The difference is in the way God's Spirit expands and uses the gifts he gives.

Is this you? Do you have the gift of Teaching? Have you made yourself available to the rest of the Body? How are you currently exercising this gift?

Teaching is one of my stronger spiritual gifts, and it led me to my life verse. I love the passage because it brings home for me and for all of us the need to use our gifts and build the character alongside it. *"Watch your life and doctrine closely. Persevere in them, because if you do, you will save both yourself and your hearers"* (1 Timothy 4:16).

Before we move on, let me jump ahead and talk about the difference between the gifts of prophecy and teaching. If you have been in church for a while, you know many churches assume that they are two names for the same gift. In a later chapter we will look specifically at prophecy, but I'd like to focus for a moment on the helpful comments by Wayne Grudem regarding this issue. He wrote:

As far as we can tell, all New Testament "prophecy" was based on this kind of spontaneous prompting from the Holy Spirit (cf. Acts 11:28; 21:4, 10-11; and note the ideas of prophecy represented in Luke 7:39; 22:63-64; John 4:19; 11:51). Unless a person receives a spontaneous "revelation" from God, there is no prophecy. By contrast, no human speech act that is called a "teaching" or done by a "teacher," or described by the verb "teach," is ever said to be based on a "revelation" in the New Testament. Rather, "teaching" is often simply an explanation or application of Scripture (Acts 15:35; 18:11, 24-28; Rom. 2:21; 15:4; Col. 3:16; Heb. 5:12).

All of this means that "prophecy" actually has less authority than "teaching," and prophecies in the church are always to be subject to the authoritative teaching of Scripture. So the distinction is quite clear: if a message is the result of conscious reflection on the text of Scripture, containing interpretation of the text and application to life, then it is (in New Testament terms) a teaching. But if a message is the report of something God brings suddenly to mind, then it is a prophecy. Neither prophecy nor teaching can be accepted that directly contradicts what God's Word says.[4]

If you do have the gift of teaching, let me speak quickly to its dark side. First, be careful not to make secondary issues primary all the time. By this I refer to matters such as: gifts, women in ministry, church structure, and many others. Remember they do not hold the same weight as the virgin birth, the divinity of Jesus, or the call to a holy Christian life. Second, hold your hands open to God and say, "Teach me before I teach, I'm willing to hear where I have been wrong or off base." I have told many young leaders I am fully prepared on judgment day to hear Jesus say to me, "Well, you sure got *that* wrong." I will also look over at some other teacher and will have to say, "Sorry, you did get that right!" Third, read lots of people who really bother you and rub you the wrong way. Jesus is working in and speaking to so many in the family and the more broadly you read, the more you will understand. By hearing the voices of Christ-followers across 2,000 years, the more you will realize that none of us are all that amazing or insightful, we have much to learn and God has already spoken to others what you need to say.

This might be a good time to remind all of us that each of God's amazing 21 spiritual gifts and the infinite combinations of them are given to us for a purpose. All of us will be accountable before God for what we use or don't use! But this particular gift of teaching is even more scary and exciting. This is one of the only gifts for which there is a direct warning: *"Not many of you should become teachers, my fellow believers, because you know that we who teach will be judged more strictly"* (James 3:1).

Exhortation/Encouragement

This gift is widespread in our church. A case can be made for this abundance based on the fact that it often shows up in Scripture often; it may be particularly needed for these times, or is simply an ever-needed gift within the Body of Christ. I'm speaking about the spiritual gift of exhortation, or what others call the gift of encouragement.

This gift is referenced in Romans 12:8, *"If it is to encourage, then give encouragement; if it is giving, then give generously; if it is to lead, do it diligently; if it is to show mercy, do it cheerfully."* Note that each of the other gifts in this passage is treated with an encouraging refinement. The gifts of giving, leading, and mercy are spurred on to generosity, diligence, and cheerfulness. These are encouraging statements. But, Paul begins, if your gift is encouragement, just do it! In a way, we could say that Paul's letters in the New Testament were driven by the fact that part of his spiritual gift was encouragement. Note, for instance, what he told the Romans early in his letter to them: *"I long to see you so that I may impart to you some spiritual gift to make you strong—that is, that you and I may be mutually encouraged by each other's faith"* (Romans 1:11-12).

Unlike the gift of teaching which is to *clarify* truth, this gift's focus is to *apply* biblical truth and to help others live out the faith practically. This is spiritual cheerleading with a specific purpose; calling other believers to begin or continue rightly applying what God has said in His Word. Here is a comprehensive description of the gift, *"The gift of exhortation is the capacity to urge people to action in terms of applying Biblical truths, to encourage people generally with Biblical truths, or to comfort people through the application of Biblical truth to their needs. "*[5] In other words, believers with this gift call others' attention to Scripture, urge fellow disciples to keep going in the faith, and come alongside the discouraged and defeated with direction from God's Word that will help them get moving again.

There are basically three expressions of this gift, and they may be exercised in subtle ways. This is important to grasp because many of us think we don't have this gift when in fact we do. The three ways this gift comes alive are to correct (to rebuke gently), to encourage, and to comfort. Exhortation is like mercy with a kick!

My dad has the gift of exhortation. Time and time again he ends up one on one with people from all backgrounds. Unlike me, he is drawn to spend personal time, hearing each story, listening with an intensity I could never fully learn, and then speaking God's truth. When you walk away after meeting with my dad, you feel really listened to and encouraged. But I also look back on those moments and realize, *Hey I just got slapped for my own good and did not even really know it was happening!*

Others with this gift are hard-core, all-the-time cheerleaders. They are always writing cards, texts, and emails, letting you know they praying for you. There's a woman in our church named Chris. Her spiritual gift of encouragement is off the charts. It's obvious that she derives great spiritual joy from encouraging others. She continually writes notes and letters of encouragement to those God lays on her heart. She even carries stickers with her and will stick one on you at a moment's notice.

If you are more cognitive or intellectual, you might observe her and conclude her actions are trite or shallow, but I can bear witness to the effectiveness and Spirit-led nature of her practices. The results of her gestures of encouragement are far more impactful than you might think, which are clues to the source of her impulses. What may appear as random kindnesses on her part turn out to be Spirit-targeted words that make a difference to others. Never underestimate people with this gift. They are faithful and mean what they say, every single time. Never dismiss their actions as fake duty or habit but genuine care. I love Flynn's explanation the gift of encouragement:

> The gift of exhortation involves the supernatural ability to come alongside to help, to strengthen the weak, reassure the wavering, buttress the buffeted, steady the faltering, console the troubled and encourage the halting! Just as the Holy Spirit is an instrument of help, so the Spirit uses this fit to make us instruments of encouragement to fellow saints![6]

The needs mentioned above are often obvious, and all who are followers of Jesus are called to assist where we can. What differentiates this gift is the supernatural way in which those who have been so gifted seem to effortlessly impact the lives around them with needed encouragement. Watching someone with this gift will also give us clues about ways we can encourage more effectively even without that gift.

What is amazing is that the word for *encourage* is actually used in Scripture to describe aspects of the ministries of both the Holy Spirit and Jesus himself. In John 14:16, Jesus described the One who would be sent in his place to work within his followers: *"And I will ask the Father, and he will give <u>you another Counselor</u> to be with you forever"* (underline added). Later, in pointing to Jesus' ongoing role as our mediator in God the Father's presence, the apostle John wrote, *"My dear children, I write this to you so that you will not sin. But if anybody does sin, we have <u>an advocate</u> with the Father—Jesus Christ, the Righteous One"* (1 John 2:1, underline added).

Here again is a compilation adapted from J. Robert Clinton[7] of the evidence that indicate the presence of this gift of encouragement. Depending on the spiritual condition of their own souls, people generally react strongly (sometimes for, sometimes against) what you say. After observing or listening to people, you frequently find yourself giving advice to them that demonstrates unusual understanding of their situation. You often feel like you have been given a message to share with someone in need and that person receives it as a comforting word from God. People frequently confide their inner thoughts to you because they sense that you have an empathetic ear and they are comforted in the process. People like to be around you because you often cheer them up simply by your attitude or demeanor. One of the roles you play when working with others is promoting urgency to get something done and you are willing to communicate that urgency to those whose energy or attention may be flagging. In various settings you love to share a truth from a passage of the Bible that means something to you. When speaking about Scripture or about life, you are not satisfied with a superficial acceptance of truth, but want people to use that truth in their lives. You seek out opportunities to share stories about God's involvement in your life because you know that God can use it to encourage others.

As is true with all the gifts, there is a dark side. Encouragers and exhorters are often lonely. They can't necessarily practice their gifts on themselves, though they need encouragement as much as anyone. Their gifts are frequently unappreciated or even resented, particularly when their exhortations are read by others as criticism or "telling me what to do," which can lead to rejection.

Let me add that sometimes this gift can be used alongside the teaching gift in a group setting or can be done one on one. Some teachers have a strong gift of encouragement as they speak, but mostly this is used person to person or in much smaller groups. The key thing to understand is that exhortation is a person-centered gift over all.

There is a great example of this gift in Scripture: *"Joseph, a Levite from Cyprus, whom the apostles called Barnabas (which means 'son of encouragement')"* (Acts 4: 36). Not only did Barnabas have the gift of giving but a very strong gift of encouragement. Think about his life. He was the one who, when Paul became a Christian, mentored him, encouraged him, and introduced him to the church leadership, the very leaders Paul had previously been fanatical about trying to kill. Barnabas was one of the first to accept non-Jewish believers and went to bat for them over how many of the Jewish traditions and laws the new Gentile Christians would have to adopt. He stayed a year in Antioch where followers of Jesus were first called Christians. He also understood his role was encouragement and exhortation and also knew that this is a key supportive gift in the grouping of gifts. You can see this in Acts when it says that Barnabas and Paul led the first missionary journey; but by the second journey, the names are reversed. We again can see a strong example of gift tension when Paul and Barabbas had a disagreement over a young emerging leader called John Mark, who had travelled with them on an earlier mission outreach but dropped out during the trip, irritating Paul. Luke tells us that once the men were all back in Antioch, the stage was set:

Some time later Paul said to Barnabas, "Let us go back and visit the believers in all the towns where we preached the word of the Lord and see how they are doing." Barnabas wanted to take John, also called Mark, with them, but Paul did not think it wise to take him, because he had deserted them in Pamphylia and had not continued with them in the work. They had such a sharp disagreement that they parted company. Barnabas took Mark and sailed for Cyprus, but Paul chose Silas and left, commended by the believers to the grace of the Lord. He went through Syria and Cilicia, strengthening the churches (Acts 15: 36-41).

I really love this honest history. But notice that this conflict was partially a gifting show down. Do we realize if Barnabas had not used his gift of encouragement, we might be missing half the New Testament books? Through his advocacy for Mark, he brought forward someone who would go on to write of one of the four Gospels, possibly the first one written. Through his cultivation of Paul, he encouraged the writer of 13 epistles. Here is something remarkable: Barnabas never wrote a book that found its way into the sacred canon, but he encouraged two men who between them wrote 14 books, over half of the 27 New Testament volumes. How much we owe this self-effacing exhorter![8]

Can you see the power of encouragement and exhortation? It does not take center stage but with God's influence ripples through lives, ministry and into eternity. Is this you, do you have this gift? If so, in Paul's words, *"If it is to encourage, then give encouragement!"* (Romans 12:8).

Apostleship

The last word gift we will examine in this chapter is the gift called apostleship. This can be a difficult discussion because this term is used for an office as well as a gift. The office of apostle is similar to elder or deacon, but was a special position Jesus gave only to a few that does not exist today.

Those with the original office of Apostle were the 12 plus Paul and they had the same authority as Old Testament prophets. They could speak and write Scripture. They had been with Jesus since the beginning and they had a personal call from Jesus Himself. They were witnesses to Jesus' resurrection, and they laid down the teaching foundation of the Church, not only recording Jesus' life and ministry in the Gospels, but faithfully following all the Holy Spirit wanted recorded in writing the rest of the New Testament as part of God's Word. This was a clearly defined and limited group from the start:

Then the apostles returned to Jerusalem from the hill called the Mount of Olives, a Sabbath day's walk from the city… Those present were Peter, John, James and Andrew; Philip and Thomas, Bartholomew and Matthew; James son of Alphaeus and Simon the Zealot, and Judas son of James. They all joined together constantly in prayer, along with the women and Mary the mother of Jesus, and with his brothers (Acts 1:12, 13b-14).

Because of the strong association between the twelve tribes of Israel and the original twelve disciples called by Jesus, the apostles took steps to complete their number following Jesus' resurrection:

Therefore it is necessary to choose one of the men who have been with us the whole time the Lord Jesus was living among us, beginning from John's baptism to the time when Jesus was taken up from us. For one of these must become a witness with us of his resurrection (Acts 1:21-22).

As you can see, there are the criteria for what I call "capital A" Apostles. We have these 12 plus Paul, yet as you read the New Testament, there are many others who are also called apostles but do not meet the requirements for the office of Apostle. They have the gift of apostleship. Timothy, Silas, Barnabas, Andronicus, and Junia are examples of those that had this gift. So the original office is finished but this gift remains very much alive today in the church of Jesus Christ.

It's worth remembering that the Greek term *apostolos* was a common term before it became an office in the early church. The word meant *messenger* or *envoy*—someone sent to represent another. You can be a gifted messenger today without claiming in any way some kind of equal standing with the original Apostles Jesus chose.

Many say that this gift is a God-given ability to create new ministries. This could be church planting, cross-cultural missions, or starting a parachurch ministry. Let's look at an example from history, the ministries of contemporaries John Wesley and George Whitefield. Yet while Wesley left behind a self-propagating church that has spread around the world, little evidence is left of the amazing impact Whitefield had. Wesley, among his gifts, probably had an apostolic gift while Whitefield had the gift of evangelism. Whitefield himself came to the end of life wishing he had taken more time, as Wesley did, to create for his followers some kind of structure that would carry them beyond his own life.

In discussing this gift, J. Robert Clinton emphasizes that the nature and purpose of apostleship requires a special kind of authority from God.[9] A person with this gifting is usually recognized by a local church and released to a new pioneering work. The gift can be experienced within one's own culture or in a cross-cultural setting. Traditionally, the apostolic gift has been associated with missionary work because the pioneering aspect was easy to see. However, all who serve as missionaries certainly don't have this gift, nor is its use restricted to cross-cultural settings.

One other nuance of gifts is that they sometimes have the same root but can be expressed in different ways and in different settings. I came across this very different idea about this gift from the pen of Peter Wagner:

The gift of apostle is the special ability that God gives to certain members of the Body of Christ, which enables them to assume and exercise general leadership over a number of churches with an extraordinary authority in spiritual matters that is <u>spontaneously recognized and appreciated</u> by those churches.[10]

The gift of apostleship is rooted in the idea of being given unusual authority, being sent or commissioned by Jesus, and having it affirmed in community. This gift could be transcultural; it could include missionaries, church planters, those called to start new ministries, or those with profound spiritual influence beyond their own ministry context. You could call the role today a bishop without title. Here is the best summary I found:

In the broader sense an apostle is one *sent, commissioned,* and therefore is not affixed to a particular location or church. Such an apostle operates in trans-local manner, but does not operate independently. He or she is church-based, representing a particular church, but ministering largely in a field beyond. *Such apostles are always essential to the life of a church that realizes its call to reach out beyond itself in the mission of the gospel.*[11]

And I would add from personal observation that this one form of the gift generates an unnatural respect and authority to speak and to influence other churches or Christian organizations even without title or formal influence in those circles. It never comes from manipulation, pride, or selling yourself. As you progress in ministry over time you may say quietly to yourself, *how in the world did I end up here, speaking or encouraging to this group of leaders or churches?*

Could this be you? Teaching, exhortation, and apostleship are three of the word-oriented gifts of the Holy Spirit. I've tried to offer a triangulated group to show you the different extremes of the word gifts: Teaching as a role that informs, trains, prepares, disciples, and equips; exhortation as a coming alongside with encouragement as well confrontation if necessary, a gift that touches on the internal life of other followers of Jesus; and apostleship which is a pure leadership and expansion gift, pushing boundaries and overcoming obstacles as the Church continues its God-given work under the Great Commission.

As you think about these gifts, allow me to remind you that humility should always be part of any effort we make to identify and employ our spiritual gifts. You should be able to say of any gift, "I would like this gift but am willing to hear the Holy Spirit say 'No, that's not part of the gift I gave you.'"

These public gifts will highlight the matter of character. The spiritual gifts do not shield you from your human capacity for sin; your constant dependence must be on the Lord, open to correction and ready with repentance even as you serve. Among the temptations we all face is the lure of bitterness over not having the gifts others have been given. This response not only reveals lack of trust in God to always do what's best for us and for His plans, but also shows we don't understand the weight that comes with other gifts. Given the struggles we have with selfish uses of the gifts we *have been* given, it becomes clear that our allotment of spiritual giftedness is exactly what we can handle—and only with God's help.

As we continue to explore these spiritual gifts, seek to maintain a disciples' attitude: attentiveness combined with readiness. An authentic disciple says,

"Show me, Lord where to go and that's where I'll go. Reveal to me the gifts You have given and I will use them for Your glory." God wants to be glorified in and through you, just as He was through Jesus.

Chapter Eight:
Spiritual Gifts– The Word Category, Part Two

In this chapter we continue our survey of the spiritual gifts that generally fall into the category of Word Gifts. For much of my life within the church, the word gifts were the only ones readily described as spiritual gifts. The love gifts were talked about as little more than emotional preferences that could almost be exercised by any Christian without the weight of it being a spiritual gift. To a degree this makes sense if we realize that many of the tasks addressed by the spiritual gifts in the Bible are tasks also charged to the Church at large. "We're all supposed to practice mercy," I was told, "why would there be a separate spiritual gift for that purpose?" Meanwhile, the power gifts, when mentioned at all, were described with suspicion as rarely real today, or more likely as gifts that had only been present in the church during the apostolic age and put out of commission once the New Testament was in place.

It always bothered me a little that the various lists of gifts in the New Testament, while not identical, listed love, word, and power gifts together without differentiating any of them as merely temporary while others were to be considered permanent. The kind of selective elimination seemed to be based more on discomfort with certain gifts than on a clear biblical reason for their absence as options the Holy Spirit would choose in equipping believers. Note the way our first word gift for this chapter is imbedded in a list of love gifts:

If it is to encourage, then give encouragement; if it is giving, then give generously; if it is to lead, do it diligently; if it is to show mercy, do it cheerfully (Romans 12:8).

Leadership/Ruling

When we think of a term like *leadership*, our first challenge is to set aside our understanding of the word outside the Church. Our Lord and model Jesus made it very clear that leadership among His followers was to be distinctly different from those called leaders in the world:

Jesus called them together and said, "You know that those who are regarded as rulers of the Gentiles lord it over them, and their high officials exercise authority over them. Not so with you. Instead, whoever wants to become great among you must be your servant, and whoever wants to be first must be slave of all. For even the Son of Man did not come to be served, but to serve, and to give his life as a ransom for many" (Mark 10:42-45).

In our exploration of the spiritual gifts at Sanctus we've spent a lot of time on the gift of leadership because we wanted first to understand the biblical picture and adjust our expectations, because our church had functioned with a certain understanding of leadership that created tension when we tried to bring other yet-unused gifts on line. One of the matters we had to grapple with is the fact that the gift of leadership or ruling is not the same as the gift of administration. Leadership is all about *what* and the *where*, not the *how*. It is vision, not implementation. Remember when we talked about administration among the love gifts? Those with the gift of administration generally will not be spiritually gifted leaders. Administration is a second chair gift; it's a supportive gift that works alongside the leadership gift that we are talking about here. The gift of leadership should be central in all churches. Here are few ways others have defined the spiritual gift of leadership:

> The gift of leadership is the special ability that God gives certain members of the Body of Christ to set goals in accordance with God's purpose for the future and to communicate these goals to others in such a way that they voluntarily and harmoniously work together to accomplish these goals for the glory of God.[1]

> The divine enablement to cast vision, motivate, and direct people to harmoniously accomplish the purposes of God.[2]

Leadership is about vision; it is conceptual. There is intense focus on the destination and the big picture. Leaders are the ones to whom God speaks and tells them what the Promised Land will look like; they see the ark before it is built, they see the Temple constructed before instructions have been spoken or the site chosen. They are the ones that are given the heaven-sent *what* and *where*, but not necessarily the *how*. Notice that there must be deep personal relationship between God and those with this gift, for they must clearly hear in order to lead. Without this hearing, vision becomes something other than heaven-sent, a good vision that bears little fruit.

Here is the first discovery moment in understanding the spiritual gift of leadership, and it's key for churches seeking a deeper application of the reality of spiritual gifts in their life together. Many people who have the gift of leadership also have the title or office of pastor, yet do not necessarily have the gift of pastor or shepherd. You may have to read that twice! This is so important for a church to understand because often leaders as well as congregations often suffer and are frustrated due to wrong expectations and longstanding traditions that have not necessarily given us the most biblical format for church organization. I'll use myself as an example since my situation applies to this gift. I, Jon Thompson, have the spiritual gift of leadership and I have the title of pastor but I do not have, nor have I ever had, the gift of being a shepherd. Don't miss the humor in the fact that my office "pastor" is actually the transliterated Latin word for "shepherd", yet my role is not a direct expression of my gift. Part of exercising my leadership gift is to see that the shepherding needs of those I lead are met. When people see this gift they often jump to the idea that it is synonymous with pastoring, but it's not.

During the first season when I taught our church extensively on the subject of gifts, I stood up one Sunday and announced, "I have a confession to make to all of you." That got their attention and silence suddenly reigned in the auditorium. I said, "Let me start over. My name is Jon Thompson, and I'm one of your pastors, though I must admit that I don't actually have the spiritual gift of pastoring." They were clearly shocked and puzzled. I continued, "What I mean is that I don't have the spiritual gift of shepherding as Scripture describes it; one of my primary gifts is leadership. In the context of all these gifts we are learning about, it's important to know what gifts someone actually has so you won't expect them to deliver in areas where they are not gifted. I'll never be a shepherd. If you want a shepherd, you may need to leave. If I visit you in the hospital, you are probably dying. If you expect me to be your shepherd, you will be disappointed. But here's the good news: there are hundreds of shepherds/pastors in this congregation!"

The fact is that we use the title Pastor as an umbrella term for a number of leadership roles in the body of Christ, and no one person can perform them all. No wonder so many pastors get into horrendous situations trying to live up to superhuman expectations, many of which they are not even gifted to do. In our church, I deeply appreciate those with shepherding gifts and am honored and delighted to lead them, because that's my gift. To get the flavor of this, think of Moses as God's visionary leader for the people, while Aaron was gifted as a pastor.

In my own interactions with young potential pastors or leaders, I often say that I lead more like Moses than I do like Jesus (which understandably makes them a little nervous). But I further explain that Moses led a movement; Jesus birthed one. Moses took over an enslaved and impoverished mega-church and led them out of captivity; Jesus called twelve men and prepared them to launch a movement that would transform the world. Jesus walked with and among His disciples; Moses walked in front of them.

As is often the case today, the average growing church may have a large percentage of members who come from very different church backgrounds, each with its own culture and worldview. If we are not monitoring the causes of our expectations, we will be in danger of disappointment and frustration when our present church doesn't deliver. If your expectations are coming from what you had in another church or what you think a pastor should be, you are being culturally driven but not necessarily biblically driven. This is why we must see people's work and participation in church through a gifting lens. Here is what Peter Wagner wrote about this matter which should send up a huge flag for many about the way they see their church now and where they assume it is going:

Many leaders dislike administration, so they make sure they have delegated that responsibility to someone who has a different gift-mix. Lyle Schaller likens skillful pastors of growing churches to "ranchers" rather than "shepherds." Ranchers make sure that their different flocks and herds get the attention they need, and they get others to do it. They take little personal interest in the problems of the individual sheep. Pastors who prefer the shepherd model will have to content themselves with small churches, and this may well be God's will for them. In them, their role of leadership will suffice without a special gift. On the other hand those who can fit into the rancher model have much greater possibilities for growth. They are likely to have the gift of leadership. God loves both shepherds and ranchers.[3]

The average church includes a number of shepherds-in-waiting, seldom encouraged to engage their gifts. But it is biblically unwise to impose what you want staff to be without looking at them and yourself through gifts. I have the gift of leadership, I love my church, and I do care for the members, but my God-given role there is to lead the whole church. This means I'm called to delegate, to pray, to preach, and to give vision. And part of the vision I see for my church is that in order to get "better at smaller" even as we grow bigger, there is going to have to be a pastoral gift revolution for many of our people, for God is calling them to shepherd each other. We will get to that in a moment.

Does this gift resonate with your experience? In what ways have you seen God work on developing your character so that your efforts to provide leadership are based on a pattern of integrity others have noted? Is there evidence in your life that you can lead from a God-glorifying Jesus- empowered place? Have you been given a vision by Jesus, or promises that you have been compelled to pray back to God?

Shepherding/Pastoring

With a fresh understanding of the gift of leadership, we are now in a better place to consider the gift shepherd or pastor. One of the strongest passages that can help us understand this gift comes from the book of Ephesians:

So Christ himself gave the apostles, the prophets, the evangelists, the pastors and teachers, to equip his people for works of service, so that the body of Christ may be built up (Eph. 4: 11-12).

Here are some helpful, different definitions that have been given for this gift:

The pastoral gift is the capacity to exercise <u>concern</u> and <u>care</u> for members of a group so as to encourage them in their growth in Christ, which involves modeling maturity, protecting them from error and disseminating truth.[4]

The gift of pastor is the special ability that God gives to certain members of the body of Christ to assume a <u>long-term personal responsibility</u> for the spiritual welfare of a group of believers.[5]

Notice words like *concern, care, model, personal responsibility*, and *welfare*. They are all person-centered, relational qualities. The idea comes from tending sheep. Shepherds are sheep-centric; they look after one flock and give personal attention to each sheep. Jesus described shepherds as people willing to lay down their lives to protect the sheep. They instruct, build unity, and heal wounds. That is why, when they serve in a leadership role, they generally lead a smaller church or small group of people. God's heart, their personalized care, and their concern for a particular group or individual to grow in Christ is more important to them than casting vision for a large group of people. In other words, the pastoral gift focuses on a limited number of people, while the leadership gift can expand to encompass a large and growing group. The pastoral gift is not a lesser gift, but uniquely needed, powerful, and significant in the Body. The effectiveness of leadership is in fact often dependent on a foundation of effective shepherding/pastoral gift people who take care of detailed needs within the body that a leader has neither the time nor the gifting to address. The larger the church, the more significant the ministry of pastors to the smaller communities that make up the whole.

Did you also notice in Ephesians 4 that teaching and pastoring could be connected? Many pastors are teachers and part of caring is teaching truth, living truth, and correcting error. When these two gifts work in tandem, they are powerful. This is because teachers are content-oriented and less focused on relationship. Pastors are highly relationship-oriented, though these two aren't necessarily mutually exclusive.

The key idea of shepherding is people, and their spiritual care, which can take the form of teaching, pastoral care, and presence. Exercising a pastoral gift is the long-term journey with people so they can just be loved through life. As one of our former care pastors used to say, "I just want people to know Jesus, to really love Him, to follow after Him in everyday life. I just want to help them to do this well and over the long haul!"[6] I hope you can hear in him the cry of a shepherd.

Others have done considerable thinking about this gift, particularly examining the extent or territory that usually goes with the gift of shepherding. One author wrote that a person who is part-time or a volunteer with this gift could usually shepherd about 8 to 15 families, tops. A staff member who has the gift in a full time role can usually shepherd 50 to100 families.[7] As I continue to have conversations with pastors and denominational heads about growth and revitalization, I've noticed that one of the elephants in the room is that most churches are led by and most seminaries and Bible colleges are training–pastor/teachers and shepherds, not leaders.

In our context at Sanctus, as well as the context of many other large and growing churches, the gift of pastoring is one of the most needed gifts at this point in Church history. I think it's fair to say that most of the largest churches on our continent are led by very able teachers of the Word with amazing leadership skills. Many of them seem like "bigger than life" people. But all of them have a shelf life. And what happens to a large church when a gifted leader leaves or comes to the end of his career is often indicative of the way other gifts have been used in that church alongside the leader's gifts. If those attending are led to believe that their primary source of ministry comes from the pulpit, not only will their personal spiritual growth be anemic, they will also feel little need to be involved in significant ministry themselves. We need people with the gift of pastoring in place for about every ten families in church!

One of the biggest expressions of pastoral gift ministry is the health and function of small groups within the church. Whether or not your church decides to call the small group leaders pastors, the gift of shepherding/ pastoring should be the gift of those who lead your small groups. This would also mean that for every ten or so small groups there ought to be a pastor assigned to shepherd the small group pastors. Everyone in the body should be in a place where their gifts benefit the church, and where they can also receive benefits from the church.

So we can see that those with this gift gravitate toward caring for a small group of people over time. Shepherds come alongside with practical actions and pointed prayer. They teach and lead, but in a smaller setting. This gift is people-centered, not vision-centered or even administrative; it is about discipleship, it can be used with teaching or other gifts but is not the gift of leadership. Are you a pastor? Are you called to be a shepherd?

Evangelism

This gift is another amazing, powerful, often misunderstood, but greatly needed gift: the gift of evangelism. The point we've made with the other gifts remains true; we are all called to talk about Jesus and give the good news to others, but this is more. The Holy Spirit does gift certain believers with a unique ability to present the gospel in a compelling way. This underscores the fact that all the spiritual gifts have an evangelistic component. They are all meant to lift

Jesus up and draw all people to him. They bring glory to God and pave the way for men and women to turn to Him.

At our church, one component of our vision was developed with the gift of evangelism in mind. Here is how we stated it: *To become a regional church of 10,000 meeting the physical, emotional and spiritual needs of people in Jesus' name.* We will definitely need some evangelists to introduce others to Christ as Savior and Lord if this vision is to be fulfilled.

This gift is specifically mentioned only three times in the New Testament:

So Christ himself gave the apostles, the prophets, the evangelists, the pastors and teachers, to equip his people for works of service, so that the body of Christ may be built up (Eph. 4: 11-12).

But you, keep your head in all situations, endure hardship, do the work of an evangelist, and discharge all the duties of your ministry (2 Timothy 4:5).

Leaving the next day, we reached Caesarea and stayed at the house of Philip the evangelist, one of the Seven (Acts 21:8).

The background of this gift is fleshed out all the way back in Acts 8:4-8 and 34-35:

Those who had been scattered preached the word wherever they went. Philip went down to a city in Samaria and proclaimed the Messiah there. When the crowds heard Philip and saw the signs he performed, they all paid close attention to what he said. For with shrieks, impure spirits came out of many, and many who were paralyzed or lame were healed. So there was great joy in that city... The eunuch asked Philip, "Tell me, please, who is the prophet talking about, himself or someone else?" Then Philip began with that very passage of Scripture and told him the good news about Jesus.

Like all gifts, you will know over time if you have this gift because when you function in it, there will be joy and results. Here are two definitions for this gift:

Evangelism is the special ability to communicate the Gospel message in relevant ways to unbelievers.[8]

The gift of evangelism in general refers to the capacity to challenge people through various communicative methods (persuasion) to receive the Gospel of salvation m Christ so as to see them respond by taking initial steps in Christian discipleship.[9]

Now that second definition brings out something very important for us. Evangelism is not just about presence but is verbal proclamation. This is a speaking or a word gift.

The famous statement attributed to St. Francis Assisi "Preach the Gospel always, and if necessary, use words," is a powerful and needed call for all of us to live an authentic Jesus-filled life. It's a call to love unconditionally in Jesus' name, giving food, water, support, counseling, benevolence, etc. It is why we say that our purpose is to meet the physical, emotional, and spiritual needs of people. But this is not giving the good news. It may lead to such proclamation and include such proclamation, but it doesn't substitute for the actual proclamation of the gospel.

No one is saved simply by living a godly life. People are saved when they hear the good news through preaching, signs and wonders, or a personal conversation to which they respond with faith. The gospel is not only lived, it must be given! Our good works, our compassion for those in need, is mercy that can open the door to what must come next. It prepares, authenticates, and creates space in the heart, but Jesus and His work must be proclaimed. It is not an either/or; it is a both/and; presence and proclamation lead to the fulfillment of the promise. Never forget that throughout the world many help and many give money, time, and food without intending or managing to bring anyone to salvation. NGO's, governments, movie stars, and organizations from other faiths are all generous sources of immediate and tangible help but those efforts do not bring salvation. Evangelism is the giving of one thing, the good news of God through Jesus by the power of the Holy Spirit. As Leslie Flynn wrote,

> The word gospel comes from two Greek words, *well* (or *good*) and
> *announcement.* Thus the Gospel is a *beneficial announcement* or *Good
> News.* The gift of evangelism involves proclaiming the Good News with
> usual power.

But what exactly is the good news? It is the thrilling report of something that happened historically, which can bring unsearchable riches presently. Because the Lord Jesus Christ, who is fully God and fully man, died for my sins on the cross over 19 centuries ago, was buried and rose the third day, God the Father can accept his Son's sacrifice as full satisfaction for my guilt. If I reach by faith to receive Christ as my personal Savior, God, declares me righteous not through anything that I do but through the merits, the work, the ability, through the credit of Christ's shed blood. No longer exposed to the penalty of the broken Law, I become a child of God. I am forgiven; I am in good standing with God because of Jesus alone; I am adopted into his family. And as I come to understand more of the good news' implications, I experience real joy for my past, strength for the present (through the ministry of the regenerating and indwelling Spirit), and a living hope for the future. This is indeed Good News.[10]

Simply put, Jesus is where shame and grace collided and through whom God has said to a really messed up world and to you personally, "It's not too late, this is not all that life has to offer. I bring you good news of great joy for all people. Today a Savior has been born who is Christ, the Lord!"

There is one more thing we must highlight here so all of us will be empowered, both those with this gift and the rest of us who must witness but do not have this gift. One author put this in a very hope-filled and truth-filled way:

First, Christians who have the gift of evangelism and who are not using their gift should be made to feel a responsibility for using it. Second, the 90 percent who have gifts other than that of evangelist should not be allowed to feel guilty if they assume secondary roles in the evangelistic process. This is where God intended them to be, or he would have given them the gift of evangelist. In some evangelical churches the guilt trip for not evangelizing is so severe that when the 10 percent do evangelize and bring new people into the church, the converts are turned off by what they find. The general tone of the body, the negative self- image of the members, the gloom and defeatism that can be felt in the atmosphere of the church, makes them think that everybody must have been baptized in vinegar! They quickly decide that they want no part of a crowd like that and soon vanish, unnoticed, out the back door.[11]

These are certainly sobering words, though I might not go so far as to call the other gifts "secondary roles in the evangelistic process." Here's the truth: the Holy Spirit has the only primary role in the evangelistic process. All other roles are secondary or support roles. The gift of evangelism is one essential component along with the other gifts that have their assigned place in the process. As he makes clear, if some of the other gifts don't create a welcoming and supportive community for new believers, the work of the gift of evangelism may accomplish far less than they could.

I agree with Leighton Ford, an evangelist who is willing to recognize his own evangelistic gift. While he admits that God makes certain people evangelists through spiritual gifts, he also says, "We must not use the teaching of spiritual gifts as a cop-out to avoid our responsibility to share Christ with others. You may not be called as an evangelist, but you and every Christian, by an attitude of love, by compassionate concern, and by well- chosen words, can have the privilege to lead others ... toward Jesus Christ."[12] When Jesus gave His great commission to the disciples in Matthew 28, He was not declaring they now all had the gift of evangelism; He was making it clear that all His followers were to see themselves as part of God's grand work of making disciples everywhere. Not all of us are gifted to evangelize but all of us are gifted to be part of the evangelistic enterprise.

This understanding of gift roles helps some of us deal with an unspoken crisis of faith. Many of us are painfully aware of family and friends who have not become Christians. Over time, our failures to share the gospel with them or even attempts that failed may cause doubt to take root in the dark parts of our soul. We begin to think, *was I lacking faith? Is the message about Jesus true? What am I doing wrong? I am a failure before the church and God!* This seed grows into a vine that squeezes faith, brings the fruit of disappointment, and even causes many to wither away.

But bring this real problem into a healthy, functioning body of Christ and a sense of hope in God's working rises. The gift of evangelism isn't a "solo" gift that works in isolation from others. The body as a whole is commissioned to spread the Gospel. Like Paul's picture in 1 Corinthians 3, the world is a farm and all of us have certain chores to do: some plant, others water, and others weed. God brings the increase and harvest. And just as we all share responsibility for our commission to evangelize, we all can rejoice as we see people set free from sin as we all use our gifts. God says to the many not gifted with evangelism that He is pleased by a faithful life, and our attempts to tell others. The more we do it, the more often we see God use those efforts. So let Jesus take the guilt, the shame, and set you free from the burden of another's role or destiny. God calls and evangelists are His hands and feet to bring in the ones He will raise to life.

To those He has gifted as evangelists, God says "Stand, be empowered, the cries of the 10,000 and beyond are being heard and they are waiting. Be my voice." Some will express this gift publically and others privately. It may be the grand declaration of C.T. Studd that expresses your heart cry; "Some want to live within the sound of church or chapel bell; I want to run a rescue shop within a yard from hell!"

Here are some common characteristics of this gift: You have the ability to talk before groups of people and easily converse with strangers, an intense concern over the thought of people being unsaved and eternally un-reconciled to God, the ability to insert spiritual truth in normal conversation with the unsaved, a freedom and joy in talking about Christian things naturally in an unforced way. You most likely have this gift if it is apparent that unsaved people with whom you have contact often pursue and ask what Christianity is all about. You have no other way to explain the fact that unsaved people actually make discipleship commitments as a direct or indirect result of your influence. You feel led to pray often for unsaved people by name, in fact, your intercessory prayer time focuses on unsaved groups of people. You will speak in an authoritative way publically or privately the message of Jesus concerning salvation. Also for some, the evangelism gift combined with a leadership gift can lead others to evangelism.[13]

Peter is a great example of this gift. What happened when he told many about Jesus the Christ? As the Spirit-filled believers who were praising God in languages they didn't know but people recognized as their own, the crowd began to murmur that they must all be drunk! Peter stood up, made a joke (Drunk? It's too early in the day!), and immediately moved into a powerful presentation of the gospel. Note that he didn't end with an invitation but a challenge: *"Therefore let all Israel be assured of this: God has made this Jesus, whom you crucified, both Lord and Messiah"* (Acts 2:36). What follows is a classic example of the Holy Spirit driving home the gift of evangelism, *"When the people heard this, they were cut to the heart and said to Peter and the other apostles, 'Brothers, what shall we do?'"* (Acts 2:37).

I wouldn't diminish the gift of evangelism that Billy Graham, Tim Keller, and Ravi Zacharias have exercised for longer than my lifetime, but it would be a serious mistake to think that they are the prototypes of the typical person chosen by the Holy Spirit for a gift of evangelism. This gift is far more often practiced in one-on-one conversations. If you find real joy in a simple conversation in which you share what Jesus has done for you, giving someone the opportunity to know Him, you may well have this gift. And if you have an insatiable desire to articulate the intellectual validity of the faith to unbelievers, you probably have this gift, too.

Let me tell you a story from the Connect small group I've been part of for about twelve years. At one point we were talking about gifts and a friend of mine said, "To tell the truth, I don't know if I even have a gift." The group responded immediately, "Well, that can't be true because the Bible is pretty clear about it." But he said, "I sure don't know what it is." There was a moment while we all looked at each other, then we burst out laughing. Misreading the situation he said, "Wow, this is a really unfriendly group! I'm dying here... Why are you laughing?" It took a moment to compose ourselves because we all knew what gift he had. I said, "Steve, every time you come to group, what do you talk about when we share concerns and pray?" He thought for a moment and then said, "Well I guess I usually come with a few people in mind that I think we should be praying for." So I said, "And what do all those people have in common?" And the light started to dawn as he answered, "I've got all these people on my mind who haven't found out about Jesus yet and I long to see that happen." "Where do those names come from, Steve?" "Well, at work and through my days I keep running into people I have great conversations with and usually end up realizing when I bring up Jesus that they don't know him yet." We all said, "Exactly. You feel called to spread the good news in a natural and persistent way. The rest of us have to be intentional; you just do it all the time." He simply had the wrong idea of what that gift looks like. Let me add this warning. Don't assume that you can't have the gift of evangelism unless everyone you talk to immediately decides to turn to Christ. That's also a wrong expectation. It's not ultimately about the reception; it's about telling the good news and finding real joy and freedom in that.

We all need to do it, but you may be among those who are gifted with evangelism, even infected with the need to share about Jesus with people around you. Is that you?

These are the Spiritual Word gifts, using speech and audible communication to convey God's message. Can you identify people in your group with this gift? Are you all chuckling over the one person in the group who has this gift written all over them because they are always fervent in bringing in the gospel to every conversation? Continue to encourage each other. Learn from those who evangelize naturally. Remember that we're all connected and the gifts are given to help us function in interdependence.

Chapter Nine:
Spiritual Gifts– The Power Category, Part 1

My hope and prayer is that you are developing a new understanding or deepening sense of how God has made each one of us and uniquely equipped each of us to serve a broken and dark world. Convergence recognizes that we are part of what God is accomplishing throughout history. This is our painfully short moment as part of his plan, and we ought to do all we can to be available for God to use. Part of the good news is that God's Spirit has actually gifted us to be useful. We don't have to generate in ourselves something to offer the rest of the Church or the world; God has given us (or will give us) what we need.

I find it valuable to continually review for my own purposes as well as for your benefit the basic breakdown we find in the gifts of the Holy Spirit for those who are in Christ. Love Gifts manifest the love of God in practical ways, Word Gifts clarify the nature, action and purposes of God, and Power Gifts demonstrate the power, presence and reality of God. In one important sense all the gifts of the Holy Spirit are power gifts. There is certainly spiritual power exercised in the love gifts and the word gifts. We might think of this third category as Working Gifts, but in the interests of reminding us that God is behind these gifts, we will continue to categorize them as power gifts.

Remember that the power gifts are the evidence of God's power in the moment to prove and demonstrate that God is actually alive and active among us. These include the gifts of tongues, interpretation of tongues, intercession, faith, discernment, healing, works of power, and words of wisdom. If you're keeping track, I know this list combined with the ones in the previous chapters, only totals 20 gifts rather than the 21 I've mentioned several times. The twenty-first gift is really a category that might be called "Others," including gifts like Chastity that does not appear in the traditional lists. Or it is "indefinable," a unique combination of many gift characteristics that it takes on a character all its own and is difficult to categorize as a mixture of known gifts or a specific gifting of God's Spirit. As we begin our study of the power gifts, some readers are cheering inside (*Finally!*), while others are thinking, *Oh no—not one of those churches with all the crazy stuff going on!* Plus, given the increasing number of people in our culture being raised in complete isolation from the Church, some might simply be wondering, *what are you talking about?* Depending on your background, you might think this drifts into cult territory where all manner of strange behavior can be expected. But don't worry. We won't go beyond what biblically motivated and directed believers have done century after century. God is up to what he's always been up to, and much of what seems strange to us is simply unfamiliar rather than truly off track. You have the opportunity to check everything I claim against what the Bible says and confirm for yourself whether we are detouring into error or following in the steps of countless other people of God who have been led to trust and obey Him even when the going was unfamiliar.

I need to say this again, no matter who you are; as you review these gifts, try to lay down your ideas, your hopes, your history, theology, expectations, fears, your controls, and embarrassments. Lay down the good and bad experiences you have had in other places and let the Scriptures lead you. Remember, we're having this conversation because we need churches to do more than just survive—we want them to thrive in the years to come. Jesus and the early church used these gifts with profound effectiveness and they not only provided ongoing hope for the church but also opened the doors of faith for the lost.

Prophecy

There's a lot of misunderstanding about the gift of Prophecy. It's found in Ephesians 4:11, 1 Corinthians 12:28-29 and 14:1-40, Romans 12:6, and 1 Thessalonians 5:19-22.

First, prophecy and teaching are quite different as gifts. Prophecy fits among the power gifts while teaching is a word gift. The gift of prophecy is exercised when someone, usually in a congregation or large gathering, has the capacity to deliver truth of a predictive nature or a situational word from God. The result is to exhort the community, edify or comfort believers, or convince non-believers of God's truth.[1] It's not the result of careful Bible study and preparation, but a message from the Holy Spirit given to an individual with this gift.

As our church struggled to address the logistics and reality of exercising this gift in a setting as large as ours, there were reasonable questions. Given the existence of such a gift, do we simply invite people to stand within our congregation and give a Scripture, a word, or an image that would serve a prophetic purpose? Does this balance the need for recognizing and allowing the gift to be exercised while testing prophesies and maintaining order in a church service? Is there a way to do both?

So we bought a cell phone. We jokingly call it "the prophecy phone," but there's definitely a serious side to what we're doing. At the beginning of a worship service we often make it a point to announce: Does anyone have a word, an image, or a Scripture that you believe is for the entire community? We encourage them to text it in to that dedicated phone. Several in our congregation who have the gift of discernment and know the Scriptures collect and read the texts and decide together which ones should be shared with everyone and which ones should remain unshared, because the Scriptures instruct us to test prophecy to make sure what is good. That's why, while teaching or preaching is often described as prophecy, (particularly by those who seem inclined to leave the power gifts locked up in the early church), the gift of prophecy may use Scripture (and will never contradict Scripture), but prophetic utterances are most often mixed, since they are situational and address immediate circumstances or needs with a message prompted by God's Spirit. Remember Agabus in Acts 21? When he prophesied he only got some of the story right:

Leaving the next day, we reached Caesarea and stayed at the house of Philip the evangelist, one of the Seven. He had four unmarried daughters who prophesied. After we had been there a number of days, a prophet named Agabus came down from Judea. Coming over to us, he took Paul's belt, tied his own hands and feet with it and said, "The Holy Spirit says, 'In this way the Jewish leaders in Jerusalem will bind the owner of this belt and will hand him over to the Gentiles'" (Acts 21:8-11).

Agabus was a man gifted by God; he was the real deal and he had the gift of prophecy. Yet this example helps us all understand the role of this gift and see where it can go wrong. He actually got two thirds right and one third wrong. Listen to what one scholar wrote about this prophecy that was nearly correct:

If one reads on in Acts we find that the Romans, not the Jews, bound Paul (v. 33; also 22:29), and the Jews, rather than delivering him voluntarily, tried to kill him and Paul had to be rescued by force (v. 32). The prediction was not far off, but it had inaccuracies in detail that would have called into question the validity of any Old Testament prophet. On the other hand, this text could be perfectly well explained by supposing that Agabus had had a vision of Paul as a prisoner of the Romans in Jerusalem, surrounded by an angry mob of Jews. His own interpretation of such a "vision" or "revelation" from the Holy Spirit would be that the Jews had bound Paul and handed him over to the Romans, and that is what Agabus would (somewhat erroneously) prophesy. This is exactly the kind of fallible prophecy that would fit the definition of New Testament congregational prophecy proposed above-reporting in one's own words something that God has spontaneously brought to mind.[2]

We start by accepting that there will be mistakes and personal agendas that mix in with God utterances. That's why Paul wrote in 1 Thessalonians 5: 20, _"Do not treat prophecies with contempt but test them all; hold on to what is good."_

Prophecy needs testing with Scripture and other gifts to see what is of God. This biblical perspective has brought such balance and humility to the use of gifts in our church. When we share with someone the part that was wrong, they now say, "Thanks; I expect to be wrong sometimes. I know I don't get it quite right every time." It removes wrong pressure and promotes interdependence and submission to leadership.

What we have found, amazingly, is that God has often given a word or a group of words through prophecy in our community that have affirmed what was about to be preached, convicted someone of sin, or singled out an individual in our church with a message of immediate value. There is any number of ways to make room for the gift of prophecy to be practiced well (which are often refined in experience), but Scripture makes it clear that we should not negate or ignore prophecy, but test it.

Tongues

Let's start with some definitions for the gifts of tongues and interpretations of tongues written by others. Bruce Bugbee wrote that this gift allows one to "speak, worship, or pray in a language unknown to the speaker."[3] Because tongues and interpretation work in tandem, here's a definition for the gift of making unintelligible tongues useful within the body through spiritual translation: "The ability to spontaneously respond to a giving of an authoritative message in tongues by interpreting this word and clearly communicating the message given."[4]

This gift has caused a lot of controversy at times and through out history. But it's there in the text quite prominently, and those who want to pull it out and segregate it with a few other gifts as having been appropriate in the days of the apostles and before the completion of the New Testament, but are no longer necessary or particularly wanted, sometimes violate their correct high view of Scripture by treating gifts like this one as somehow less than the jot and tittle Jesus said would not pass away from the Word. And, as 1 Corinthians 13 says, the perfect has not yet come.

The first time we see the gift of tongues present is in Acts 2, at the outpouring of the Holy Spirit and the birth of the church:

When the day of Pentecost came, they were all together in one place. Suddenly a sound like the blowing of a violent wind came from heaven and filled the whole house where they were sitting. They saw what seemed to be tongues of fire that separated and came to rest on each of them. All of them were filled with the Holy Spirit and began to speak in other tongues as the Spirit enabled them. Now there were staying in Jerusalem God-fearing Jews from every nation under heaven. When they heard this sound, a crowd came together in bewilderment, because each one heard their own language being spoken. Utterly amazed, they asked: "Aren't all these who are speaking

Galileans? Then how is it that each of us hears them in our native language? (Acts 2:18).

Five things happened simultaneously: 1) a loud and fierce wind filled the house, 2) what appeared to be tongues of fire hovered over the believers, 3) they were filled with the Holy Spirit, 4) they spoke in tongues other than their own, and 5) foreigners and strangers understood what was being said by these Galileans. Luke then lists at least some of the widespread linguistic origins of the crowd (vs. 9-11a), followed by some of the crowd reactions:

"We hear them declaring the wonders of God in our own tongues!" Amazed and perplexed, they asked one another, "What does this mean?" Some, however, made fun of them and said, "They have had too much wine" (Acts 2:11b-13).

Luke includes 15 geographical areas with their unique languages. God was using these first Christians as He promised by giving them the ability to speak all at once in many languages in order to begin the process of bringing the world back to God through Jesus and His people. Do you see it? This is the reverse of the Tower of Babel where God broke our unity and fractured our human family as an act of grace to preserve those people and all of us from judgment. It's why he removed Adam and Eve from the garden so they could not eat the tree of life and be eternally lost! Now God's mission through His Spirit and the Church is to reverse Babel and create a stronger unity out of our massive diversity. Or as the Scriptures teach, in Jesus a new human family is created and the old dividing walls are now gone (cf. Ephesians 2:14-16).

In the outpouring of the Holy Spirit on Pentecost, the tongues were known languages (though not known by the speakers). The speakers unknowingly voiced praise and thanksgiving to God, and the outcome was evangelistic.

People heard about the works of God in their mother tongues, and then Peter stood up and preached (in Aramaic or Hebrew) about Jesus and His work. When he finished, 3,000 came to faith. The Gospels show us it was the pattern of Jesus' ministry to include signs and wonders followed by preaching, which brought many to repentance and faith. There are other accounts of tongues in Acts 10 and 11 and also in Acts 19:6 *"When Paul placed his hands on them, the Holy Spirit came on them, and they spoke in tongues and prophesied."*

We are trying to understand this gift today in part by studying other people's experiences in the early church. A narrative can teach us, but a narrative is not necessarily teaching. One author wrote, "In Acts, the gift of tongues was given several different times. In one case, Acts 2, the men who received the gift of tongues spoke in other recognizable dialects. In Acts 10:46, either the gift was in other recognizable dialects or Peter and his friends received the interpretation because they heard them glorifying God. In Acts 19:6, it is unclear whether the tongues were understood or not. In each of the above incidents concerning tongues, the primary purpose of the gift was to authenticate that new segments of people were being added to the church and that God was endorsing them by releasing this gift."[5] So these expressions of tongues were not anticipated. In Acts, God clearly used this gift as a sign that he was starting to connect Jews and non-Jews together in a new family called the Church. It was used to speak about Jesus, to worship God, and to express deep thanks!

We need to stop here for a moment. If you have been exposed to a variety of church experiences, you have likely encountered two major teaching approaches to the subject of tongues among those who accept the historic position that tongues, along with the rest of the spiritual gifts, remain available to the Church today. One takes the view that all and any Christian, if they ask, can have the gift of tongues. The other teaching is that all true Christians *must* speak in tongues because it is the required first sign to you and others that Jesus has moved in.

Though many good and honest Christians hold this later view, it is not rooted in the whole council of God. This teaching has broken many, and some have even doubted their salvation or felt like second-class Christians because they didn't have this gift, even though there were other very real evidences of God's presence in their lives. Some have tried so hard to make this gift a reality in their lives that they have faked speaking in tongues. This must all end right now. Because tongues are falsifiable (capable of being imitated or pretended) they can't serve as the definite test of real conversion. Jesus *didn't* say, "By this will all men know that you are my disciples, because you speak in tongues." His standard was higher and more costly (cf. John 13:35).

Both of the views about tongues we just looked at can't be right. As we have learned, God gives the gifts sovereignly and none of us are called to have all the gifts or share in one particular gift. Ephesians 4, Romans 12, and 1 Corinthians 12 all say the same thing time and time again; we share God's Spirit together, we are called to have the character of the Spirit, but He gives the gifts and we get what He chooses to give. As with the rest of the gifts, we expect that some believers will be given this gift for God's purposes. The Word of God needs to direct our thinking and teaching as well as, if necessary, correct our experience in every area of the spiritual life.

There are different kinds of gifts, but the same Spirit distributes them… Now to each one the manifestation of the Spirit is given for the common good. To one there is given through the Spirit a message of wisdom, to another a message of knowledge by means of the same Spirit, to another faith by the same Spirit, to another gifts of healing by that one Spirit, to another miraculous powers, to another prophecy, to another distinguishing between spirits, to another speaking in different kinds of tongues, and to still another the interpretation of tongues (1 Corinthians 12:7-10).

God gives the gifts and we all have different gifts. Whatever gift you do have is a sign of God's blessing and presence in your life. Don't accept the pressure to insist on a gift God Himself has not chosen to give you and do not put this expectation on others.

There is still more here that we must learn to practice as believers once we know Christ. We're not taking discipleship or sanctification seriously if we ignore the role gifts play in what God wants to do in us and through us once we are part of His Body, the Church.

I think it's important to note that Paul and Luke used different words to describe these experiences of tongues. Their variety of terms helps us understand more about this gift. The word *tongues* actually refers to several expressions, not just one thing. When Paul mentions the gift of tongues he calls it *kinds of tongues* (1 Cor. 12:10). The word *kinds* can mean offspring, family, stock, race, sort, or species. The word *tongues* (glossa) is used to describe a language. But Paul uses a figure of speech that can mean anything that is spoken by your tongue. In Acts 2, the word for *tongues* means a known or recognizable language, but Luke does not use that word in the other accounts in Acts. The word he uses describes the process of explaining something to someone who does not understand what is being said. The point is that there have in fact, always been different expressions of this gift and even Luke and Paul in their language acknowledge this.[6]

Let's go back to the crucial passage in 1 Corinthians 14. Here we get great insight into this gift as well as directions in the right and wrong uses of it. Paul is teaching the church to use these gifts correctly. Don't forget that Paul is dealing with a church that had this gift but was using it in a very wrong way. Paul's concern was for the way this gift was being misused in public worship. He clarified the use of tongues in edification, the matter of intelligibility and its limitations in expressing love. Let's walk through this passage.

"Follow the way of love and eagerly desire gifts of the Spirit, especially prophecy" (1 Corinthians 14:1). Notice how right up front, he starts with character, urging the way of love. This is clearly a continuation of 1 Corinthians 13. Gifts are amazing and God-given, but without ever-growing character they will be misused or we will be discredited even though God is at work through us.

"For anyone who speaks in a tongue does not speak to people but to God. Indeed, no one understands them; they utter mysteries by the Spirit" (v.2). We learn four things about tongues from this little verse. First, tongues involve a person speaking to God by the Holy Spirit, not to fellow Christians. Second, it is mysterious in the sense that it lays outside of our understanding. That is, neither the speaker nor the hearer knows what is being said. Third, it edifies the speaker and this is really important. This is not about ego, or being self-centered, it is about a person being built up through private praise, thanksgiving, or prayer. Let me suggest a parallel in the physical world with those who practice the discipline of running. They will agree that running can be hard, exhausting, and painful, and yet they derive a sense of well being from moving across the landscape, often alone, hour after hour. Those who watch can't understand, and the runner herself may not be able to explain exactly what happens, but may quote the well-known words of Olympic track star Eric Liddell, "When I run, I feel His pleasure." Fourth, tongues can, but don't need to be a known human language. Some argue that tongues must be a known language but let's continue reading and reflecting. Within the scope of 1 Corinthians 14, all that is said is that tongues cannot be understood. First Corinthians 13:1 makes reference to "the tongues of men or of angels," in order to underscore the point that neither is more effective than love.[7]

But there is more to be resolved in this matter. As Wayne Grudem pointed out in his writing:

Some have objected that speaking in tongues must always consist of speech in *known* human languages, since that is what happened at Pentecost. But the fact that speaking in tongues occurred in known human languages *once* in Scripture does not require that it *always* happen with known languages, especially when another description of speaking in tongues (1 Cor. 14) indicates exactly the opposite. Paul does not say that foreign visitors to Corinth will understand the speaker, but he says that when someone speaks in tongues *'no one'* will understand and the outsider will not know what the person is saying (1 Cor. 14:2, 16). In fact, Paul explicitly says that something quite the opposite of the phenomenon at Pentecost will happen in the ordinary conduct of church life. He warns that if "all speak in tongues" and "outsiders or unbelievers enter," far from understanding the message, they will say, "you are mad" (1 Cor. 14:23).[8]

He is doing what he did earlier in chapter 12 by pointing out the ludicrous idea of everyone in the Body of Christ insisting on being a certain member or claiming to function as an independent operator—an eyeball rolling down the street finally freed from the limitations of the rest of the body!

Moreover, we must realize that 1 Corinthians 14 is Paul's general instruction based on a wide experience of tongues-speaking in many different churches, whereas Acts 2 simply describes one unique event at a significant turning point in the history of redemption (Acts 2 is historical narrative while 1 Corinthians 14 is doctrinal instruction). Therefore it would seem appropriate to take 1 Corinthians 14 as the passage that most closely describes the ordinary experience of New Testament churches, and to take Paul's instructions as the standard by which God intends churches to regulate the use of this gift.[9]

Chapter 14 continues:

Anyone who speaks in a tongue edifies themselves, but the one who
prophesies edifies the church. I would like every one of you to speak in
tongues, but I would rather have you prophesy. The one who prophesies is
greater than the one who speaks in tongues, unless someone interprets, so
that the church may be edified (vv4-5).

Again this is about what's best for the church in a worship gathering. Yet,
we do learn other things about the gift of tongues. As I have mentioned, many
argue from this passage that all people can receive this gift. But 1 Corinthians
12:30 makes clear that's not true. Notice his language about tongues is "I wish, I
would like," it is not "you will, you can, or you must." His point here is that
intelligible prophecy is better and is God's will for corporate gatherings. If there
are speaking in tongues in a small group or a public worship time, then it must
be interpreted, in this example, by someone else. Don't forget that Paul allows
tongues to be publicly interpreted but he prefers prophecy. His concern is over
unintelligibility, which leads to a non-edifying environment. He continues:

Now, brothers and sisters, if I come to you and speak in tongues, what good
will I be to you, unless I bring you some revelation or knowledge or
prophecy or word of instruction? Even in the case of lifeless things that
make sounds, such as the pipe or harp, how will anyone know what tune is
being played unless there is a distinction in the notes? Again, if the trumpet
does not sound a clear call, who will get ready for battle? So it is with you.
Unless you speak intelligible words with your tongue, how will anyone know
what you are saying? You will just be speaking into the air. Undoubtedly
there are all sorts of languages in the world, yet none of them is without
meaning. If then I do not grasp the meaning of what someone is saying, I am

a foreigner to the speaker, and the speaker is a foreigner to me. So it is with you. Since you are eager for gifts of the Spirit, try to excel in those that build up the church (vv. 6-12).

Again, Paul is not saying that speaking in tongues is wrong, but that by itself it's not helpful in public. You will not build up or help anyone if you practice the gift of tongues but misuse it. By using tongues in public without interpretation you will alienate Christians, seekers, and particularly those who want nothing to do with Jesus. The question is: What is more important, your gift experience or the community? That's why he says, *"Excel in those [gifts] that build up the whole church."*

Paul then adds, *"For this reason the one who speaks in a tongue should pray that they may interpret what they say"* (v.13). Notice again, he gives an out, if you speak in tongues and it is interpreted, all is well. Back in verse 5 he refers to interpretation by others but here he says the speaker can do it. The point is that another or the speaker must have the gift of interpretation. Both are options.

Then Paul keeps going with an extended teaching on the subject of tongues:

For if I pray in a tongue, my spirit prays, but my mind is unfruitful. So what shall I do? I will pray with my spirit, but I will also pray with my understanding; I will sing with my spirit, but I will also sing with my understanding (vv. 14-15).

If the gift of tongues is given to you, when you use it you will know God is being praised or thanked or that you are praying into a situation, but you will not know what is fully being said. And that is okay. This is about prayer, about praise, and about thanksgiving. You will be moved and changed. You will know the presence of God. So Paul essentially says, "If you have tongues, good! Pray in tongues. But when you are with others, pray with a language that everyone around you knows." The point is for those with the gift of tongues it is not either/or, but both/and. It deepens the way we pray in different ways. For example, some with this gift will sing in tongues as worship. But when we gather together, let us use the language we commonly hold together. In other words, I will pray and praise in a known language for the sake of others! Do you see the humility, the willingness to serve others over self? *"Otherwise when you are praising God in the Spirit, how can someone else, who is now put in the position of an inquirer, say "Amen" to your thanksgiving, since they do not know what you are saying? You are giving thanks well enough, but no one else is edified"* (vv. 16-17). This is not saying that if a word in tongues expressed publicly is interpreted, it necessarily becomes prophecy for the community. If tongues are interpreted, then we can agree to what you are saying to God, what is being prayed for, what you are thanking God for, or what are you praising God for. The gift of tongues tends to be person-centered while prophecy is community centered. Let me simply say, AMEN.

Paul brings this conversation about tongues to an evangelistic conclusion:

I thank God that I speak in tongues more than all of you. But in the church I would rather speak five intelligible words to instruct others than ten thousand words in a tongue. Brothers and sisters, stop thinking like children. In regard to evil be infants, but in your thinking be adults. In the Law it is written: "With other tongues and through the lips of foreigners I will speak to this people, but even then they will not listen to me," says the Lord. Tongues, then, are a sign, not for believers but for unbelievers; prophecy, however, is not for unbelievers but for believers. So if the whole church comes together and everyone speaks in tongues, and inquirers or unbelievers come in, will they not say that you are out of your mind? But if an unbeliever or an inquirer comes in while everyone is prophesying, they are convicted of sin and are brought under judgment by all, as the secrets of their hearts are laid bare. So they will fall down and worship God, exclaiming, "God is really among you!" (vv. 18-25).

Reading this again in this moment is really scary for those who take the Scriptures seriously. Gordon Fee articulated the situation Paul is describing best:

Because tongues are unintelligible, unbelievers who hear receive no revelation from God; they cannot thereby be brought to faith. Thus by their response of seeing the work of the Spirit as madness, they are destined for divine judgment just as in the OT passage Paul has quoted. This, of course, is not the divine intent for such people; hence Paul's urgency is that the Corinthians cease thinking like children and stop the public use of tongues, since it serves to drive the unbeliever away rather than to lead him or her to faith.[10]

Moving back toward the subject of worship, Paul writes, *"If anyone speaks in a tongue, two—or at the most three—should speak, one at a time, and someone must interpret"* (v.27).[11] We learn three things from this verse. First, the goal here is to say that tongues should not and may not dominate a worship service. Second, those speaking in tongues should take turns. This is especially important because it shows control and demonstrates that this practice is different than what happened with false tongues in their old pagan worship services. Third, someone must interpret. And so there is no misunderstanding, Paul adds, *"If there is no interpreter, the speaker should keep quiet in the church and speak to himself and to God"* (v.28).

So if you speak in tongues but neither you nor anyone else, as far as you know, has the gift of interpretation, or no one translates in the moment, stop speaking in tongues out loud unless you are given instruction from the leadership regarding the availability of an interpreter. Go privately before God by yourself and pray, giving thanks. That means at your home, or after a service, go off by yourself to a private place to pray, give praise, and deeply cry out to our God.

Here is a summary of the teaching we have covered in the last few pages: Tongues can be a known or unknown language given to some, but not all Christians. The gift can be used evangelistically when it is a known language. Tongues can also be used to authenticate the addition of new people into God's church; it can be used for edification in small groups or worship. Privately, this gift can be used to worship God by singing in tongues, to pray for others, to be thankful, to give inner assurance of communion with God, and as an affirmation of the personal presence of God in your life. This gift can bring joy and allows you to cry out to God over others when words do not come. You can be deeply changed and moved by this gift.

Tongues provide a special spontaneous message that can be given, but if there is not someone present to interpret the message then the speaker must not go on. Remember Paul was not angry that two or three spoke in tongues, but that there was no pause to interpret. I'll tell a story in the next section about how we addressed this tension of handling the speaking of tongues when we didn't know if anyone among us could interpret.

If not interpreted, continual use of tongues will break church unity and impede God's work in those that need to meet him personally. If you have the gift of interpretation, when you hear someone speaking in tongues you will know in your mind what is being said supernaturally. Those with the gift of interpretation may or may not have the gift of tongues.

Interpretation

Our discussion of tongues naturally leads to a biblical on the power gift of interpretation, since we have mentioned its importance several times in describing the use of tongues. This gift is exercised when someone speaks in tongues and another person understands what is being said and can interpret for the audience. Paul is clear—the presence and practice of this gift will humble or bring someone to conviction, it will deepen unity and bring significant encouragement to a church body. On occasion the interpretation is directed to a non-Christian who suddenly realizes God is speaking to them.

The effective use of both tongues and interpretation brings up the practical issue we struggled with in our church. If we never allowed speaking in tongues in public, then the gift of interpretation would also go largely unused. The two gifts work in tandem; one can't flourish without the other.

I was in a young adult service and a large percentage of our morning worship congregation had joined us. During the service I had this overwhelming sense someone was supposed to speak in tongues. This was early in our journey into embracing all the spiritual gifts and we had not had someone use tongues publicly. So I stood up in my pastoral role and asked, "Does someone sense they are supposed to speak in tongues?"

This was new territory and everyone looked around for a moment. Then sheepishly, a woman in her twenties that I knew well raised her hand and said, "I think I'm supposed to."

So I said, "Would you please stand and speak in tongues as loud as you can." As she was rising, I could feel the "Oh my goodness, what will happen now" current of curiosity/anticipation/concern move almost audibly through the room. She stood and spoke unintelligibly but loudly for fifteen or twenty seconds. When she was done, she sat down again. I waited to say something. The questions were written on everyone's faces—"Now what? What's happening in this conservative church?" After a few moments of silence, I asked, "Did anyone understand what she just said?" One, two, and then a third hand went up from different parts of the auditorium. We brought these people forward and we didn't let them talk to each other. Here's the amazing thing: each one of them had the same message. We let them share with the congregation, enjoyed the sense that God was speaking to us and interested in what was happening, and then we continued with our worship service. Please hear me: the power gifts aren't more significant or supernatural than the other gifts; they are just another way we to experience the presence of God in ministry. Often their apparent extraordinary nature is more in their unfamiliarity than in greater results or impact compared to the other gifts in action. The power gifts need all the other gifts as much as all the other gifts need the power gifts.

Is this you? Do you find words coming into your mind and mouth that you don't understand but usher you into God's presence? Have you ever had the uncanny experience of listening to someone speak a foreign language or an unknown tongue that you never studied or heard before, but you understood what was being said? Perhaps you've never talked about this experience with other Christians. And maybe, because you have never been around people who speak in tongues, you have a latent gift of interpretation, waiting to be used.

Intercession

The gift of intercession is actually a gift of prayer. Though not included in any of the formal lists, it is inferred in Scripture and is a very strong gift we need to consider. Here is the best definition I have found:

> The gift of intercession is the special ability that God gives to certain members of the Body of Christ to pray for extended periods of time on a regular basis and see frequent and specific answers to their prayers, to a degree much greater than that which is expected of the average Christian.[12]

All Christians are certainly called to pray for others. "When we move from petition to intercession we are shifting our center of gravity from our own needs to the needs and concerns of others. Intercessory prayer is selfless prayer, even self-giving prayer... It is priestly ministry and one of the most challenging teachings in the New Testament is the universal priesthood of all Christians. As priests, appointed and anointed by God, we have the honor of going before the Most High on behalf of others. This is not optional; it is a sacred obligation (and a precious privilege) of all who take up the yoke of Christ."[13]

So, we all pray, and we all "stand in the gap" through prayer, but certain of our brothers and sisters in Christ have been gifted with the ability to pray for extended periods of time on a regular basis and see specific things occur as a result of their praying. This isn't about driving on a crowded street and asking God to open up a parking place, or joining a throng of thousands in a stadium more or less praying that your team's player will make the impossible shot... Intercession is entirely about bringing the needs of others into God's presence with passion. This not only going boldly before the throne of grace (Hebrews 4:16) but also staying there until you see God's answers. Think of Anna, who is mentioned by Luke as someone with a lifestyle of prayer, *"She never left the temple but worshiped night and day, fasting and praying"* (Luke 2:37b). In 1 Timothy 2:1, Paul instructs Timothy that the life of the church must include a persistent encouragement to prayer, *"I urge, then, first of all, that petitions, prayers, intercession and thanksgiving be made for all people."* The apostle doesn't give Timothy this task, but tells his protégé to make sure the task gets done.

The more we have embraced spiritual disciplines and spiritual gifts in our church, the more I have discovered the number and variety of intercessors among us.[14] For example, some of them I'm tempted to call "phone book" intercessors. Give them a list; they want a column of names to pour over in prayer. They don't even need a lot of details about the needs of the persons they are praying for—they understand that God knows those needs better than they ever will—but they will lift a list of names before God for hours, an exercise I find absolutely exhausting just to describe, much less participate in. They do it without breaking a sweat or falling asleep. It must be a spiritual gift!

Then there are the "crisis" intercessors. They're like medical first-responders when disaster strikes or there is an urgent need. They go about the routine of their lives, like washing dishes after a meal and suddenly they are sharply aware of a need to pray for a situation or a person. Everything else is put on hold and they pray until they are released from that call to prayer. The desire comes with intensity and eventually goes.

There are also "assignment" intercessors. They feel strongly called to pray without ceasing for a specific movement, person, need, project long term. There's a woman in my life; now over 75 years old, she has been praying for me for sixteen years. She would tell you that her primary role and calling as part of our church is to pray for me. Though when we first met, she didn't like me at all. She thought I was running the youth ministry in a bad way and dealt with those perceptions by dragging me in front of the senior pastor for a confrontation. After that awkward encounter, she went home and was confronted by the Spirit of Jesus who informed her that she was "assigned to that guy you don't like." Since then we've come to know and love each other over the last decade and a half. She is now a gracefully aged woman who has lived through a lot of stuff in her own life, but the one constant that has marked her entire experience of walking with Jesus is prayer. I'm simply the latest assignment in a life-long pursuit of the presence of God on behalf of others. We now meet every week for half an hour and she prays for me, my marriage, what I'm preaching on, and other aspects of the ministry. If I'm speaking somewhere she can travel, she will be present in the classrooms or preaching venues to pray for me as well as those in the audience. She says I'm still her assignment and I can tell you by observation and the experience of answered prayer in my life that she has taken her duties seriously.

I can write about her like this because I know that no amount of personal willpower will make me into an intercessor the way the Holy Spirit has gifted her to be. Her commitment to pray humbles me and at the same time reminds me that having that gift would necessarily mean that I wouldn't have the time or be able to do what the Spirit *has* gifted me to do. We need each other. And I know that in reading the description above, some who have picked up this book have felt profiled. This is you. You may have been puzzled that you have been hounded and haunted by the need to pray for someone or something for years and you never realized this very longing is part of the Holy Spirit's gifting in your life! Welcome to what God has designed and gifted you to do. Now get on with it, because there are so many people who need you to pray for them.

What we've learned at Sanctus is partly an error of assumption on my part. I thought that all these intercessors (and we discover them all the time) would naturally get along. I jumped to the mistaken conclusion that if we gathered all our intercessors in the same room that there would be great unity. But not so fast. Consider the categories I described above. The "list" people wanted lists for everyone, the "crisis" people wanted to get everyone in crisis/warfare mode, and the "assignment" people kept asking others who or what their personal assignment was. Three very different prayer languages were being spoken—and I don't mean tongues. It was holy chaos! Like me, many of them had assumed (a common issue in spiritual gift management, it turns out) that everyone else with the same gift would be practicing the gift in the same way. It took a while to realize that we needed to cluster our intercessors by their "style" or "priorities" within their gifting. Once they discovered there were others with the gift of intercession that *were* very much like them, they found it much easier to understand and appreciate those with the same gifting but a different way of exercising their gift, all to the glory of God. And we all learned more about the way expectations and assumptions affect the way we get along and work together.

Chapter Ten:

Spiritual Gifts– The Power Category, Part 2

To keep things fresh in our minds, in the last chapter we looked at the spiritual power gifts of prophecy, tongues, interpretation of tongues, and intercession. We're moving together through what the Bible says and illustrates about these gifts, recognizing that some of them may take us into unfamiliar territory. In this chapter we will focus on the spiritual power gifts of faith and discernment of spirits. Let's remember that others have gone where we are going, and ultimately we seek to follow Jesus as our Savior, Lord, *and* model in every area of our lives.

Faith

Let me begin with a personal disclosure. Of course we are all called to have faith, and our very relationship with Christ is based on salvific faith, but the spiritual gift of faith falls into a category of its own. Faith is an amazing gift. It is an area I'm weak in, but both my wife and the lead pastor of our church are gifted this way, and I'm blessed to watch it exercised in their lives. I certainly benefit from their gift of faith. People with this gift bring oxygen into a room. I love this definition: "the gift of faith is the ability that God gives certain members of the body of Christ to discern with extraordinary confidence the will or purpose of God for his work."[1] A person with this gift recognizes "it" and knows God is going to do "it". When the Church at large is considering an action, those with the gift of faith often become the tipping point in the decision-making process—with God we can do this! And when skepticism and doubt is rampant, people with the gift of faith speak up, "No, I know God is about to do this." They breathe life into intercession, preaching, and vision. We need people with this gift to exercise and verbalize it. They need to know the rest of us who don't have this gift are counting on them. They don't have to cross their fingers in cautiously hopeful anticipation; they confidently say, "I know this is true." And it's worth noting that faith people are not simply "yes" people. Sometimes their gift of faith causes them to say, "No, God is not going to do that." Identifying and accepting such people within the church adds a deeper level of confidence (meaning "with faith") to your congregational and leadership decisions, both in choosing "yes" as well as "no."

The Spiritual Gift of Faith is included in 1 Corinthians 12:9, *"To another faith by the same Spirit, to another, gifts of healing by that one Spirit."* Faith could also be translated *informed trust*. It is not just pie in the sky or I-hope-this-is-true thinking; it is trust in a person who has proven Himself and thus His written Word and situational promptings are trustworthy.

Because of who God is, we can trust in what He says and what He does. All Christians are called to have faith. The Scripture is clear: *"And without faith it is impossible to please God, because anyone who comes to him must believe that he exists and that he rewards those who earnestly seek him"* (Hebrews 11:6). And Ephesians 2: 8-9 adds the big picture, *"For it is by grace you have been saved, through faith—and this is not from yourselves, it is the gift of God—not by works, so that no one can boast."*

If you are a Christian, you have had a faith encounter. Your faith radically shifted from trust in yourself, another religion, or another worldview and is now fixed on Jesus. You have been lifted from darkness to light (Colossians 1:13-14), from a dead-end existence to life itself, freely given by Jesus through His Holy Spirit. Salvation is the opposite of religion. Religion says, "Trust in others or in yourself and you'll be okay." But that's an example of blind and dead faith. Our faith is trust in Jesus alone, in His work alone, in His Word alone; for we do not have enough in ourselves alone to ever do what must be done. We can never bridge the gap between a God who is fully holy and fully love and ourselves! That's why Jesus came for us when we could not get back to God.

Salvation is about all of us trusting in God, His character and His revealed will. As Elizabeth Elliot wrote:

Faith is not an instinct. It certainly is not a feeling - feelings don't help much when you're in the lions' den or hanging on a wooden cross. Faith is not inferred from the happy way things work. It is an act of will, a choice, based on the unbreakable Word of a God who cannot lie, and who showed us what love and obedience and sacrifice mean, in the person of Jesus Christ.[2]

But the spiritual gift of faith is not saving faith, or walking out our Christianity in everyday life. Here are some definitions of this gift:

The gift of faith is the special ability that God gives to certain members of the Body of Christ to discern with extraordinary confidence that will and purpose of God for his work.[3]

The gift of faith is a Spirit-given ability to see something that God wants done and to sustain unwavering confidence that God will do it regardless of seemingly insurmountable obstacles.[4]

The spiritual gift of faith is a key gift in any local church. These people are not naive as others sometimes think; they are God-inspired visionaries who have *"confidence in what we hope for and assurance about what we do not see"* (Hebrews 11:1). This kind of faith is the life-blood of the church. Many believers want so much to exercise greater faith but life, history, personal loss, and unmet expectations have made them cautious at best and jaded or unbelieving at worst. Yet God gives this gift to some among us so we can keep going with heaven's blessing and unnatural confidence. Yet do not forget, the purpose, reason and true source of faith is God and His glory.

Here are a number of possible symptoms of this gift as identified by Clinton.[5] You have an unusual desire to accept God's promises at face value and to apply them to given situations until God fulfills them. You can receive a vision of some future work of God and are deeply trusting God for it until it comes to pass. When you hear a God-given vision, you resonate with it. You have the recurring experience in the midst of various situations to sense that God is going to do something unusual even though most of the people around you don't have this kind of assurance. You have an unusual desire to know God in His fullness and to be cast on Him and Him alone for solutions to problems. You love the thrill of knowing time and time again that God is real because He and He alone has specifically in a detailed way intervened on your behalf. You have an attitude that declares not only that God *can* do something but also that He *will* do something in the situation; in fact, in many cases you understand that God has already done it.

There are hundreds of examples of this gift throughout the Bible and church history. Think of the roles of Caleb and Joshua in the Old Testament. This gift is being put to use all around you, yet you may not have taken time to notice it. And you may not have even paid attention to the evidence of its presence in your own life. One of the most historically known exercisers of the gift of faith is George Müller. Yet generationally his story is being lost. Let me include a summary of his life to show the impact of the gift of faith in and through his life:

Almost every book that discusses the gift of faith refers to the life and ministry of George Müller, who by faith operated an orphanage in Bristol, England. He cared for 10,000 orphans over a period of 60 years, receiving $5 million in the process. He began the work with only two shillings in his pocket. Without once making known any need, he received enough to build five large homes, able to house *2,000* orphans, and to feed the children day by day, all by faith and prayer. Never did they go without a meal. Often the pantry was bare when the children sat down to eat, but help always arrived in the nick of time.

One story that best demonstrates Müller's faith is documented this way:

A trans-Atlantic sea captain, after 22 hours on the ship's bridge in a dense fog off the banks of Newfoundland, was startled by a tap on the shoulder. It was Müller, then in his 70s. "Captain, I have come to tell you I must be in Quebec on Saturday afternoon." This was Wednesday. When the captain said it was impossible, Müller replied, "If your boat can't take me, God will find some other way. I've never broken an engagement in 57 years." I'd like to help," responded the captain, "but what can I do?" "Let's go below and pray," Müller suggested. "But Mr. Müller, don't you know how dense the fog is?" "My eye is not on the fog, but on God who controls the fog and every circumstance of my life." Down on his knees, Müller prayed the simplest prayer the captain had ever heard. In his opinion it fit a child of nine. "O Lord, if Thou wilt, remove this fog in five minutes. Thou dost know the engagement made for me in Quebec for Saturday." Putting his hand on the captain's shoulder, Müller restrained him from praying. "First, you don't believe God will do it, and second, I believe he has done it, so there's no need for you to pray. Open the door, Captain, and you'll find the fog gone." And so it was. Müller kept his Saturday engagement in Quebec. Modestly, Müller wrote, "It pleased the Lord to give me in some cases something like the gift of faith, so that unconditionally I could ask and look for an answer."[6]

We love these stories, but they cannot only be about history. When we read these great accounts, we are tempted to think *I wish that would happen; I hope God does it, would that not be great*? But then, with a shrug, we move on. But we should not be willing to move on! Who among us will be the George Müllers for our church? Who in this generation will rise up with selfless and radical faith; who will stand and say to the rest of us, "Your imaginations are not the Lord's; what you see is not what heaven sees"? And when this happens will we be ready? Will we listen when the Calebs among us say, "Let us enter the Promised Land? Many of you will say that the giants are too big! They may look big, but our God is bigger!" But those among us with faith, leaders by the gift or behind the scenes will be hope-filled, confident, steadfast, unwavering, and full of unnatural peace. If you have this gift, what a gift you are to the rest of us doubting people!

Yet here is a word of caution for the many of you that have been gifted with faith by the Holy Spirit and some needed understanding for the many without this gift. Like all gifts, there can always be a dark side; there will always be gift tension for those who are consciously exercising this gift within the Church. So hear these words of caution from another thinker and pastor:

People with the gift of faith are usually more interested in the future than in history. They are goal-centered possibility thinkers, undaunted by circumstances or suffering or obstacles. They can trust God to remove mountains as 1 Corinthians 13:2 indicates. They, like Noah, can build an ark on dry ground in the face of ridicule and criticism, with no doubt at all that God is going to send a flood. People with the gift of faith are often highly irritated by criticism, much more, for example, than those with the gift of teaching. They can't bring themselves to understand why anyone would criticize them since they have such complete assurance that what they are doing is God's will. They interpret criticism of them as criticism of God, and therefore they often become impatient with Christian friends who do not go along with them. They typically have difficulty understanding the "system" and why it works as it does to slow down progress. Usually people with the gift of faith have a large amount of courage because they feel deeply that they are in partnership with God, and "if God be for us, who can be against us?" (Rom. 8:31). In other words, you without faith do not be quick to dismiss what the Lord has said and you with faith not all that question are against God. They could be using their gifts! But all be careful lest we miss what God is doing and we wander in the wilderness when we do not need to personally or as a church!"[7]

As mentioned, much of the time faith is connected with the gifts of leadership, intercession, works of power, healing and other permission-based gifts. Do you have this gift? Is this you? If you are gifted this way, oh how the rest of us need your Jesus-centered, God-given courage, your heaven- filled understanding and childlike trust!

Discernment of Spirits

The spiritual gift of discernment is at its heart a God-given sensitivity to truth, error, or evil. It really is about sensing the often-hidden source of a situation beyond what appears on the surface. This gift is mentioned in 1 Corinthians 12 and 1 John 4. If you have been given this gift, you have the supernatural capacity to recognize the source of what's in front of you. People with the gift of discernment see behind the curtain of appearances, which can be misleading. As with the gift of intercession we discussed in the previous chapter, there are also different styles to this gift. Some with discernment simply know when God is present and acting. Others with this gift understand the hidden motives of people, good or bad. And others are tuned in to situations in which the demonic is present. Often, it's a combination of discernment areas. Let me put it another way: people with the gift of discernment are like the spiritual eyes of the church. They simply "see" or "sense" what others around them don't.

Of course we are all called to be discerning. As believers we are urged to know God more and more deeply, to recognize His truth, and to know what is non-negotiable. Every Christian is called to give his or her full allegiance to Jesus, to allow His truth (the Scriptures) to permeate our lives, and to walk in heaven-given power. We are called to be rooted in the *living* Word and hear Him through His *written* Word. As the author of Hebrews wrote, *"But solid food is for the mature, who by constant use have trained themselves to distinguish good from evil"* (Hebrews 5:14). And look what Luke wrote about some rapidly growing disciples: *"Now the Berean Jews were of more noble character than those in Thessalonica, for they received the message with great eagerness and examined the Scriptures every day to see if what Paul said was true"* (Acts 17:11). Even Jesus' best friend John brought this home in such a powerful way. *"Dear friends, do not believe every spirit, but test the spirits to see whether they are from God, because many false prophets have gone out into the world"* (1 John 4:1). John was saying, "Look everyone! We live in a supernatural world and we are called to discern, to see, to test all teaching and supernatural experiences. Why? Because many false prophets empowered by unholy spirits have gone into the world." Think about the context of what John was facing. The Gnostics were all about secret knowledge and experience. These leaders were active in public worship and in small groups, prophesying and speaking in tongues on behalf of God, involving real supernatural experiences that ended up with a message not from God though it looked and sounded genuine.

What John is teaching us here is to evaluate experience and teaching, words and deeds. We must look at the utterance that comes from a person and assess a person inspired by any spirit. And by the way, every person speaking within the faith community and displaying supernatural evidence then as well as now is also connected with that spirit. Behind the speaker is not just a distant influence but also a symbiotic relationship between person and spirit. For some it is from God and for others it is evil.

Growing up in conservative churches, I was taught that all that supernatural experience stuff is dangerous, it's made up, physiological, evil, and God does not act that way anymore. The basic tactic when it came to supernatural experience was to dismiss it all with the absolute statement: "We don't do that here, good or bad!"

That approach is tempting because it makes life easy for leadership, avoiding involvement with the messiness of the supernatural, though not necessarily dealing with reality. Ignoring evil is the spiritual equivalent of pretending to be an ostrich and sticking our heads in the sand. We don't overcome evil by pretending it isn't there; we overcome it with goodness that only comes from God (Romans 12:21).

John's instructions offer us godly guidance. He doesn't tell the churches under his care that since spiritual power could be abused they shouldn't expect God to work in power. He doesn't make something out of the norm automatically evil—He tells us to test, question, and not easily accept. For Him, the origin and source of power mattered. We need to understand this: on the surface, the experiences can look the same. Teaching, speaking in tongues, prophecy, whether done under the control of the Holy Spirit or under the control of evil, will not necessarily appear immediately different. That's the power of counterfeits. The danger of the spirit of the Antichrist is that it looks, acts, and sounds right, but is not. The false angel of light can still create a blinding effect (2 Corinthians 11:14). The question is what outlet are you plugged in to? The source matters, and in time the results will reveal the source.

John's words remind us we are all called to be discerning and not dismissive when it comes to spiritual evidence and expressions. Notice, John is directing his instructions to individuals within a framework: "all of you; test the spirits!" The implication is that spiritual discernment is an obligation of the gathered church and its leadership. But let's go further. When we read Paul we also find that discernment is a spiritual gift given specifically to some individuals. Remember these are not natural talents, but divine abilities that enable us to do ministry. Here are a couple definitions to help our conversation:

The *discerning* of spirits gift refers to the ability given by God to perceive issues in terms of spiritual truth, to know the fundamental source of the issues and to give judgment concerning those issues; this includes the recognition of the spiritual forces operating in the issue.[8]

The gift of discerning of spirits is the special ability God gives to some members of the Body of Christ, which enables them to know with assurance whether certain behavior purported to be of God is in reality divine, human or satanic.[9]

Again, like all the spiritual gifts, the focus of this gift's expression is within the body of Christ. There's a certain level of discernment that comes from experience, and a deeper level that comes from those whom the Spirit has given the capacity to go beyond by observing patterns over time. The exercise of the gift appears to be intuition; a response not necessarily directly connected to observations.

Here are some indicators of this gift that are widely recognized: a keen sense for recognizing inconsistencies; a good grasp of Scriptural truth in general with ready and practical applications; a deep underlying sense of conviction which will not allow you to rest when you know people are being given half-truth, misapplied truth, or false teaching, and are asked to act upon those errors; an unusual sensitivity or intuitive grasp of people and situations—you often and usually quickly notice when public speakers give wrong interpretations or misapply the Scriptures; you will get a glimpse of the behind-the-scenes supernatural reality in a situation, either by mental picture or in reality; you notice physical symptoms that lead you to know something is wrong. You will see or sense demons in people, places, or situations.[10]

As consistently applied throughout history, the gift of discernment is used to distinguish truth from non-truth in terms of verbal utterances like prophecy. Also, today with the entire canon of Scripture before us, this gift can be used to discern whether teaching is on target or consistent with the revealed truth of the Word. Its use can help to protect the church from heretical tendencies in either teaching or in practice. In other cases this gift can be used to discern whether the source of a particular activity or power is the Holy Spirit, the person, or the demonic realm.

Notice the gift of discernment is multifaceted. I find that people that have this gift tend to primarily function in one of the three ways. You could say that some primarily see up, some see down, and others see to the side. First, many with this gift will know that God is really in a situation; they discern God's active presence in a person or a circumstance that isn't obvious to others. Have you ever been sitting in a church service and suddenly became aware of Jesus' presence? If it happens often, you may have this gift. Second, some with this gift will know when things look good on the surface, but the motives are not pure. They listen to a sermon and everything is right, orthodox theology and all, but they sense a problem with the motivation of the preacher. Some with this gift will say "Amen" to the message yet stop from full endorsement of the messenger. Sometimes it isn't about the "what" of a message, but the "why" it is given. A true message given out of hatred or for the purpose of manipulation isn't always apparent. Conversely, some with the gift of discernment will be able to distinguish truth from error, even if the motives are proper. When you are listening to someone teaching, you will understand that though they are sincere and convinced of what they are saying, the message is not true. When you sit with a Mormon, a New Ager, or even a fellow Christian and understand that though they have no wrong motives they are sincerely wrong, this gift will come into play.

As I mentioned earlier, some styles of this gift involve a special awareness of motives. Let's say that I preach my heart out one Sunday morning. My theology is flawless, my presentation is engaging, the illustrations have everyone crying or laughing, and my application is practical for almost everyone. But internally, there's a knot of anger in my heart, and almost unconsciously I'm directing the edge of my message toward one person—I hope he or she really gets this, because I'm sick and tired of their resistance to the message. (Upon reflection, what I'm sick and tired of is my perception they are resisting me, rather than God). But someone with the gift of discernment might approach me afterwards (believe me, it has happened) with a gentle question, "So, great sermon, Pastor, but where was the anger coming from?" Or "Everything was right in your words today, Jon, but what was happening in your heart?" Let me tell you, having been on the receiving end of this, the first time is disconcerting. Then it becomes deeply humbling and convicting. Once you identify those in your congregation with this gift, you can see them coming and you almost know what they are going to say. You also realize God has given you a gift of people to help guard your heart and intentions—a priceless gift for anyone who might ever be tempted to put up a good front.

Let me speak briefly to those of you who are discerning. This gift can be destructive in a person who isn't continually seeking humility and improved character. First, express this gift with gentleness, particularly in approaching someone who has done his or her best. Second, realize that while you may have this gift, you can also be wrong. Sometimes the impression comes from your own bias or last night's tacos, so exercise caution and ask permission to share. Third, don't respond immediately; wait at least twenty-four hours and then approach with gentleness. Fourth, stop, drop, and roll—just because God gave you an impression doesn't necessarily mean you're supposed to act. Ask Jesus why He showed you something and what you should do next. Fifth, use phrases like, "I think I discern… I'm wondering if… it could be… not, God told me so deal with it!"

In the third expression of this gift, some know when demonic powers are present. They will sense and perhaps even see the presence of the demonic in people or in situations; they will know that it doesn't matter what is happening. When the actual presence of the demonic is discerned, it needs to be dealt with.

Both Jesus and Peter had this gift:

Jesus and his disciples went on to the villages around Caesarea Philippi. On the way he asked them, "Who do people say I am?" They replied, "Some say John the Baptist; others say Elijah; and still others, one of the prophets."
"But what about you?" he asked. "Who do you say I am?" Peter answered, "You are the Messiah." Jesus warned them not to tell anyone about him. He then began to teach them that the Son of Man must suffer many things and be rejected by the elders, the chief priests and the teachers of the law, and that he must be killed and after three days rise again. He spoke plainly about this, and Peter took him aside and began to rebuke him. But when Jesus turned and looked at his disciples, he rebuked Peter. "Get behind me,

Satan!" he said. "You do not have in mind the concerns of God, but merely human concerns" (Mark 8:27-33).

Twice Jesus discerned in Peter the presence of influence beyond the disciple. In the first case, Peter's declaration of Jesus' identity was the result of the Holy Spirit's revelation to him, as Matthew's account makes clear (Matthew 16:17). This was quickly followed by Peter's bold challenge of Jesus' declaration regarding His coming death and resurrection. Jesus realized that response in Peter was being prompted by a demonic power (v.33) or was spoken by it through Peter.

Amazingly, Peter himself was later given this same gift as part of his role in the early church:

Now a man named Ananias, together with his wife Sapphira, also sold a piece of property. With his wife's full knowledge he kept back part of the money for himself, but brought the rest and put it at the apostles' feet. Then Peter said, "Ananias, how is it that Satan has so filled your heart that you have lied to the Holy Spirit and have kept for yourself some of the money you received for the land? Didn't it belong to you before it was sold? And after it was sold, wasn't the money at your disposal? What made you think of doing such a thing? You have not lied just to human beings but to God." When Ananias heard this, he fell down and died. And great fear seized all who heard what had happened... About three hours later his wife came in, not knowing what had happened. Peter asked her, "Tell me, is this the price you and Ananias got for the land?" "Yes," she said, "that is the price." Peter said to her, "How could you conspire to test the Spirit of the Lord? Listen! The feet of the men who buried your husband are at the door, and they will carry you out also." At that moment she fell down at his feet and died. Then the young men came in and, finding her dead, carried her out and buried her beside her husband (Acts 5:1-10).

This couple was trying to have their cake and eat it too. Publicly, they were acting as examples of generosity when their motives were selfish. They were not being compelled or coerced into giving; they chose to attempt to defraud the church and God. Do you see both gifts? Words of knowledge (we'll get to that in the next chapter) "you have lied," and discernment, recognizing Satan is present. The result of the Spirit's discerning intervention had a powerful effect on the rest of the church: *"Great fear seized the whole church and all who heard about these events"* (Acts 5:11). Could we not agree that the absence of the use of this gift throughout the church today is part of the explanation for the lack of intentionality, holiness, and fear of the Lord so prevalent among us?

There is one other huge lesson we all need to walk through especially with power gifts like discernment. At this point you may be thinking, *yes; that's me, especially the last description about sensing and seeing non-physical beings, presence, or powers around people or places. Okay, I believe the gift is real but does that mean the spiritual ability is from God?*

Excellent question! We have to understand and remember that from our side and from the demonic side spiritual gifts will look, sound, and even seem the same much of the time. Other groups like Muslims and Hindus speak in tongues and it sounds and seems the same as when followers of Jesus practice that gift, but those expressions are not a gift from the Spirit of Christ. They look and sound the same, but have a different source. One source is genuine; the others are counterfeits. However, the existence of counterfeits doesn't mean we should stop using what is genuine. It means we need to take care that what we use *is* genuine.

Here's a needed warning. Most of us have been taught to evaluate things based on what we see, not what we discern. We often assume that something evil will appear overtly evil. But that's not true. The demonic are called angels of light and a convincing lie is always made up of 90% truth. Or, to recognize another danger, we think that God would *never* do something so out of the box that it violates our comfort or history, which is not true either. Looking at Jesus and Peter; it was where the thoughts, statements, and actions were coming from; it was the source (good or evil) that provoked their response. The statements or actions they responded to did not look evil or dark on the surface, but they definitely were.

I remember a woman came into my office one day and began to describe a wide assortment of experiences. They were all examples that I recognized as similar to my own understanding and experience of discernment. She talked about seeing spirits and knowing when evil was present. But the longer she talked, even though superficially our experiences had a lot in common, inside me everything was going sideways. So I asked her this question, which is an important question to keep in mind throughout all this conversation about gifts: "How long have you had this gift?" She answered, "Oh, I've had it since I was born." Red flag number one became apparent. You see, you are not born with gifts of the Spirit; they are a byproduct of being born again. When the Holy Spirit takes up residence in you at the point of salvation, He brings your gifting. If you have spiritual gifts before you are converted, they are not from God, no matter how benign or helpful they may seem or how they have been used. You must give those gifts back to Jesus and ask Him to cleanse them because they didn't originate from His Spirit. Red flag number two showed up when I asked her, "Have you had other confirmations of this gift?" She said, "Yeah, I went to this spiritist church and they laid hands on me." I thought, "Oh, no…" At that moment our eyes met and I watched her whole face change. I realized I wasn't dealing with God, but with demonic power in a person. Yet the whole time she thought it was from God. She wasn't trying to deceive; she was deceived and didn't know it.

Here is the lesson: If you realize you have had supernatural insight, that is, seeing demons, knowing emotions or thoughts of people, and this ability has been with you since *before* you were a Christian, that ability or "gift" is *not* from God. No matter how benign, helpful, or "good" that gift may have appeared its source is highly questionable. All Spiritual gifts are given *after* we become Christians. By that I mean you have established a personal relationship with Jesus that resulted from you asking Him to be your Savior and Lord. Spiritual gifts are not given just because you grew up as a Christian or in a Christian environment. It doesn't matter how strong, how vivid, how real your experiences are. This is all about source. The spirit of anti-Christ will do everything it can to look and act like Christ. One of the great dangers of the current fascination with all things "spiritual" and the assumption that spiritual powers are self-authenticating is evidence of the degree to which our world today is under the spell of demonic powers.

As a pastor, many have approached me and said, "Jon I can do this, I see that, I know things!" And I will ask, "When (did this start?); where (did this "power" come from?); how (did you come to have this?); with whom (did you first become aware of this power?); and who (benefits or gets glory from this power?). Often the answers to these questions make it very clear that the "gift" being exercised is not from Jesus.

So the question is, are you willing to give up any ability you have to Jesus Christ, who died, rose again and now sits at the Father's side? Are you willing to give up anything that you have relied on, that you have made a part of your identity, so you can be truly free? Are you willing to forsake all and accept only what Jesus would want to give you by His Spirit's presence? Remember the gifts are given in order to bring God glory and to build up the church.

As a last thought on this gift, many times people ask if they can have discernment in more than one of the directions I mentioned. Yes. I find sometimes people will have two out of three, others one, and others all three. It is an important and helpful gift within the Church to avoid error and evil.

Chapter Eleven:
Spiritual Gifts– The Power Category, Part 3

This is the third chapter unpacking the spiritual gifts categorized as Power Gifts, even though, as we've admitted, all genuine gifts of the Holy Spirit are ways He empowers or enables us to carry out tasks in the spiritual realm that bring glory to God and strengthen the Church. Part of our purpose here has also been to develop a common script or language and understanding of what the spiritual gifts are, what they look like, how they feel, and how they are used. I've said more than once that using the same, even biblical vocabulary, but meaning different things leads to confusion, division, and falls far short of all God longs to accomplish in and through his Church.

This chapter focuses on the gifts of healing, works of power (miracles) and words of knowledge or wisdom. Again, all of these gifts revolve around God's glory and His promise of a new heaven and new earth that breaks into the now. They are all power gifts in that they demonstrate the effectiveness, presence, and reality of God at work in the here and now. At their heart they are all about healing–physical, emotional, spiritual, and even directional healing.

Why do we need healing to such an extent that several gifts are given by the Holy Spirit to address that need? The answer is because we are *all* broken and we live in a world that is full of brokenness. Unfulfilled dreams, poverty, disease, war, lack of basic necessities, oppression, injustice—the pain of brokenness forms great pools of pain from which people either find belief in God or reject his existence. Most of us some times and some of us all the time find the existence of suffering to be an open-and-shut case against the possibility of a great, good, and all-powerful God. Genuine faith always has a response, if not an easy answer, for suffering. Suffering as the argument that turns us away from God doesn't do anything to answer the problem of suffering itself.

Suffering invades and infects our own lives in so many ways: pain, disease, anxiety, loss, disappointment, failure, family breakdown, abuse, and the influence of the demonic. In all of this—the global human family dysfunction—creation itself groans deeply in bondage longing for freedom. Our suffering is experienced physically, emotionally, mentally, sexually, and spiritually, which are all connected to relational breakdown with ourselves, others, and God Himself.

All this had its beginning long ago in a lost garden at the fall. When Adam and Eve sinned, death entered our experience, and thus sickness, brokenness, and suffering were also introduced into the created order. Sin marred the goodness of God's creation, and creation has lived in a state of frustration ever since. Suffering continues throughout the world in you, in me, in us. This brokenness comes from many streams, forming one great river which floods over us all, good, bad, evil, religious, or indifferent.

Satan and the demonic are real. They participated in the original fall of the human race and have been working ever since to bring and perpetuate suffering in our lives and the lives of our families. They are actively involved in society building communal worldviews and intellectual deception.

But it's not just about the reality of the demonic. There is also the reality of our own often deliberate, sinful choices. We are not islands and our choices are not made in a vacuum. Our choices and our actions always affect us, others, and the world around us.

So much, if not all, of the suffering and darkness can be connected back to sinful choices where a person, a nation, a community, or a business (you fill in the blank) breaks God's heart and His law. We cry out to God, "Why don't you do something? Why do you allow these disasters and all the suffering?" And He says, "But you want a choice; you would rather die than give up your right to choose. Because you are made in my image you must have choice. And so you choose, and every day as the human family you continue to choose. And it is so many of your choices that bring so much of the darkness that you blame me for."

The question is, with all our bondage and self-destructive behavior, is there any relief? If we can't help ourselves, is there any hope? Thanks be to God, there is. Joy to the world the Lord has come! God has intervened, and a Savior has been born! We couldn't solve our problem, so God physically stepped in. Through the birth, life, death, and resurrection of Jesus, our enemies—death, sin, and Satan—have been overcome. History is now being reversed. The dawn has come and day-by-day light is breaking through the darkness. Listen again to the grand promises written about Jesus hundreds of years before He came:

Surely he took up our pain and bore our suffering, yet we considered him punished by God, stricken by him, and afflicted. But he was pierced for our transgressions, he was crushed for our iniquities; the punishment that brought us peace was on him, and by his wounds we are healed (Isaiah 53:4-5).

Each time someone meets God through Jesus there is healing. And we know the promise to all who trust in Jesus is that we will be fully healed at the final resurrection. Indeed, all of creation will be healed. The "not yet" contains our great longing for the great healing to come; it is what we must cling to in both good and terrible times. Hear the Word of God that does not lie!

So will it be with the resurrection of the dead. The body that is sown is perishable, it is raised imperishable; it is sown in dishonor, it is raised in glory; it is sown in weakness, it is raised in power; it is sown a natural body, it is raised a spiritual body (1 Cor. 15:42-44).

"He will wipe every tear from their eyes. There will be no more death or mourning or crying or pain, for the old order of things has passed away" (Revelation 21:4).

As we wait for this amazing new heaven and earth, as we wait to be physically raised to new life with no sickness or death, the question is: Does God ever set anyone free in the now? Or do we just continue to deal with life the best we can, sing, "This world is not my home, I'm just passing through," and suck it up? Of course not. For some of us he will heal and for others our suffering will become the place where our joy grows the most.

God has given some among us gifts that help bring into the now what's to come in the future. That taste of the future comes through the gifts of healing, works of power, and words of knowledge.

There is also quite a bit of confusion in today's church about these last few Power Gifts. First, let's acknowledge all the fake stuff: TV lights and cameras, and requests for money but with no real action. This can cause many of us to become so jaded and skeptical that we end up as Christian atheists, passively believing all the right stuff but expecting nothing, seeing nothing, and readily dismissing those times when we do see God move.

If we step beyond the fake spirituality and scientific idolatry, we are left with the possibility of divine action. This is typically when some churches will declare that all that stuff only happened in Bible times but doesn't happen today. On the other hand, some churches wrongly assert that everyone can be healed and wealthy; that God has promised wholeness and prosperity to every Christian in every way, immediately. Just have faith and you will always receive is a promise to every Christian to be healed, delivered, and set free.

Both views can't be right and actually they are both sincerely, or not so sincerely, wrong. It is not *never* (as in God never does these things now), and it is not *always* (as in God has committed himself to always do what we want as long as we have faith); it is *sometimes* (as in the God who always works doesn't always work the way we expect or want Him to work. He's in charge; we are not). The answer to the question of miracles and healing today is, "Yes, they happen when God sovereignly chooses."

You see, these Power Gifts we are about to discuss (healing, works of power and words of knowledge) function within situational permission. The decision about when and how to work is always God's. We can see this in Jesus' life. Jesus knew, healed, and delivered with authority (the blind, deaf, mute, bleeding, dead, demonic, and mentally ill). Notice also that Jesus did not always ask God for help, "If it be Your will." He often simply took the authority God had given Him and acted on God's behalf. But it was not just because He Himself was God; He asked permission and then acted. What approach did Jesus teach?

"Jesus gave them this answer: 'I tell you the truth, the Son can do nothing by himself; he can do only what he sees his Father doing, because whatever the Father does the Son also does'" (John 5:19).

This pattern of permission is seen in Jesus' life again and again. He would go, pray, and listen to the Father, line up His will with the Father's, then act. He prayed before He did his deeds, not during them. One the best examples of this is the way Jesus handled the death of His friend Lazarus. After he was dead for four days this is what Jesus said when He told them to open up the grave:

> *So they took away the stone. Then Jesus looked up and said, "Father, I thank you that you have heard me. I knew that you always hear me, but I said this for the benefit of the people standing here, that they may believe that you sent me." When he had said this, Jesus called in a loud voice, "Lazarus, come out!" The dead man came out, his hands and feet wrapped with strips of linen, and a cloth around his face. Jesus said to them, "Take off the grave clothes and let him go"* (John 11:41-44).

Our task if we have any of these Power Gifts is to get our will lined up with the will of Jesus and the Father. Only on that basis can we then exercise the authority God has given us. If we have these gifts, then, like Jesus, we are also to spend time exercising the spiritual disciplines like prayer and solitude with God to receive instruction and to line up our will with His, or to get permission, and only when we receive the "Yes," to act.

As Charles Kraft wrote:

> Jesus prayed before he did his deeds. But what he did during them should not be called prayer... We are to imitate Jesus and take authority as he did. When Jesus said that whoever believes in him would do what he did, I believe he meant to include the way he did things in the what of that verse. Like him, we are not to ask God to do the works, but to line up our wills with his and talk not to the Father but on his behalf, speak authoritatively to correct the situation.[1]

So, will God heal, will He direct us, and will He deliver us? Of course, that is ultimately guaranteed by the resurrection. Will He do this for us in this life? The answer to that specific question of timing is, "Maybe." God's will, His glory, His sovereignty and our willingness to listen matter so very much. For if He says "Yes," we must act! And if He says "No," we must then ask God to use our brokenness and suffering to bring Him glory and produce in us unnatural joy.

With these factors in mind, let's turn to this chapter's gifts as listed among those in 1 Corinthians 12:

Now to each one the manifestation of the Spirit is given for the common good. To one there is given through the Spirit a message of wisdom, to another a message of knowledge by means of the same Spirit, to another faith by the same Spirit, to another gifts of healing by that one Spirit, to another miraculous powers" (1 Cor. 12:7-10).

Words of Wisdom/Knowledge

There are those who hold that these are two distinct gifts, and others who believe they are really two aspects of a single gift. Observing those who practice this giftedness, I personally think that they are two expressions of the same gift. But there is more to consider, since the original language helps us understand the wisdom and knowledge facets of the same gem. In illustrating this gift, lots of people want to say that the gift of knowledge just means you are good with facts and data that can help the Church such as seminary professors or historians. In contrast, they describe the gift of wisdom as simply helping people live out their Christian life in very applicable ways. That explanation misses the point here. Clinton is helpful:

The use of the Greek word *logos* prefacing both wisdom and knowledge suggests that these gifts are situational communications given by the Holy Spirit for that moment. Thus, we are not just talking about people who are knowledgeable about the Bible or God but are talking about a word which comes from God as wisdom or knowledge for a certain specific situation."[2]

The key idea in understanding this gift is that it functions like the gift of prophecy but not in a communal setting; it's one on one. It is God giving a very direct word about an issue that needs to be dealt with, or a word of encouragement, or situational insight in which someone with the gift supernaturally directs another believer how to walk in God's way and will for that moment. Among the classic spiritual disciplines is the practice of exercising spiritual direction, or submitting to it. Those with the gift of words of wisdom/knowledge excel in the role of spiritual direction. But notice it is situational, it's prompting based, it's a Power Gift, and when it is given you know God is speaking. It's not just another lecture, sermon, or small group study.

The church in which I grew up made these gifts (when on rare occasions spiritual gifts were discussed at all) into very static qualities or capacities. Words of knowledge basically meant you were a good theologian who could "rightly divide the word of truth", and words of wisdom meant you were simply a wise person in matters of the faith (even if you didn't have a long white beard). But that's not what these gifts are about, because as we've seen, those descriptions actually fit other gifts like teaching and evangelism more exactly.

So how do these two "words" describe unique areas of gifting? First, these two gifts are dynamic and situational. Having these gifts doesn't mean having a spiritual "switch" you can turn on at any moment as a teaching or evangelism function, or schedule, as in, "Come tonight for a special gathering to be enthralled by words of knowledge and wisdom among us." No, the use and timing of these gifts to a large degree remain under the ongoing control of the Holy Spirit, and he enables those he has empowered in the moment to exercise these gifts. In other words, you may be very aware you have this gift but not be free to use it in every situation.

The word of knowledge functions when God gives you information about someone you have no direct access to any other way. The right exercise of this gift and the information God gives you always humbles, always helps, and never humiliates. It can bring healing to others, but never hurts them. So words of knowledge are similar to prophecy, but are directed to individuals.

I discovered the power of this gift early in my growing awareness of the Spirit moving among us. I was participating in a large youth retreat held in a hotel in Niagara Falls involving 1,400 people. One of our objectives was to include a strong prayer component to the entire event. The idea of prayer wasn't new, but doing it in some intentional fashion was something none of us had ever done before. At one person's suggestion, we went to the hotel and prayed over every room that would be used by the young people. Frankly, a number of us felt less than comfortable about this while others in the group reported this finally filled a desire they felt had been unmet. So despite the unfamiliarity we all participated.

Next we got out the list of every person who was registered and began to pray over those names. Again, although most of us involved in this effort believed in prayer and some of us were actually gifted in this area, we noticed a variety of responses that we later realized were related to a gifting style that varied between list/assignments, crisis/spontaneous, and promptings. Eventually we came to understand that every gift has a variety of expressions, some of which function with a little tension between them. List people are drawn to the systematic, relentless engagement of praying over assigned names or groups without needing to know details— confident that God knows those and simply invites us to pray without ceasing. Spontaneous or crisis pray-ers, are driven a little crazy by lists—they want to be called into significant intercession for specific needs or people. Promptings are an unexpected and undefined call to pray for people or situations for which few specifics are known. The reality is that all types of prayer expressions are needed.

Back then we were about to discover even more about words of knowledge. As we prayed through the list of names that for the most part represented people we didn't know, some of us began to receive mental images, words, or information connected with those names even though they were strangers to us. During prayer, words like "self-injury" or "divorce" would occur to several of us. We knew what church these kids were from, but usually nothing else. Frankly, we didn't know exactly what was happening among us, and yet it seemed clearly to be something God was doing for His purposes. Once we recognized this was a pattern, we decided to take sticky notes and, when someone's name stirred a thought, write that person's name on the front of the note and what we "saw" or "heard" on the back. These were then organized on a large board in the prayer room.

When the conference started, young people were encouraged to visit the prayer room if they had specific needs for prayer. As they came and identified themselves and their churches, we were shocked to realize that we had placed a sticky note on the wall with their name on it. We would ask them to wait while we retrieved it and then tell them, "While we were praying for you before this retreat began, several of us connected this word or image with your name. Does this make any sense?" And we would turn the note over and read it to them.

Then it was their turn to be shocked, for time after time, the word we had been given was directly connected to the need they had in mind as they came for prayer. Their natural question was, "How did you know? There wasn't much we could say except, "This is of God" and then pray for those kids.

Now we know we were receiving words of knowledge, information given by the Holy Spirit to encourage someone by helping them realize God is very much aware of their situation and needs. This, along with a fuller understanding of intercessory prayer and words of wisdom came to us organically as we followed the Spirit's leading into areas we had not explored before. We discovered what believers in previous generations knew and practiced, the practical outworking of the gifts of the Spirit, expressed in brightly colored yellow and turquoise sticky notes.

Words of wisdom are similar in character, but have a different focus as a gift. This gift is in action when God gives a situational word or a message acutely applicable in a moment that provides insight for people into the next steps of their spiritual journey. These are practical instructions like "go to this place" or "read this book." Wisdom is knowledge applied, and in this case, every time the supernatural, situational word is given, you recognize it came from Jesus' lips to you.

There is a key aspect of the use of these gifts that should be emphasized, and that is the importance of permission. We have learned as a church that we don't impose the practice of gifts on others; we make it a practice to ask for permission before exercising any gift for another. Why is this crucial? Because permission invites a small step of faith it allows someone to be willing to take a step and open the door to the Spirit's work without knowing exactly what might happen.

There's a fascinating episode in Jesus' ministry that demonstrates this in Matthew 13:53-58.

When Jesus had finished these parables, he moved on from there. Coming to his hometown, he began teaching the people in their synagogue, and they were amazed. "Where did this man get this wisdom and these miraculous powers?" they asked. "Isn't this the carpenter's son? Isn't his mother's name Mary, and aren't his brothers James, Joseph, Simon and Judas? Aren't all his sisters with us? Where then did this man get all these things?"

And they took offense at him. But Jesus said to them, "A prophet is not without honor except in his own town and in his own home." And he did not do many miracles there because of their lack of faith.

Why didn't Jesus do many miracles in Nazareth? They wouldn't give Him permission. They even knew about His "wisdom and these miraculous powers" (v.54), but because they thought they knew Him, they refused to accept the possibility that God was gifting Him for His work.

Here's another story about the word of knowledge gift in operation. I was in church one day and had a distinct prompting from the Spirit to pray for a particular woman. There was another pastor with me, so we approached her and asked if we could pray with her. We began by asking her for permission: May we pray for you? We are so careful about this in our church because there is so much opportunity for spiritual abuse and we know we need to recognize and give God's Spirit room to work in a person's heart and mind even as He works in ours. If we feel the need to lay hands on the person, we also ask for permission, explaining if necessary the importance of human contact both for them and for us. We might also mention that Jesus often touched people, which was remarkable in a culture where so many people were considered untouchable. He's our model. One of the most painful bi-products of abuse of many kinds is that it robs people of the easy acceptance of meaningful touch, when the longing to be touched is one of the deepest needs we have as humans.

In addition to permission, we also told this woman something we make a practice of saying in situations of gift-use:

What I'm about to tell you isn't necessarily right. I'm only a human being, seeking to be used by God, and I've learned that I don't always hear or respond correctly, but I also know that God often does speak in these situations. As you listen, I want you to test the truth of these words rather

than assume because I'm a pastor I know more, or because you have a need
and this is the answer to that need. Let's be open together to what God has
for you in this moment.

These practices of humility in the exercise of the gifts are particularly
significant when it comes to the use of the power gifts. The last thing we want to
do is scare people inappropriately or further abuse them by making a harmful
mistake.

Also note one other aspect of this setting that is an important characteristic
of healthy and holy use of the spiritual gifts. I was acting in community not only
with another pastor, but also with the awareness of others who have confirmed
and encouraged the practice of my gifts and are quick to pray in any situation
where my gifts, or the gifts of others are being exercised.

We knelt and prayed together. Moments into this, I received a clear picture
in my mind of this woman, sitting in bed with her Bible open and she was
singing to Jesus. Jesus himself was sitting at the corner of her bed, listening to
her sing words that flowed out of her reading of the Scriptures. It was a scene of
both great peace and great power. I asked her, "Do you regularly do your
devotions in bed?" She answered, "Yes. How do you know that?" I had to
answer, "Well, I'm not sure. Do you often sing to Jesus as part of your
devotional times?" Her eyes got big with surprise and she said, "I do, but I've
never told anyone that!" I knew in that moment why I had been prompted to
pray with her. I said, "I need to tell you that when you do that, Jesus hears you.
He loves you and what He hears coming from your heart." This woman
responded with instant tears of joy as emotions flowed through her, and after a
few moments she quietly said, "And I've been thinking lately that Jesus has
stopped listening to me. God's Word continues to speak to me in ways that
inspire my singing, but I also wondered if I was just singing to an empty room."
The moment was so humbling and edifying for her because she received an

unexpected confirmation that Jesus was listening to her; that He was with her even in those times when she felt alone. This was an instance in which a word of knowledge contained information that I didn't have from any source other than the Holy Spirit, and was exactly what this woman needed at that point on her journey. Though I hardly knew her, God allowed me to affirm her faith and encourage her to keep going. This is a great example of a Power Gift in action because it demonstrates God's presence and interest in our daily experience.

This is a wonderful story of encouragement, but I must add that they aren't all like that. Another time, when a young married man asked for prayer, I said to him, "No; I won't pray for you." He was shocked and bewildered; twice more he insisted I should pray for him. Finally I said, "You don't really want me to pray for you, because Jesus is standing right behind you and He's about to undo you." He said, "I still want it." So I looked at him and said, "You're having an affair. You must repent; then go home and tell your wife." That word of knowledge exposed great pain and ultimately brought great healing. The man's marriage was restored and that couple serves Jesus together today. I did not know this information other than by revelation.

One part of this gift offers a supernatural "what," the other offers a supernatural "when" or "where." The gift helps someone understand that *what* has happened must be dealt with in the way God instructs. It also directs another believer: this is *where* and *when* you need to do it.

Here are several evidences and experiences connected to these two expressions of the gift. Clinton explains:

You have a sensitivity to the Holy Spirit's prompting, which allows for the recognition that certain thoughts or impressions are from God. A recognition that in certain situations the Holy Spirit wants to do something and gives you knowledge that could not have originated with you. This knowledge helps release the activity of God in the situation. When this gift is effectively exercised, the person to whom the word is given often realizes what they are hearing settles a question, helps make a decision they were facing, or shows them a way forward they had not considered... In your mind's eye, a person with this gift might see words written like newspaper headlines or ticker tape; they could hear God speak in an inner voice; in their mind's eye they might see the sin or the situation that needs to be confronted or healed. This gift may allow a person to see pictures or visions in healing situations. They might actually feel pain or other symptoms of a condition that God wants to heal. The person feeling the symptoms does not have the condition. Rarely, a person opens his/her mouth and utters accurate information without a prior access to the situation.[3]

The key idea is that this knowledge or wisdom helps release the activity of God in the situation. Since it is so specific and so on track, a response is demanded. It's like prophecy for the church but one on one.

Much of the time these gifts are given and used with other gifts. In the case of dealing with the demonic, the gift of discernment lets you know evil is present while a word of knowledge can show how they came into a situation. They both can be used to expose secrets in people's lives that God wants to deal with and allow people to know in the moment that they are called to do this or that in a very specific way.

Is this you? Do have this gift? Does the description of this gift in action resonate with what you have experienced in various situations, though you may not have known how to respond? Realize this is a way God has gifted and equipped you to be of real help and encouragement to people in or out of the Church.

Healing

The word *healing* refers to bringing wellness of many kinds; including all types of illnesses, physical, emotional, and mental. Here is how some have defined and described this gift:

> The gift of healing is the special ability that God gives to certain members of the Body of Christ to serve as human intermediaries through whom it pleases God to cure illness and restore health apart from the use of natural means.[4]

> The divine enablement to be God's means for restoring people to wholeness.[5]

The focus of the gift of healing is human illness, and not with demons or their side effects. This is really important. If you survey the Gospels, those who are mentally or physically sick call Jesus "Lord," "Teacher," "Son of David," or "Master," which all denote humble and proper respect for the Lord. Yet demons addressed Jesus as "the Holy One of God" (Mark 1:24), "the Son of God" (Mark 3:11) or "the Son of the Most High God" (Mark 5:7). The contrast in modes of address is an important characteristic that distinguishes ordinary sickness from demonic possession. Sick people came to Jesus with hope; demon possessed people saw Jesus as a threat. So even the language of people and demons shows which gift Jesus was about to use, healing or works of power.

This spiritual gift has been at the center of much of the Church's historic hesitance to engage in careful examination and exercise of the gifts. Given the amount of craziness that has sometimes been associated with healing, it's not hard to understand the temptation to deny the gift as a whole rather than accept it, even though it is often misunderstood and counterfeited. One of the important decisions we have made at Sanctus is to accept the challenge to "have conversations" about everything and anything that God has said or done, no matter how out of the norm it may seem. We have identified in Scripture and experienced two types of healing that we now look for in our church. One is discussed in some detail in James 5:13-15.

Is anyone among you in trouble? Let them pray. Is anyone happy? Let them sing songs of praise. Is anyone among you sick? Let them call the elders of the church to pray over them and anoint them with oil in the name of the Lord. And the prayer offered in faith will make the sick person well; the Lord will raise them up. If they have sinned, they will be forgiven.

The process described here is not necessarily the gift of healing; it's an office-based responsibility carried out by elders in the church. Part of eldership is the authority to pray for those in need, anointing them with oil. James is not setting up the church as an alternative care option for those who are sick, rejecting the notion of healthy practices, medicine, and doctors. In fact the oil present is an indicator of the importance of a medicinal component to healing. The reference to sins in verse 15 points to the elders' role in questioning the sick person regarding what care has already been pursued to make sure every God-provided resource on the medical front has been consulted. It also gives the sick person the opportunity to consider whether their sickness is related to sin, since sometimes sickness can be the consequence of sinful behavior. It makes little sense to pray for physical healing when the spiritual violation that contributed to the problem goes unaddressed. In our church, partly because of our size, we schedule a time of healing prayer with the elders at least once a month and walk people through these biblical steps. We do this at the end of our services by reading James 5, and then have our elders be available at the front of the church post service. In many ways it feels like communion, worship or singing–a normal part of church and common faithfulness that's public and available. And by the way, that last point matters. In the past we did it only once in a blue moon, when someone would call and ask. Providing this opportunity publicly post service as a normal routine encouraged and facilitated God's help for those who were seeking.

Think about it; we've seen this same pattern with most of the gifts. There's a general expectation, for instance, that all believers will pray regularly and seek to improve their prayer habit consistently, yet others are gifted to pray. All are called to make disciples; some are given the gift of evangelism, we're all encouraged to give generously; some have the gift of giving. And we all are called to take seriously God's willingness to heal and involve church leadership in seeking healing with us.

There are also some people who actually have a spiritual gift of healing. This gift is exercised when God's Spirit chooses and gifts certain of His children to be healing intermediaries within the body of Christ. God heals people through them. The model we see practiced by Jesus, who clearly had this gift, is that He touched people or people touched Him, and God healed. He demonstrated how a person with the spiritual gift of healing might go about practicing their gift. This gift is about sickness.

Does this mean the gift allows someone to heal indiscriminately? Are all healed when they are touched or prayed for? Does a person with this gift simply walk through life passing out healing left and right? We all know from experience that doesn't happen. But does that mean the gift isn't part of God's ongoing plan?

I grew up as a Baptist. When it comes to praying for healing, we do kind of. Our prayers were mostly phrases designed to minimize any confidence and maximize giving God an out for not healing: "O God, if it is by some chance your will, perhaps, and not trying to put You under any pressure, or assuming You would actually intervene—would You heal this person, maybe? And if not, Your will be done." I can contrast my upbringing with some of my Pentecostal friends who come down heavy on the name-it-and-claim it approach to healing, where the appeal to God is assumed to have been answered and the failure to see that answer is entirely the fault of the sick person's lack of faith. I realize those are extreme examples of a biblical position on the gift of healing and God's promises to heal. But here's the point: in the middle of the conversation about healing we really need to connect a view of history and convergence with the present.

Let's begin with our ultimate model, Jesus. Following Him through the Gospels we see Him healing as He used spiritual disciplines like prayer. The impression is that part of His prayer life with the Father was devoted to getting permission or authority for healing, because the accounts, particularly in John 5, show Jesus in places with many sick people where He didn't heal everybody. Here is the key and the power of the gift of healing; it also has to be tied to permission. How does one get permission? By the spiritual disciplines of asking and listening: Lord, do You want me to pray with Your authority or not? This gift is often exercised in conjunction with the gift of words of knowledge and best performed in community.

One author really brings needed understanding as he wrote:

The gift of healing does not give a person supernatural power over disease. He or she is simply a channel through whom God works. There were several uses of this gift in the New Testament. In addition, to the humanitarian element, showing God's love and compassion to people in need, there was also, releasing healing power gave authority to the message and the messenger who brought God's word to the people, it was a way of demonstrating the love and compassion of God to people.[6]

Here are some clues that might reveal or confirm that you have this gift. You experience a deep desire to see God alleviate physical problems in people and the willingness to be used by God to do so, an unusual ability to sense the power of God when it is present for healing, and the ability to trust God and believe that He wants to heal. You have the willingness to take risks for God... The principle of contagion probably applies here. Those who are around people operating in this type of healing ministry are likely to be drawn into it and be open to God releasing this gift in them so that they can release the healing to others. It is not about a show, it's not about a big, dramatic display; it is about God healing people to either bring the person or others to Jesus in whose name the healing took place, or it is to heal followers of Jesus.[7]

Some with this gift speak of sensing heat or power in them or their hands, and after the healing it leaves. Before you dismiss that as New Age or crazy, I remind you that Jesus used the same language. A women bleeding for years was so desperate, she touched Jesus' clothes and was healed. And Jesus immediately noticed that power had left Him, and He asked, "Who touched me?" (Mark 5:25-34).

But then Wagner writes:

It seems that in the exercise of this gift that faith plays a crucial role. However, faith to be healed does not always originate with the person needing healing although this is often the case in the New Testament. Sometimes the faith originates with the person doing the healing. Other times it appears as if it depends totally upon God and not upon the healer or the person receiving the healing. The phrase, the power of the Lord was present for healing, occurs several times in the New Testament. When the power of the Lord is present for healing the quality of faith in the one being healed and the quality of faith in the healer seemed to be overshadowed by the sovereign work of God.[8]

Does this mean we should not go to doctors or refuse medication? Of course not. It's not an either/or choice. If God says, "Heal," then do it, but if not, of course we can and should use all medical help for both physical and mental illness. Those are clearly means God also uses to bring about healing. Is this you? Do you have the gift of healing?

Before we end this discussion of the spiritual gift of healing, let me include a copy of the script we read before we provide healing prayer in our services. I thought it would be a helpful example after what I have already said about this gift, to give you an idea of how we facilitate the use of this gift in a local church.

1. Spiritual Gifts: Here at Sanctus, we believe the Bible teaches all the gifts are for the Church body today. If you've been sensing a prompting from God during the service—maybe a Scripture, a image, or a word—that you feel is for the whole church, please text it to the number on the screen or come see me at the front. Our team will test and discern the word to see if it is for the wider body.

2. Context for Healing Prayer: There's a growing sense among the leaders of this church that God wants to do more among us through signs and wonders, and part of that is physical healing. This is a new thing for us as a community—to pray for this—so be gracious with us as we learn, but we want to step out in obedience and faith and see what the Lord wants to do among us.

3. We want to make room for a word of knowledge at this time if available. "We have a sense, or we wonder if there might be someone with..."

4. Instructions and Invitation: If that's you (or, if there's no word of knowledge ready to give at this point, say, "So if you are seeking physical healing tonight, and if you sense that God is prompting you to come forward to receive prayer for physical healing,) then we would welcome you to come to this prayer area over here where a trustworthy team of pastors and volunteers—with the right mix of spiritual gifts—would be happy to pray

with you and seek the Lord's will for physical healing. Let's see what Jesus will do.

5. Setting expectations: Let's remind ourselves what Scriptures say about healing: The Bible is clear that not everyone will be healed in this life, but all believers will be fully healed when Jesus returns. However, God sometimes chooses to miraculously heal some of us now, according to His sovereign will, and for His glory. So we want to be open to that, to follow the prompting of the Holy Spirit, and to ultimately seek God's sovereign will above anything else. When we align ourselves with God's will, that's when His power will come.

To summarize what I've said about healing, Elder prayer is simply what should be practiced as a matter of course in the church body. The church should be reminded that the Elders can be asked to anoint and pray for healing. The gift of healing is also permission-based. There must be heightened awareness and listening developed through spiritual disciplines, and at times the cooperation of those with the gift of knowledge can urge the use of the gift of healing.

As part of a Connect group I had a very good friend who was dying of cancer. It was a terrible situation. I remember sitting in a hospital not knowing what to do. This young mom's husband was a first generation Christian and I felt helpless as her life slowly faded away. So I prayed, "God, do you want me to ask for healing?" I didn't have the gift as far as I knew. And I heard an unbelievable answer: "No. I'm going to take her home." This is why permission matters. If you under-promise, you'll expect God to do nothing, and if you over-promise, you can shipwreck someone's faith. Permission from God is critical when it comes to healing.

Miracles

The last of the Power Gifts is workings of power, also known as miracles. This gift involves the release of God's power to demonstrate His utter uniqueness. As Jesus demonstrated, it involves casting out demons, raising people from the dead, and changing the course of nature. Here are some great sample definitions:

> The gift of miracles is the special ability that God gives to certain members of the Body of Christ to serve as human intermediaries through whom it pleases God to perform powerful acts that are perceived by observers to have altered the ordinary course of nature.[9]

> The term may refer to any kind of activity where God's mighty power is evident. It may include answers to prayer for deliverance from physical danger... or powerful works of judgment on enemies of the gospel or those who require discipline within the church... or miraculous deliverance from injury... But such acts of spiritual power may also include power to triumph over demonic opposition...[10]

> The workings of powers, refers to the releasing of God's supernatural power so that the miraculous intervention of God is perceived and God receives recognition for the supernatural intervention.[11]

We see these workings of power in Jesus and many of His followers time and time again. Its uses are two-fold. It can be used to bring people to Jesus for the first time or to build up or set free those that already follow Jesus.

Where we find reported miracles in the New Testament, they often highlight or confirm the witness given by those spreading the gospel. They drive home the weight of the message. Particularly in places where the power of darkness has been active, God's mighty power demonstrates the defeat of evil. We see in Hebrews 2 an indication of this gift in action:

We must pay the most careful attention, therefore, to what we have heard, so that we do not drift away. For since the message spoken through angels was binding, and every violation and disobedience received its just punishment, how shall we escape if we ignore so great a salvation? This salvation, which was first announced by the Lord, was confirmed to us by those who heard him. God also testified to it by signs, wonders and various miracles, and by gifts of the Holy Spirit distributed according to his will (Hebrews 2:1-4).

There are several evidences of this gift. God has put you in situations in which you saw the power of God demonstrated in order to vindicate God's character. Others have noticed that you have an ability and sensitivity to discern what God wants to do in a given situation, a willingness to risk your reputation and trust God in unusual circumstances. You often find it relatively easy to exercise a deep trust and faith in God. You are ready to deal with demons directly and when you pray, they leave people or strongholds they have held. Through these acts many come to faith in Jesus or are set free to walk in a deeper way in their relationship with Jesus himself.[12]

Notice some key things as a summary. Healing is God using someone to heal people physically or emotionally. Works of power are about dealing with the demonic, with nature, or performing actions that cause all to know God is truly involved. Words of knowledge are God giving information or specific calls to action that the person giving them would not otherwise be able to know, and which lead to God working and his Lordship growing. Notice that a word of knowledge is spontaneous, situational, specific, and must be authenticated. And unlike prophecy, it will not be obviously effective 100% of the time, which is okay. It needs to be tested.

With healing, with power, or a word for a person, you must ask Jesus, "yes or no?" and this request should be made in community. Permission to speak or act is key in seeing God work. Stop and ask God: "Why have You told me this?"

"Am I to pray, am I to consult with leaders, am I called to act?" Just because you know or are gifted does not mean you own what you have been given. Think about Jesus, His will and His work, not your ego, your identity, or your fame. It is about God's glory; about Jesus bringing people to Himself and then releasing them so they can be free and the world will see Him.

I cannot stress this enough: character is key, authority is essential, and relationship with others is foundational. We all need to have grace with each other. We all need to know that as we learn to use these gifts we are going to make mistakes. We all need to give each other space, encourage one another towards right use of the gifts, and let Scripture continually guide our steps.

Does what I've described match experiences you have had as a follower of Jesus? Those vivid moments of awareness of other people's lives may be important clues about the role God's Spirit has built into your life as a Christian. Just remember that the principle of permission gives you some room to discover whether these impressions are part of your gifting. One other thought; how will you and your church know if gifts are present if they are never acknowledged or given room to operate—either situationally or proclamationally?

Let me also encourage those who are discerners or gifted with words of knowledge. Just because God allows you to see something (and don't downplay the role God plays here), you are not the oracle of spiritual knowledge. This gift is counterfeited on the other side by people who act like they own the power they wield, using it to manipulate and harm others. Your practice of these gifts must be saturated with humility and eagerness to continually listen to God. When you are given some kind of special knowledge, respond by prayerfully asking, "Lord, I acknowledge You are the source of this knowledge. I'm eager to understand why You have shown me this."

This response has been very helpful in learning to manage my own gifts, which seemed strange and maybe even crazy to me at first, so I tended to handle them as information that required immediate and significant confrontation. I had to learn that a proactive approach often got me in trouble because I lacked permission—not only from God but also from those I intended to help. If you find you have been gifted with one or more of the power gifts, take time to understand your gift, ask God to work on your character, particularly humility, and remain in proper relationship with the leadership of your church as you learn in practice how to use your gifting well.

All this may begin by opening a conversation with other believers. Ask them what they have seen in your responses and actions in various settings. Be willing to respond with your own perceptions of them. Share your experiences, even the strange ones that have caused you to wonder what God was doing in your life, or if it was God at all. And remember that all the gifts have been ultimately given for the benefit of the entire Church and as a vehicle to bring non-believers to Christ. Be ready to encourage those with gifts that are clearly different than yours. Recognize that God's Spirit is composing an amazing musical piece that He wants played by a symphony of the Body of Christ, made up of many instruments that don't play the same notes but together create a majestic harmony of glory to God.

As I come to the end of these chapters about the gifts of the Holy Spirit, I want to emphasize the power of all this related to our task of evangelism. The spiritual gifts matter. We can all feel overwhelmed by the task before us, and the complexity of the needs all around us. We feel we can't individually, or as a local church pivot quickly enough to respond to these needs, or, we try to reach so many groups of people that our efforts become unfocused and confused. All this is why convergence matters so much.

Our world is looking for love, and God has provided His church as a conduit of His love to the world. If the world does not see and find love in the Church, they won't find it anywhere else. When people are empowered with love gifts, they become passionate about social justice and other arenas for God's love. People with word gifts become the great thinkers of the Church, able to argue brilliantly and compellingly for both believers and unbelievers about the beautiful rationality and meaning of the gospel. People with power gifts can demonstrate the power of God for people who access the faith through power.

We must also remember that unlike us, much of the world comes to faith this way—they experience spiritual power before engaging their intellect. Here in the west, I suspect a good part of our reluctance to accept the spiritual gifts is that we try to begin with rationality and logical conviction before we can embrace them as manifestations of God's power.

The Church has been historically healthiest when the spiritual gifts have been engaged through believers. The effective functioning of all the gifts creates the most compelling evangelistic impact on the watching world, drawn by profound experience, profound thinking, and profound love. This was God's plan all along. When all the gifts are affirmed and growing and people and groups are engaged in their spiritual giftedness, the power to reach many grows exponentially. The intellectual curiosity of skeptics, the power of experience, and love of community all give answers, all open doors which lead very different people to the same place, the Lord Jesus Christ.

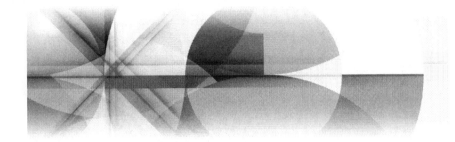

Chapter Twelve:
Convergence and Revival

We've been having the conversation about convergence at Sanctus for a long time. The conversation started before I was even on the scene. In fact, the conversation goes all the way back to a brief exchange between Jesus and Peter, during which Jesus said, "I will build my church." Believers across the centuries have continually asked, "How, Lord; how will You build Your church?" And over and over, Jesus has answered the question through how he modeled the reality of the spiritual disciplines and spiritual gifts for His followers. You and I are simply some of the latest participants in the conversation around discovering what generation after generation has found: how faithful Jesus has been in building and preserving His church. If you've learned anything from this part of the conversation, that understanding ought to bring the profound sense that God has been consistently and intentionally at work for a long time, and He has accomplished more than we will ever really know this side of eternity. We only get glimpses along the way, and we actually have our moment to participate. This should alleviate our fears and our instinct to run and hide in the middle of today's surrounding, dangerous storms. Jesus' life and ministry was surrounded by both controversy and power. So was the early church, and so it has been ever since. Convergence should give you hope.

Revival

There is a unique spiritual experience that can descend upon a local church and sometimes impact an entire region, which we call *revival*. Revival is, more than anything else, those moments in history when God sovereignly chooses to break into our common faithfulness and create healthy spiritual upheaval.

In retrospect, as a church we have been on a journey of genuine historic revival though it was not always immediately obvious. At one point early on I was engaged in my regular devotions without any unusual signs: nothing fantastic or shocking; Gabriel wasn't present; lights weren't flashing; the room didn't shake. I was by myself, reading my Bible as a worship song played in the background.

Unexpectedly, a heaviness entered into the room that I recognized as neither psychological nor evil, yet it left me unable to move. I simply knew God was present and as I waited, my mind was told, "Read 2 Chronicles 5," a passage whose contents I couldn't remember. Immobilized because the presence of God was so strong, I couldn't even reach for a printed Bible. All I had was a Blackberry (from which I have been subsequently set free by an iPhone), which at that moment was my only immediate access to the Scriptures. When I opened my YouVersion app, it offered me an update. The voice within me said, "I'll wait for the update," which even at the time seemed funny and shocking. As soon as I started reading 2 Chronicles 5, I realized it was the account of Solomon dedicating the Temple in Jerusalem he had constructed to honor the Lord.

In that moment the Lord said, "I have decided to sovereignly bring a movement of My Spirit in My church like you've never seen, and you're going to start praying this passage from My Word back to Me."

That starting point began a journey that significantly changed the trajectory and experience of our church forever. In the immediate months that followed, myself and several of our church staff were given five or six promises of God, which led to a period of three years of multiple encounters with God that had nothing directly to do with spiritual gifts or disciplines but were simply palpable visits from God among us. Time and time again it was like Jesus would come shockingly close and sin and pain would be exposed. We traced much of this back to the promises God had given us to pray back to Him.

At one point, I was with one of the other pastors (Dave) and a few others, and we strongly sensed the Lord was going to approach, although not able to explain how we knew. We were gathered to pray and again sensed the weight of God's presence in the room to the point that for the first time in my life the holiness of God so overwhelmed me that I felt I needed to die.

I remember feeling as if I needed to dig myself into the ground. Yet at the same time I felt terror, I also felt completely loved. That's how I knew it was God. Out of that intense moment I experienced God begin to undo me. Over a period of six months, under the watchful care of other pastors, God's Spirit fundamentally confronted me on everything from my theology to the practical matters in my life of defending myself, hurting others, sexual sin, self-sufficiency, engaging in church politics, focus on my own needs, fear, and more. And every time, Jesus moved closer and I simply could not resist Him.

The point is that all these unusual events were initiated by Christ, not programmed or planned by us. These encounters with the living God happened not only with me but also to our lead pastor Dave, our prayer pastor and eventually spread throughout the church at large. Hundreds and hundreds of people had encounters with Christ that cannot be explained as normal experiences. Since 2011 our church has had several moments of this, where Jesus seems to draw close, then steps away only to return again. Many of us liken these experiences to waves of God's presence that come in with intensity and then recede. And each time we sense the receding; we're tempted to wonder, "Is it over? Are we done?" but Jesus lets us know, "No, no. I have other things to do, but I'll be back. In the meantime, continue to pray the promises I have given to you."

We have collected the accounts of over four hundred incidents of encounters with Christ from these last several years that left the people in our church radically changed. One of our takeaways from all of this has been a theology of the weight of God's presence, which is what the origin of the word "glory" really means in the Bible. We discovered that reality firsthand as God dealt with us.

During much of 2011, I was preaching a series on the spiritual gifts. The results and parallel experiences of God's presence were not planned. We were doing our best to faithfully declare the entire counsel of God but weren't expecting to see God move us toward revival. Once things began to happen, one of the most shocking occurrences for Dave, the rest of our staff, and myself was the way God kept "going ahead of us" and leading us into new experiences. We noticed a remarkable pattern in which several of us would be simultaneously given the exact same name of a person for whom we were supposed to pray. So we began to approach these people and ask, "May we pray for you?" We learned to ask permission in order to exercise humility and to build safety in these relationships. With their permission, we also asked, "In general terms, what have you been asking God for in your life?" "Would you be willing to lay down your expectations of what you would like the Lord to do in favor of simply asking Him to do what He wants for you?" When they agreed, we prayed simply and the outcomes were amazing. People of all ages and backgrounds with whom we went through this process all said, in one way or another, "I have been asking God to do a new thing in my life. In my devotional times I have longed to sense God moving." We saw Scripture promises confirmed in obvious ways as those who sought Him found God. This has continued among us as a pattern as we continue to be given names of people to pray for. God still from time to time meets the deep hunger of people for Him by encountering them in encouraging and life-changing ways.

Here's another example. One day during the week both Dave and I were in our offices at church. As he was working, Dave was given a name and when he mentioned it to me, I realized the same person's name had been clearly on my mind. We discovered almost immediately that this particular woman was actually in the building at the time, taking part in a women's Bible study. We contacted her and, in private told her we had both been given her name as someone we should pray for, and could we have permission? Was she willing to lay down any expectations? She responded by saying she felt the Lord had been preparing her for something. As Dave and I prayed, both of us were given the strong sense that the need in her life was about a lack of forgiveness. When we told her, she immediately burst into tears. She said, "Yes, there is a person against whom I've been harboring bitterness and un-forgiveness, and the Lord has been speaking to me about it but I've been resisting Him. Now that you have confirmed it I can't do that anymore." She left us and went to reconcile with that person right away.

The lessons about God's working can be delivered in almost any setting. I was teaching in a Seminary class and a middle-aged woman put up her hand. She was Reformed in background and not charismatic at all. She told a story about a very dark time in her life when a friend of hers who was more charismatic prayed for her. During the prayer time her friend shook like a leaf, which scared her, but her friend's prayers were powerful and they revealed that she knew information about her that she had no access to at all. The friend knew background details about the need that made her prayers very pointed. She was also able during her prayer to inform this woman of what Jesus was doing in her life during the dark time. The information brought healing and humility, not humiliation, and Jesus did move. My questioner was wondering how to integrate what seemed undeniably true about that experience with a lifetime of spiritual teaching that downplayed that kind of direct involvement by God in a personal situation.

I realized as I was listening to her account that this Reformed woman presumed that if you had the gift of Words of Knowledge then you had to shake for it be real! She fused the practice of a real gift with a non-essential experience. It wasn't so much the realization that God was showing her His intimate awareness of her situation; it was the way that knowledge was given that she found difficult to process. And frankly, it was for me, too! Right in the class I stopped and asked her why she paired one (shaking) with the other (word of knowledge) and she said, "I don't know I just did!" So much confusion was cleared up regarding people's reluctance to exercise spiritual gifts.

This matters because the model or experience of a gift with other incidental factors (right or wrong) can become a stumbling block in recognizing a gift, walking in it, or even accepting it. As I thought further about the process of gift recognition, a much larger, more significant issue for the church came up. What is the difference between gifts and disciplines, which are normal and guaranteed, and the non-normal, unusual moves of God?

If you take time to read the stories in the Bible, you'll see something if you look closely. Many that knew God, lived for Him, loved Him, and were faithful in the boring, bad and good times, suddenly met their God in a more profound, more tangible, more unexpected, more overwhelming way. Those who were faithful in a little suddenly got a whole lot more! From the shepherds at Jesus' birth to the Transfiguration, from Elijah on Mount Carmel to Isaiah's call, all are examples of heaven touching and changing earth, a foretaste of what is to permanently come.

The modern word for this in Christian vernacular is *revival*. To have the God we worship, sing to, give to, live for, and speak about suddenly and manifestly come upon His people with such power and palpable presence that them, the lives of people, and the church are so changed that those in the community also begin to experience (searching or not) dramatic encounters with the God—that's revival! Suddenly, life is not business as usual. You will know heaven has touched earth and revival is happening when everything changes, or when all that is known is suddenly and fully experienced.

Listen to some different descriptions people give of this work of God, of this hope!

"The sovereign act of God, in which he restores his own backsliding people to repentance, faith and obedience." --Stephen Olford

"The return of the Church from her backslidings, and the conversion of sinners." --Charles Finney

"An extraordinary movement of the Holy Spirit producing extraordinary results." --Richard Owen Roberts

"A community saturated with God." –Duncan Campbell[1]

Are there distinctions between renewal, revival, and awakening? At Sanctus, we would say, "Yes." This is the common script we've chosen: RENEWAL is when God touches the heart of a single individual. REVIVAL is when God touches a community of faith at large. An AWAKENING is when the wider society is impacted through mass conversion and life change.

One of the Bible passages that best describe God's unique work in this area is the event we call the Transfiguration of Jesus. The account is recorded in three of the Gospels (Matthew 17:1-13; Mark 9:2-13; and Luke 9:28-36). Let's follow Matthew's account and see what Jesus was trying to show us and tell us through the lens of revival.

What had happened just before this event is very important. Jesus was walking with Peter and the other disciples and He asked them a question that every individual must answer. The answer given leads to eternal life or death; it's the answer that changes one's life trajectory.

When Jesus came to the region of Caesarea Philippi, he asked his disciples, "Who do people say the Son of Man is?" They replied, "Some say John the Baptist; others say Elijah; and still others, Jeremiah or one of the prophets." "But what about you?" he asked. "Who do you say I am?" Simon Peter answered, "You are the Christ, the Son of the living God" (Matt 16:13-16).

Think of all the answers Peter *didn't* give that have been offered to manage Jesus: you are just a prophet, just a spiritual teacher, just a political revolutionary, not an incarnation of God, one great religious teacher among many, one of several paths to God, you are crazy, you are a liar, or, you are Satan the deceiver. He confessed the correct one: "You are the Messiah, the long awaited One and You are Son of God. You are the only one who has seen God face to face because You and the Father are One, so You can speak with authority from Your identity, all You are is grounded in Who You are, God in flesh, Immanuel, God with us!"

Since Peter's confession, that truth that has rocked the ages, brought hope to millions and been a stumbling block to many more. But at the Transfiguration the Father and the Son choose to pull back the veil just a little more to show three of the disciples that the one they really do know, the One they have served with, eaten with and seen heal; the one Peter now has claimed is the Christ, is actually the One they have heard and read about from Genesis to Malachi. For the One they hang out with is none other than the God of Adam, Noah, Abraham, Isaac, Jacob, David, Isaiah, and Jeremiah.

"It's time," heaven says. So the Son of God, Jesus of Nazareth, in obedience to the Father, sets the stage for a revival of sorts. It is first only for a small group, Jesus' inner circle of 12: *"After six days Jesus took with him Peter, James and John the brother of James, and led them up a high mountain by themselves"* (Matthew 17:1).

"After six days." This should send up an Old Testament flare for us. It was in six days that God created all of reality, beauty, color, and life, and then said it was good. In six days God spoke and existence came to be. Yet another new creation was about to happen through Jesus' perfect life, death, and resurrection, a new creation that would not only bring us back into a relationship with God but was the signal of the beginning of the end which will culminate in the restoration of Eden, the new heavens and the new earth.

There is still more to understand about the significance of the six days. What is about to unfold is connected to Moses' personal encounter with God at the giving of the Ten Commandments. Read the words of Exodus 24 and notice the time frame as well as words like *fire, cloud, glory* and where they show up as we walk through the passage in Matthew.

> *The Lord said to Moses, "Come up to me on the mountain and stay here, and I will give you the tablets of stone, with the law and commands I have written for their instruction."... When Moses went up on the mountain, the cloud covered it, and the glory of the Lord settled on Mount Sinai. For six days the cloud covered the mountain, and on the seventh day the Lord called to Moses from within the cloud. To the Israelites the glory of the Lord looked like a consuming fire on top of the mountain* (Exodus 24:12, 15-17).

Notice back in Matthew 17:1 that it says Jesus led them up. He started the process. They didn't know where they were going, and they didn't know what was going to happen, but they agreed they would follow Him, wherever He led.

So here are Peter, James, John, and Jesus up on this mountain. Luke's account notes they went to pray and to connect with the Father, until like all of us sometimes, they fell asleep. It says in Luke 9:32 that Peter and his companions *"were very sleepy."* As their eyes were closing and dreams were coming into their minds, as yawning turned into a losing battle with slumber, everything suddenly changed. The heavens ripped open and the mountaintop was consumed with unnatural light, fire, and brilliance. Terror and fear came in milliseconds as the three wondered if this was dream or reality; they were so scared they lost their ability to move. Sleep was gone as all five senses were overwhelmed, and they were transfixed, frozen, and full of wonder. Matthew simply said of Jesus, *"There he was transfigured before them."*

Transfigured– what does that mean? Jesus was changed in appearance. The original word in Greek is where we get the word *metamorphosis*. He was transformed so that in the moments that followed He was seen as fully human and fully God. These three men got a glimpse of Jesus, as He will be seen in heaven! Jesus the Christ, the Son of God was manifest and revealed so Peter, James, and John saw Him in heavenly splendor. As R. T. France wrote "This transformation is not so much a physical alteration as an added dimension of glory, it is the same Jesus, but now with an awesome brightness 'like the sun' and 'like light.'"[2] Peter's confession 'you are the Christ' is now fully realized!

Matthew continued by describing this beyond-yet-present experience as best he could, given the stunned testimony of his three witnesses. *"His face shone like the sun, and his clothes became as white as the light"* (v.2b). Mark, probably listening to Peter struggle to verbalize the unspeakable, recorded it this way, *"His clothes became dazzling white, whiter than anyone in the world could bleach them"* (Mark 9: 3).

For a brief moment the veil was lifted and they saw fully. Jesus and His clothing gleamed and glittered, shining brighter than any modern light we have ever seen or invented. This light was coming from *within* Him and descending from above Him. As Peter, James, and John looked on, and their vision adjusted to heavenly light, they suddenly saw two others, the most famed personages in Jewish faith and history. They are called the fathers of faith, great men that these three had heard about since they were little boys: *"Just then there appeared before them Moses and Elijah, talking with Jesus"* (v.3). Both figures now conversing with Jesus had their lives ended in supernatural ways and both were great leaders who talked with God at Mount Sinai. Moses was the great lawgiver, the one that led Israel out of Egypt. Elijah was the greatest miracle-working prophet who came to represent all of the prophets. They were present to witness and to testify that the One with whom they were conversing was the fulfillment of the Old Testament.

The entire unfolding of God's plan in history, allegory, in poetry, and in prophecy was to prepare the world for the coming of Jesus. The Law and the Prophets show us our sin, our need for an external Savior; they give us hope. Now, at this moment, time was shattered, heaven and earth kissed, and Jesus, God in flesh, was about to start the process that would lead to greater miracles and a greater second exodus.

Remember that Peter, James, and John were orthodox Jews. They must have been thinking, *Moses and Elijah; are you kidding me? I have heard about and revered you my whole life and now here you are! And this is the long-awaited Messiah! I am seeing more in this moment than any Jew has ever seen before! It cannot get better than this, the kingdom has come, heaven on earth, and all Jewish hopes and fears are now dealt with!*

So, how *did* Peter respond? He said to Jesus, *"Lord, it is good for us to be here. If you wish, I will put up three shelters—one for you, one for Moses and one for Elijah"* (v.4). Notice again that although Peter usually called him Rabbi, Teacher, or Master, he now went much, much further and calls him Lord, the name of God from the Old Testament.

In confusion and amazement, Peter basically said, "Let's stay here! This is great; our prayers are answered, we want it all now, let's plant a flag and declare this the kingdom of heaven right here and now!" Peter wanted the momentary experience of the long-anticipated reality to be fulfilled. "We want to live here, to commune with you. We don't want to go back to the mundane, the boring, the 7-day workweek, sickness, the family fights, the Romans, politics, war, and dealing with diseases and demons. You keep talking about dying and death, but you don't need to do that when there's *this* alternative! Let's go buy some tents from Cabela's and make camp!" Do you really think you and I would think something different?

The suggested placement of the shelters also shows us something. One old preacher said, "Peter, bewildered by the heavenly vision and not knowing what to say, proposed to build three shelters, one for Christ, one for Moses and one for Elijah. He seemed, in fact, to place the lawgiver and the prophet side by side with his divine Master, as if all three were equal. At once, we are told, the proposal was rebuked in a marked manner."[3]

As Peter was working on a strategic plan to camp forever with Jesus and His heavenly posse, another act of heaven interrupted Peter's thoughts, desires, and human agenda: *"While he was still speaking, a bright cloud enveloped them, and a voice from the cloud said..."* (v.5).

"A bright cloud enveloped them..." The history of the cloud is central to everything we're talking about throughout this book. The cloud is a form of the Shekinah glory (which means "dwelling of God"), referred to often in the Old Testament. A supernatural cloud is always connected to the brilliance, glory, fire, and overwhelming presence of God. That presence was experienced at the giving of the Ten Commandments, but also throughout the wilderness wanderings when a pillar of cloud led Israel by day and a pillar of fire at night. It was experienced at both the dedication of the Tabernacle (Exodus 40:34) and of the Temple (1 Kings 8:10- 11). It was the same fire that came down and consumed sacrifice and altar on Mt. Carmel when Elijah invited God to display His power. It was seen at the call of Isaiah (Isaiah 6:1-4) and Ezekiel (Ezekiel 1:4). It is the glory that shone around the shepherds when the angels sang and announced the birth of Jesus (Luke 2:9). That same cloud appeared at the Transfiguration of Jesus and at the birth of the church in Acts 2:2-3 when the Spirit came as tongues of fire. It was also seen at the death of Stephen and at the conversion of Saul on the road to Damascus. And it is out of that cloud, on the mountaintop, from the fire, that the voice of the Father speaks, *"This is my Son, whom I love; with him I am well pleased. Listen to him!"* (v.5).

The Holy Spirit, now in the form of a cloud, was given to affirm Jesus' identity, so His life, death, resurrection, and accession would be valid. Here we see God in his Trinitarian fullness again, as at Jesus' baptism. There is the Father's voice, the Son of God in flesh, and the Spirit in the form of a cloud. We see the reality of the God who is one, found in three Persons forever and ever, amen! And what does God say? "Listen to him, obey him" (v.5).

The disciples' response is far too rare among people who claim to seriously follow Jesus today: *"When the disciples heard this, they fell facedown to the ground, terrified"* (v.6). How often are we "facedown" in God's presence? Assuming that He was manifest before us, this response from us would be immediate. *Terrified*: in that shocking and sudden exposure to ultimate reality, they knew that only God is God and they most definitely were not. At that moment they knew their own sinful, imperfect condition before the Holy God— and that they were invited and allowed guests with no other right to be there. During unusual moves like this, our omnipresent God becomes palpably present; He who is transcendent comes near. In those terrifying moments, there is not only a spiritual response, but also a physical one.

When God moves in such ways, and He still does, it is for His glory, for our freedom, and to empower us to move forward in our ministry for others. This is what Isaiah experienced as God prepared him for the challenges he would face

Jon Thompson

as God's prophet: *"'Woe to me!' I cried. 'I am ruined! For I am a man of unclean lips, and I live among a people of unclean lips, and my eyes have seen the King, the Lord Almighty'"* (Isaiah 6: 5).

Encountering God in all aspects of relationship is always full of terror and euphoria, fear and adoration. The Transfiguration story concludes, *"But Jesus came and touched them. 'Get up,' he said. 'Don't be afraid.' When they looked up, they saw no one except Jesus"* (vv. 7-8). As soon as it happened, it was over. Moses and Elijah had vanished and the cloud was gone, and they were returned to reality. What a letdown! All the emotion, adrenaline, terror and euphoria, was here and then gone in an instant. And what does Jesus say? "Let's go. Time to go down the mountain, back to real life, to the Romans and politics, the diseases and demons and struggles of faith, back to the everyday. And yes, back to ministry, now in a deeper, more empowered way."

As we think about revival and convergence, we personally, and as churches, must first be willing to be led up the mountain by Jesus; that is our only part. We don't know what He will do when we reach the top. That is why we must continually seek His presence and practice common faithfulness in the low country while we pray for revival. Secondly, if God in His sovereignty wants this, then He is the one who leads us up. The preparation for revival is often marked when God gives a promise that we must start praying back to Him. Then, in His time, He sends the Holy Spirit and He reveals Himself fully. He moves from omnipresence to palpable presence. We will be terrified, we will confess sin, we will know our need, and we will see all our pain exposed. Much of the time, if we will let the witness of history speak, there will be accompanying physical manifestations like falling over, shaking, weeping, and trembling at the presence of God. Every time God moved in great power in the Scriptures there were physical reactions by the people or the leader. Study church history; accounts from Jonathan Edwards, Wesley, and the Welsh revivals are all full of the unusual work of God from holy laughter, to weeping, to falling over. Do these always happen? No. Do they make you more holy or spiritual? No, but when God moves very close, strange things do happen. The results prove if God's move was real and if that move was accepted and internalized.

Think about John the disciple. He was Jesus' closest friend; he walked with Him and saw all He did. John was there at the Transfiguration, he was there when Jesus died, he held his newly adopted mother as Jesus bled out, he was there when Jesus was resurrected, and he was there when Jesus ascended to heaven. Yet much later, John had another remarkable encounter. At this time, John was the only one of the twelve left; the rest had all been martyred for their love for Jesus. He was ministering in Ephesus, but was exiled at age 90 to the island of Patmos, and there he met his friend again, but now saw Him fully glorified—transfigured again:

> *I turned around to see the voice that was speaking to me. And when I turned I saw seven golden lampstands, and among the lampstands was someone like a son of man, dressed in a robe reaching down to his feet and with a golden sash around his chest. The hair on his head was white like wool, as white as snow, and his eyes were like blazing fire. His feet were like bronze glowing in a furnace, and his voice was like the sound of rushing waters. In his right hand he held seven stars, and coming out of his mouth was a sharp, double-edged sword. His face was like the sun shining in all its brilliance. When I saw him, I fell at his feet as though dead. Then he placed his right hand on me and said: "Do not be afraid. I am the First and the Last. I am the Living One; I was dead, and now look, I am alive forever and ever! And I hold the keys of death and Hades* (Rev 1:12-18).

At age 90 John fell over like he was dead even though he had been Jesus' closest friend! Picture a 90-year-old senior prostrate before Jesus. If you read the encounters of Ezekiel or Isaiah with God, you will see there is a physical reaction to the proximity of the Divine. You will know it is the glorified Jesus and that the Spirit of Christ is among you in a new and close way when you feel that you must die because of your sin, yet you are loved and assured of forgiveness at the same time. Holy love and terror held together is an overwhelming experience. The Holy Spirit comes in full power: the cloud, the fire, and the dove come to give the church, for a period of time, an extraordinary movement of himself, producing extraordinary results in lives, families, the church, and then the community.

During this time we will be pointed to Jesus only; He will be all we can see and He will be the only one we will care about. His will, His agenda, His glory will become central. We will be able to read the following verses and know they are true: *"We live by faith, not by sight. We are confident, I say, and would prefer to be away from the body and at home with the Lord. So we make it our goal to please him, whether we are at home in the body or away from it"* (2 Corinthians 5:7-9).

Convergence is the ongoing, guaranteed reality of God's persistent work in and through His Church; revivals are occasional and intense moments God gives His people. Revivals always include mass conversions of people to Jesus, and a true awakening takes place. But a common mistake many make is to pair the outworking or unusual manifestations of the Spirit during revival with the gifts that are always present in the daily Christian life. No, the revival settings I've described above are not about gifts or disciplines. As we have learned, spiritual disciplines are for all to exercise at any season of life. Spiritual gifts are sovereignly assigned and are normative, day in and day out. But revival is not normal, is not always, and neither are the results. Much of the time during revival there is greater power and presence of God, which means the disciplines are used more and the power behind the gifts is stronger. But revival is started and ended only by God. Otherwise, we all would want to build tents, and historically some have tried but were not allowed because God does not dwell in temples or monuments built by human hands. These seasons are given to send us out and to sustain us over a lifetime. Don't pair one experience with the other. Some revivals last days, some last years.

Should we pray for, ask for, and expectantly wait for God to move in revival? Absolutely. But if He says, "No," or "Not yet," that does not affect the gifts He has given or the disciplines He has modeled. This should help leaders set right expectations about manifestations and outworking. This distinction is not abstract.

On the one hand, many churches that *did* have a real work of God in the past keep trying to replicate it. We must accept that time is done, and we must go back to gifts and holy habits and the last part of Acts 2–good old, common faithfulness. God can do something new in His own timing.

On the other hand, too many of us have never asked to see if Jesus wants revival, to see if a promise would be given to pray back because of fear and ungodly control. My point is that there is one set of experiences and overarching expectations for a revival and another for everyday ministry. For a time they can fuse together if God so chooses, but not necessarily. It would be wise for all pastors and leaders to understand this and never confuse these factors so that expectations are neither too low nor too high. We must keep our expectations anchored to Jesus, who never disappoints.

By history, Sanctus is not only a very conservative congregation; we are also involved in a conservative association with a number of other churches. As word got out that unusual things were happening among us, Dave, a staff woman named Beth, and I were asked by the head of the association to give a report at the national gathering of the board of the association. Naturally we were a little nervous, but the three of us went and for two and a half hours shared what had happened to us personally as well as what had happened throughout our church.

Much of that time was my tearfully recounting the painful process by which God had undone me.

Two remarkable things happened that day. First, as we were sharing, all three of us had the profound sense that the Lord wanted us to pray for one particular administrator on the board, though we had no specific information. We approached her and invited her to join us during the lunch break in a separate room, where we sought permission to pray for her. When she agreed, we were immediately aware that something was wrong between her and her husband and that an inappropriate violation had occurred as an issue of unfaithfulness, though not in a sexual way. We were given an Old Testament passage in which God declares that he is Israel's husband. We asked, "Has something happened in your marriage; has your husband left you? Has something wrong taken place?" She immediately burst into tears. We responded, "We have been commissioned to assure you that Jesus is your husband. He is going to take care of you." We confirmed what God had directly conveyed to her the day before in her devotional quiet time. Between the four of us there was a profound sense of God's love and nearness in that moment.

The second thing that occurred was a contact between Dave and the association's head of doctrine and credentials. We only knew him in his official capacity but Dave's best friend was a member of his church. He asked Dave, "Do you actually think you are hearing God's voice, not just the way Scripture speaks?" When Dave answered yes, he added, "And do you believe that when you hear God speak you need to obey?" Again Dave said, "I do." The man then said, "While all of you were speaking this morning I felt God's Spirit telling me something and I believe I should obey." To which Dave said, "So do I; what has he told you to do?" He said, "I want to confess to you that I have hated you for twenty years." He quickly explained that Dave's longstanding friendship with the member of his church had provoked a jealousy in him during all that time because he felt he was competing with Dave. Neither Dave nor his friend had ever been aware of the problem. But it was resolved that day.

Both these encounters are examples of revival spreading, because God's Spirit was leading people into radically different behavior patterns that were not normal for them. We witnessed vulnerability, repentance of sin, and confessions that were not natural outgrowth of the disciplines or gifts but were sovereign moves of the Spirit. In these situations we had the privilege of letting others know what God was doing among us, and have God confirm it by drawing near in a powerful way. These were ever-widening concentric circles of spiritual impact that we could trace back to that odd moment when God's Spirit met me in my living room and instructed me to read 2 Chronicles 5.

Chapter Thirteen:
Final Notes

In this final chapter, I would like to share and perhaps review for emphasis a number of discoveries we've made at Sanctus that may help you implement and see convergence in the place God has you. For the most part, these are not matters spelled out in Scripture, though as you think of them you will probably note that they have always been part of the life of the Church.

Gift Tension

I realize I've mentioned this throughout the spiritual gift chapters, but it deserves another comment here, because it is relentless and makes an appearance at the oddest times. I want to describe some of the unexpected and hard-to-manage aspects of life in the Church when the gifts are being widely exercised and the disciplines are being intentionally pursued. After tracking these matters in my own life as a follower of Jesus for years, and now with hundreds of fellow Christians, I have repeatedly confirmed the fact that tension and even conflict among believers can often be traced, not to personality differences (which *are* a factor at times), or depravity and demonic resistance

245

(which always resist God's work), but the friction and heat created by the gifts at work. Unless we add this to our list of possible reasons for tension, we may miss something important or address an issue the wrong way.

Here's an example of gift tension. When you spend time with someone whose spiritual gift includes mercy (and that's not your gift), you will note that they are deeply moved and passionate about helping that one person or that marginalized group. When everyone else doesn't rally around the current need provoking them to an outpouring of mercy, they can easily wonder, *what's wrong with this church? Can't they see this need? Can't they feel the desperation? Don't they care for the poor and love the marginalized enough to want to give their life for them?*

The questions aren't wrong, but they can lead to the wrong conclusions if the person fails to remember that their gift is only one of at least twenty- one others. The passion flows in twenty-one different ways—all of them significant. When Paul wrote his extended explanation of the Body of Christ and gifts, he not only inserted the chapter on Love in the middle (1 Corinthians 13), he dedicated a major part of Chapter 12 to the matter of gift tension. He talked about the parts of the body such as the ear, hand, and eye and noted that none of these, as important as they are in themselves, can act alone. They all rely on the other members in order to function. Every member serves all other members, and the only truly essential one is the Head—Jesus Christ himself. In 1 Corinthians 12:21, Paul put the matter bluntly: *"The eye cannot say to the hand, 'I don't need you!' And the head cannot say to the feet, 'I don't need you!'"* That's true, but those of us who have been around church for a while can tell you that this actually does happen. We can become so focused on our gifting that we minimize the gifting and role of others. The visual image of an eyeball rolling down the street without connection to the body presents both a funny and deadly serious image of the crucial truth that God has given everyone gifts to serve everyone in the Body and be sustained by the rest of the church.

This is gift tension. Our spiritual gifts make us respond almost instinctively (or better, with supernatural, spiritual sensitivity) to a situation that places us in a position to alert or encourage others to take action even though they may not perceive the need in the way we do.

Perhaps you've had the experience of spending time with someone whose spiritual gift is intercession. In the course of interaction, you might ask them about their prayer life. Their response is, "Well, I admit today was pretty bad... I only prayed three hours and I can't wait to get back to it." Your jaw drops as you think, *Three hours? I managed three minutes and was running out of stuff on my list.* If you happen to think that out loud, or you mention your frank amazement at their commitment to prayer on behalf of others, they may respond by asking, "Well, don't you love Jesus? Isn't it a special part of walking with Him to spend a lot of time talking with Him? Is something wrong with your spiritual life? Why are you such a Martha instead of being like Mary? How can I pray for you?" The awkward moment that follows this exchange is gift tension. Most of us don't pray out of gifting, we pray out of obedience—and we can all do better. It's wise in that situation to appeal to their strength—"Yes, do pray that I will find greater joy in prayer and a persistent longing to participate." But the person whose gift is intercession also needs to realize that the Holy Spirit has not gifted them to be guilt or shame generators, but to be encouragers and the consistent prayer core of a local church even as others pursue their gifts.

As mentioned earlier, here is one of the greatest examples of gift tension from the early days of the Church, recorded in the books of Acts:

In those days when the number of disciples was increasing, the Hellenistic Jews among them complained against the Hebraic Jews because their widows were being overlooked in the daily distribution of food. So the Twelve gathered all the disciples together and said, "It would not be right for us to neglect the ministry of the word of God in order to wait on tables.

Brothers and sisters, choose seven men from among you who are known to be full of the Spirit and wisdom. We will turn this responsibility over to them and will give our attention to prayer and the ministry of the word." This proposal pleased the whole group. They chose Stephen, a man full of faith and of the Holy Spirit; also Philip, Procorus, Nicanor, Timon, Parmenas, and Nicolas from Antioch, a convert to Judaism. They presented these men to the apostles, who prayed and laid their hands on them. So the word of God spread. The number of disciples in Jerusalem increased rapidly, and a large number of priests became obedient to the faith. (Acts 6:1-7).

The use of "complained" in the first verse is a little misleading. A better translation of the phrase would probably be, "the Hellenistic Jews among them lodged a complaint against the Hebraic Jews." What brought about the complaint? Here you have two groups following Jesus but at odds with each other! The Hellenists were Jews that spoke Greek and attended Greek synagogues while the Hebraic Jews spoke Aramaic and Hebrew and were in synagogues that spoke those languages. Many of the Hellenistic Jews lived all over the Roman world; in fact Paul was a Hellenistic Jew. So there were language barriers, and social tensions because one group sometimes considered themselves more Jewish or more faithful than others.

This was all taking place while both groups lived in the area of the Hebraic Jews, so the Hellenist Jews had little in the way of a social or economic network to care for their widows who were in need. At the same time, wealthier people had been giving money and land to the young church, so no one would be in need. In lodging a complaint that their widows "were being overlooked," the Hellenist group was essentially saying, "Our widows are not getting any food because your widows are getting it all!" They were not just saying, "Hey; this isn't fair." The word used here actually comes from the story of Moses when the people *grumbled* against God and Moses. In other words, the early church, only three years old, is about to split and fracture along ethnic lines. An "us versus them" spirit can crush a church. And this was all happening during a powerful move of God, at a time when "the number of disciples was increasing."

The response by the Twelve to this crisis shows us that there was need for confrontation or correction as well as a need for an assignment of gifts. Their actual statement is a fascinating, correct response to gift tension: *"It would not be right for us to neglect the ministry of the word of God in order to wait on tables"* (v.2). Now if you have the gift of mercy, your immediate thought is, *what's wrong with waiting on tables? That's where real ministry happens!* But note that the apostles didn't say something was wrong, they said it would *"not be right for us"* because to do so would mean turning away from or neglecting their own gifting and as well as crowding out those who *were* gifted to respond to this need. Their response of leadership created the office of deacon in the church. These are special roles of supervisory service that should be given to those gifted to carry them out. Rather than demeaning the service of "waiting on tables," the apostles saw these as ministries worthy enough to lay hands on and commission those identified by the rest of the church for that task. This wise resolution of gift tension brought about a fresh round of revival as the word of God spread (v.7).

Gift tension reminds us that we're part of an organism. We are neither independent actors, nor merely dependent parts (like parasites on the body), but are interdependent. The rest of the church needs us as much as we need the rest of the church. It's like Paul talks about in Ephesians 5 in his discussion of marriage as a parallel for the relationship between Christ and his bride, with mutual submission to one another, even though we have distinct roles.

Let's look to Acts 15 one last time:

Some time later Paul said to Barnabas, "Let us go back and visit the believers in all the towns where we preached the word of the Lord and see how they are doing." Barnabas wanted to take John, also called Mark, with them, but Paul did not think it wise to take him, because he had deserted them in Pamphylia and had not continued with them in the work. They had such a sharp disagreement that they parted company. Barnabas took Mark and sailed for Cyprus, but Paul chose Silas and left, commended by the believers to the grace of the Lord. He went through Syria and Cilicia, strengthening the churches (Acts 15:36-41).

This is gift tension. One of them wasn't wrong and the other right. This isn't arrogance on Paul's part or stubbornness on Barnabas' part; both these leaders in the early church were functioning within their giftedness in working through the tension. Paul was an apostle/leader/teacher gifted with a large vision for spreading the Gospel throughout the world, Barnabas, whose very name means "son of encouragement" was a one-on-one nurturer. In fact, Barnabas was committing himself to do for John Mark what he had previously done for Paul, when Paul first showed up in Jerusalem as a new believer and the Church at large wondered if they could trust their former persecutor. Barnabas took the heat for standing with Paul.[1]

The failure to recognize and acknowledge gift tension can cause intense disagreements and even destructiveness. Mature believers watch for gift tension and adjust expectations to manage these gift-based responses and approaches. That kind of response fosters unity and amazing harmony in ministry. God is able to orchestrate the gifts He gives to the Body in such a way that the various parts produce results that amaze us and bring glory to Him to a degree we could never accomplish on our own. But like the example above, sometimes the disagreement is so sharp there's no immediate resolution.

By the way Pastor, is this your story? Has gift tension now or in the past created a rift between you and another that needs to be reconciled now that you see it through this lens? When it comes to forgiveness and confession, are others watching to see if you actually practice what you preach?

Grace

If you are excited and motivated by what you're learning about convergence, let me caution you about the desperate need for grace anytime believers deliberately begin to seek their spiritual gifts and exercise them within the church. As you know I come from a more conservative evangelical background, one not strongly charismatic (particularly at the beginning). Here's what I've experienced in churches firsthand, including the one I now help lead. Everyone is grace-filled when it comes to the love gifts and word gifts as a rule. If I have an off Sunday and deliver a somewhat less than dazzling sermon with a theological point that may have been unclear, I will usually be approached with gentle questions and encouraging suggestions. "Hey, did you really think that one point all the way through? It seemed like you lost the thread about half way through the explanation. Maybe there's a better approach for getting that point across?" If something I do or say appears to reveal a character issue (an angry tone or impatient gesture) people will come to me and say, "Look; love you, but couldn't help but notice that one slip...what's going on there?" They *wouldn't* say, "Jon, you don't have the gift of teaching at all," or "Jon, you are a false prophet!"

What I'm saying is that people with the word and love gifts tend to function at the relational end of personal interaction. Those with the power gifts—not so much. In other words, I've found that people who have been given a gift in the power area have to learn and be intentional about grace because those gifts tend to be heavy on truth, which can easily impact someone like a hammer or a brick, so the pain of the delivery actually takes away from the needed corrective or instructive side of the gift.

For example, if someone speaks in tongues, but don't do it correctly within the community, the response by others is too often a quick, "See? It's just fake; it's not real"—rather than asking, "How could we do this better?" We assume there's room to grow and learn in the use of the love and word gifts but often don't extend that assumption to the power gifts. Those are assumed to be delivered "fully functioning," when in fact, just like the other gifts, people with power gifts have to grow into their gifting. Because we're talking about community gifts—spiritual capacities given for the benefit of the whole body—it makes sense to think in terms of all of us needing mentors who have the same gifting we have, but who have been exercising the gift longer. We also need mentoring from believers with other gifts who can help us see the impact of a proper or improper use of our gift within the church.

If we are discounting the reality of gifts in general or selecting only certain gifts as acceptable, we are seriously handicapping the Body of Christ from functioning at full capacity. We prevent parts of the church from growing up in Christ and their Holy Spirit enablement to serve the rest of the Church. When one part of the body is kept undeveloped or ineffective, the whole body suffers just as much as when one part of the physical body suffers. Please hear my plea for all of us to be hesitant in dismissing any of the gifts simply because they make us feel uncomfortable or not entirely in control.

Remember, especially as a church leader, that what you legitimize from the pulpit will be seen in action. Pastors ask me all the time, "Why in your church and not in mine?" This underlines the suspicion that we're inventing or making up these stories. My answer is, "You've not had the courage to openly talk about this and allow the many people in your church to step forward and share their experiences." Dear pastor, you ignore the grand river of Spirit-given experiences flowing through your church at your peril. How can you shepherd, evaluate, disciple, and really lead if you ignore what God wants to do among you?

I've also found that the theological accusations against some of the spiritual gifts as too emotional or experiential are themselves often based on emotion and experience rather than the witness of God's Word and the accumulated history of the Church. We all need to ask ourselves regularly, "How do I do a better job of giving grace to brothers and sisters in Christ who struggle to understand and practice the gifts the Holy Spirit has given which are meant for the benefit of all of us?" Those of us in leadership roles and responsible for explaining the parameters and "constructing the sandbox" will not do our best if we eliminate or discount gifts rather than seek to understand their purpose within the church (particularly if we don't have those gifts ourselves). Too many of us make the all-too-easy decision to dismiss gifts with the unintended consequence that we weaken the whole church by excluding resources that are truly from God.

Alongside the exciting and somewhat (at times) turbulent process of discovery in our own church, I've had the opportunity to interact widely with believers in other churches. I have found that many deeply committed followers of Jesus don't really know what to do with the gifting they sense in themselves since it seems to be covertly or overtly rejected by others in the church that they respect. They want to be led but know they aren't gifted that way; yet also want to contribute their part to the body. Leaders in the church often function with significant confidence in their spiritual gifts and are even open to the need for constant improvement in the way they exercise their roles, yet may at the same time hamper, hinder, and hurt other believers as they move in to significant service through gifts on behalf of the whole church. No, as Paul asked rhetorically, we don't all teach or pastor, but all of us have been gifted by the Holy Spirit for some purpose within the church that those who teach or pastor are *not* equipped to do. There's nothing unscriptural about establishing mentoring relationships so that those who are discovering their gifts can meet with others who are already practicing those gifts, and confirm as well as improve their use of those gifts. We all (even pastors) need mentors. I'm simply pleading that you choose to offer grace to those discovering their power gifts just as readily as you dispense grace to those who are exercising the love or the word.

How Do We Lead The Church?

As solo pastors or pastor teams, many of our churches operate based on programs. This is true of mega, large, small, and in-between churches. Let me add immediately that this isn't intended to denigrate programs; we need people-structures to function well. HR, strategic planning, age-appropriate programing, governance—are all good things and even necessary. But don't let programs be the end of the conversation about being the Church together. The Church is not some kind of neighborhood fitness center where people show up and select from a menu of programs they think will help them get spiritually healthy—basically a self-directed, self-motivated, consumer view of the Body of Christ. No, once a newcomer has been converted and born anew by the Holy Spirit, or gives evidence they have been previously converted, they are expected to take an active role in the church.

Yes, we have as many programs as most churches our size, but the difference we actively pursue is to staff every program, every role (even the most apparently inconsequential) with people clearly gifted for that role. Our approach to volunteers is not "any warm body will do," but "there are no 'along-for-the-ride' cells in the physical body nor in Christ's body—so what has the Holy Spirit gifted you to do within the Body of Christ?" It's not necessarily the task itself. Parking cars is not on the list of spiritual gifts, but there are certain people whose gifts make them far more able to enjoy parking cars as the platform for their ministry and contribution to the life of the church. We've found that the rate of burnout goes way down when people are filling roles in the church that actually fit their gifts rather than serving in ways they have been made to feel guilty about or pressured into.

We are a church presently made up of about 2,600 people. We systematically ask ourselves, "How can we identify gifts more quickly and effectively?" "How are we mentoring gifts that have been identified?" And "How do we match the gifts and gifted people in our church with the roles that need filling?" Serving takes on a different tone, energy, and life when people whom the Holy Spirit has gifted do it. We haven't by any means perfected this yet, but the changes have created a whole new atmosphere for ministry and a greater sense by people at large that they have a God- designed role in our church that they have been equipped to fill.

This approach helps create a setting in which programs are not perpetuated if the Holy Spirit has not enabled enough people to carry them out. The opposite is true. You need to launch programs that make use of the gifts you do have, discern opportunities, and be willing to close ministries that have run their course. Jesus never said, "By their programs you shall know them." Programs are a necessary means not the end goal of ministry and life in the Body of Christ.

Using a Common Script

When I was doing my graduate studies in Leadership and Spiritual Dynamics, I came across a book that talked about "common scripting" as a key ingredient in developing organizations and change management. It makes profound sense when you think about it; if you don't share the same language or agreed vocabulary, especially about the important things; the results are confusion, miscommunication, and disunity. I touched on this in Chapter One, but it's worth revisiting. We live at a time in which growing churches are often made up of people from various different denominational or spiritual backgrounds. Each of those backgrounds has words in common but not necessarily common meanings to those words. Mix them with a significant percentage of people today who have little or no religious upbringing or a spiritual but non-Christian upbringing with a different, wrong, or no language at all to describe their experience, and you have a setting ripe for confusion, discord, and conflict.

Convergence in our church partly came about when I devoted thirteen weeks to an extended study of spiritual gifts. Among other things, it was intended to give us a base line vocabulary to use in clarifying, identifying, mentoring, and employing spiritual gifts. We didn't relegate a discussion of spiritual gifts to a Sunday school class with a handful of attendees; we brought the conversation front and center before the entire church. We determined that the shared understanding of spiritual gifts was so important that we made it our central focus for a period of time. It was not an easy process nor was it universally well received. Some found the conversation so uncomfortable they chose to leave. I was doing my best to be biblical, clear, and complete in those messages, but none of us took them as the final word. We agreed to recognize them as the basic vocabulary for an ongoing discussion, not the "end of discussion." Newcomers to our church are still encouraged to listen to those messages as part of joining our church and gift discernment process. We want them to understand not only *what* we mean when we talk about spiritual gifts, but also *how* we talk about it.

The conversation continues. Discussions take a lot longer when we say what we say, followed by saying what we mean, followed by making sure others understand what we meant to say; but the resulting clarity is worth it. We've all had to learn that very familiar words from someone else's mouth may have a different meaning than they do in our ears. It doesn't necessarily mean we disagree; we may be talking about two different things using the same words, or using different words to describe the same reality. It takes listening and patient discussions to figure this out. But out of those discussions comes a common script.

Food for Thought

As a church we have discovered that common scripting opens the way for a lot of other understanding. When we were first clarifying and identifying spiritual gifts as a major part of our life together in 2011, we thought it would be helpful to hold some gatherings where those in each of the three gift groups (love, word, and power) could gather and get to know each another. We planned three meals, one for each of the groups.

Week one was the Love Gifts potluck. I cannot fully convey just how amazing that meal was—it was like hospitality, great eating, and caring, all on steroids. The dishes, the serving, the decorations, the organization, the welcome—it was the kind of meal you would pay a lot of money for, yet it was lavished on one another by people eager and excited to exercise their gifts. It was a feast of caring! During the meal we celebrated and encouraged those gifts. We urged them to mentor one another. We also talked about the dark side of their gifts, and the challenge to remember that those with the word and power gifts needed to be loved as well as understood by those with love gifts. We gently warned them how easy it is for those with love gifts to feel misunderstood and stepped on by others, which makes those gifts less lighthearted than they sometimes seem. We reminded them that their gifts actually needed training from those with word gifts, and targeted application from those with power gifts, because all the gifts are necessary. And we encouraged them to find more experienced mentors who shared their gift to help with their development, and also to seek out ways to help younger practitioners with this gifting.

Week two was the Word Gifts potluck. Right from the start we could tell this was an entirely different group. It was like a role play of Jesus's words to His disciples in John 4:32, "I have food to eat that you know nothing about." Compared to the previous week, the food was terrible. Most of the preparation and presentation was merely functional and secondary. Clearly, the emphasis at this meal was not on eating; it was on talking. There was some great caring, but the conversations were definitely at a higher level of intensity and theological precision than the previous week, where lighthearted banter and laughter flowed freely. During this lunch, there was more of an "iron sharpening iron" tone to the discussions and a lot more watching and suspicion. Again it was my privilege to challenge their commitment to practice their gifting with increasing wisdom, and to be mindful of the dangers of discounting or mistreating those with the love or power gifts. I reminded them that sometimes actions do speak louder than words, and if our words are true and accurately reflect God's Word, we will need those with the other gifts to put actions to our teaching.

Week three was the Power Gifts potluck. It was our first public gathering for people who had discovered that their gift involved this category of power. We were in uncharted territory but excited to see what would happen given the eye-opening experiences of the previous two weeks. The results were as hilarious as they were refreshing. As people arrived, the initial conversations quickly followed a familiar pattern, "Oh, you have this gift? Wow! Me, too. That makes so much sense! No wonder you did this or said that in those situations! And I thought it was just me." The discernment people were obviously intent on sensing whether or not everything that was going on was really of God. So many who attended were astounded and deeply relieved there were others in our church that shared their gifting. They had assumed they were part of a minority, when it turned out that our church had a healthy contingent of Power Gift people. Again, the food was secondary (and no one volunteered to re-enact the miracle of the feeding of the 5,000), but during the evening there was so much mutual affirmation, encouragement, and challenge to practice their gifts well. We again focused on the importance of the need to go the second mile in extending grace and recognize the crucial importance of both the other groups to establish a foundation and context for the Power Gifts to have effect. We also spoke a lot about humility and timing in using these gifts.

The point of these meals was this: Think creatively about ways to get people in these groups together, but do get them together. The basis for mentorship requires that those with each of these gift categories know each other and encourage each other. Talk to them, be honest with them and affirm them, but also be direct and firm with them about what you expect as this broad expression of body life becomes part of your common script and practices as a church. Model an openness to flexibility as all of you exercise your gifts and learn to function together, always emphasizing the need for grace as you make mistakes and learn together.

If you are reading this as a senior pastor or other ministry leader I realize that the conversation about spiritual gifts often feels like a Pandora's Box with hidden dangers and inevitable problems, and to a degree that's true. You might be thinking *if I allow this, there's no going back.* And you're right- it *will* cost you. It will challenge theology, culture, and perhaps a lot of your history. But is the alternative free of problems? Does the body of Christ really function in a healthy and effective way when significant resources given by the Holy Spirit are left hidden or rejected? Are you tired of trying to sit on a three-legged stool that has only one or two legs? And can the church survive in such a weakened state all that we face today?

My experience as a pastor, teacher, part-time seminary professor, and leader has caused me to be deeply convicted in my own church and especially in my exposure to many other Christians from a wide variety of backgrounds. There is, in your church, a surprising wide and deep underground river of experience that is currently neglected and undefined. If you don't legitimize those experiences from God's Word in the pulpit publicly, all those people will be left thinking that you either don't believe in what they have experienced or that you suspect what they are sensing is something wrong or even evil. If you're the leader, they are waiting for your permission to talk about it. If our stated desire is for personal renewal and outright revival in the Church, the outpouring of the Holy Spirit has to be part of the conversation.

The Matter of Guarantees

Some of you may have been put off or concerned that I use the term "guaranteed" when I describe the gifts of the Spirit and the spiritual disciplines of the Christian life. Someone gently questioned whether I might have placed the gifts over the Holy Spirit. Let me assure you I have not, though I acknowledge I have been bold in my view! The spiritual gifts are one of the ongoing evidences of the Spirit and are the only guaranteed place of power from which to serve.

Spiritual disciplines are a place of ongoing transformation post-conversion. As I've shared consistently, salvation is not earned by these acts or habits. These disciplines provide space for the Holy Spirit in personal and communal moments to strengthen, encourage, rebuke, correct, help, and to speak so we are able to understand our role in what we are called to do next! The role of holiness and character are so critical because the power behind the gifts, the person that meets you when you walk in the holy habits, can be grieved. Thus his power and presence can be muted and damped. Paul wrote in Ephesians 4:30, *"And do not grieve the Holy Spirit of God, with whom you were sealed for the day of redemption."*

Don't live in a way that contradicts what you already are and what you will be forever. Don't push down, attack, ignore, or grieve God's Spirit in you. If you allow habitual anger, un-forgiveness, lust, coveting, and lying, not only will you break the unity of the church, but you also grieve the Spirit by giving ground to the devil himself. And let me tell you; the thoughts, impulses, and actions he will use to tempt you are nothing but life draining, church breaking, victory stealing, and darkness invoking. His evil work removes Sabbath, removes sanctuary, removes peace, removes knowing presence, and removes holy power to serve. When we grieve the Holy Spirit, our gifts aren't revoked, but they dim greatly, and the spiritual practices become powerless to transform.

The Holy Spirit convicts us of sin, helps us see Jesus, gives us the ability to accept Jesus, allows us to walk like Jesus, and lets us understand, desire, and be molded by Scripture. Every time you truly meet the Holy Spirit you will meet Jesus Christ Himself and will be given the opportunity to become more like Him. The Spirit baptized us into Jesus, He teaches us, seals us, and prays for us. He is not a force; He is God Himself. Every encounter you've had with God in any way is through and by the Holy Spirit. John 16:13 says, *"But when he, the Spirit of truth, comes, he will guide you into all the truth."*

In writing this book, I presume a common faithfulness. That is to say, Acts 2:42-47 is what every church is called to pursue. We are to praise, sing, be thankful, love each other, say no to sin, practice communion, prayer, accountability, serve the poor, give our time, talent, treasure, use our spiritual gifts, and share the Gospel. We are to preach, worship, break bread and pray in community, and experience God's presence, signs and wonders, real relationships, transformed lives, and the opportunity to invite people to gather in guaranteed places of meeting with God, This is a normal Christian life. This, no matter what the denomination or cultural expression, is a normal Christian church.

There are other guaranteed places to meet God. The Scriptures are a guaranteed place of encounter between God and His people. The Holy Spirit is always present, always overshadowing its words. As the author of Hebrews wrote, *"His powerful Word is sharp as a surgeon's scalpel, cutting through everything, whether doubt or defense, laying us open to listen and obey. Nothing and no one is impervious to God's Word. We can't get away from it—no matter what"* (Hebrews 4:12-13). Or remember Paul's famed words on Holy Writ, *"All Scripture is God-breathed and is useful for teaching, rebuking, correcting and training in righteousness, so that the servant of God may be thoroughly equipped for every good work"* (2 Timothy 3:16-17).

The Holy Spirit is always leading us into God's truth, the holy faith passed down. In fact, the Holy Spirit who leads us and teaches us is actually the author of the Scriptures. There might be 66 books and numerous writers, but behind them all is one author. The Holy Spirit will lead us, speak to us, and form us through the Bible.

Another place of guaranteed encounter is the actual Gospel. As Paul wrote to the church in Rome, *"I am not ashamed of the gospel, because it is the power of God for the salvation of everyone who believes: first for the Jew, then for the Gentile"* (Romans 1:16). The word "power" is where we get our word *dynamite*. The gospel has sheer power, it is dynamic, it the place where the Holy Spirit brings the whole of the God the father's calling and the whole of Jesus' work past, present and future into effect within a life. As John MacArthur said, "The gospel carries the omnipotence of God, whose power alone is sufficient to save people from sin and give them eternal life."[2] And this power brings salvation. The Holy Spirit is always around, above, below, behind and in the giving of the gospel. No matter the results He is always present.

Gathered worship is a wonderful guaranteed place of encounter. One week I was preaching to our community about this and I asked this question, and made the following comments:

What happens when we worship, what is happening when we sing, give, or read together? Honestly, sometimes it's great, sometimes it's boring, sometimes I'm inspired, and sometimes not! A thousand things– personality, music style, my day, or my week–all can affect my experience! Sanctus Church, if we want to be marked by passionate worship over the long haul, then we must actually accept and believe what the Bible says is happening as we use our voices and our hearts. See, ten minutes ago when we were singing, we actually drew near to God Himself and entered the place where angels fear to tread. If it is genuine worship of God Himself, we walk right into the place, the Holy Place. Remember these words *"Therefore, brothers and sisters, since we have confidence to enter the Most Holy Place by the blood of Jesus"* (Hebrews 10:19).

And what does it look like? What does every service look like, small or large, great production or very note of key? What does it look like, what does the real environment truly encompass, whether in a cathedral or house church, bells and smells, speaking in tongues, hymns or choruses, loud or soft, traditional, transitional, contemporary or new? When we gather, together we walk into and join this eternal chorus:

Then I saw a Lamb, looking as if it had been slain, standing at the center of the throne, encircled by the four living creatures and the elders. The Lamb had seven horns and seven eyes, which are the seven spirits of God sent out into all the earth. He went and took the scroll from the right hand of him who sat on the throne. And when he had taken it, the four living creatures and the twenty-four elders fell down before the Lamb. Each one had a harp and they were holding golden bowls full of incense, which are the prayers of God's people. And they sang a new song, saying: "You are worthy to take the scroll and to open its seals, because you were slain, and with your blood you purchased for God persons from every tribe and language and people and nation. You have made them to be a kingdom and priests to serve our God, and they will reign on the earth." Then I looked and heard the voice of many angels, numbering thousands upon thousands, and ten thousand times ten thousand. They encircled the throne and the living creatures and the elders. In a loud voice they were saying: "Worthy is the Lamb, who was slain, to receive power and wealth and wisdom and strength and honor and glory and praise!" Then I heard every creature in heaven and on earth and under the earth and on the sea, and all that is in them, saying:" To him who sits on the throne and to the Lamb be praise and honor and glory and power, for ever and ever!" The four living creatures said, "Amen," and the elders fell down and worshiped (Rev 5:6-14).

This is not metaphor or poetic license at its heart! When we sing, we enter right into God's holy presence, with all the angels, with all that already have died and are with Jesus, we enter the place where without Jesus' covering you would die! We are in the presence of God right now! Do we together believe this? Do we say this is true before we come to worship? Right now this is happening, felt or not, see it or not, God is among us and we are in the Holy Place of God. Would you sing differently, would you give differently, would you prepare for Sunday differently, would you pray differently if you read this before church and said, "I am about to enter this place?" Let it begin today! I want to be part of a church marked by passionate musical worship. That only happens when we come expectantly and believe whom we are about to meet in this environment no matter feelings or preferences. And what does the Bible teach? *"Come near to God and he will come near to you"* (James 4:8); *"But thou art holy, O thou that inhabits the praises of Israel"* (Psalm 22: 3). We draw near, he draws near, and we host his presence as we gather in worship.

Worship is a guaranteed place of meeting God. Yes, He is everywhere, but in times of worship when people truly come to meet with Him, when they are prepared and ready and seeking God, He moves from omnipresence to palpable presence. Are we not truly the temple of God? Is not the Holy Spirit the Spirit of Christ? What did Jesus say? *"For where two or three gather in my name, there am I with them"* (Matthew 18:20).

Another guaranteed place to encounter God is Communion. The breaking of bread–communion, the Lord's Supper, the Eucharist–is a place of *remembrance*. We stop and remember, think about and reflect on Jesus' death and resurrection. *"For whenever you eat this bread and drink this cup, you proclaim the Lord's death until he comes"* (1 Corinthians 11:26). As one author wrote, "The past is not a golden age to be rehearsed with nostalgia. Rather, it is a retelling of those events of the past that matters. The telling of the past instructs, informs, and encourages us to live in the present in the light of the past."[3]

Do I believe Jesus is in the actual elements? No, the juice and bread is not Jesus; they don't turn into anything; they are only symbols that focus our attention, but Jesus is at every table when we meet!

It is actually *communion*. Think about what the word means. This is a place, an environment where we really are together with Jesus and each other. We are not called to be alone; it's not good for us to be alone, especially at this meal hosted by Jesus Himself. It is here that we declare, experience, and know God's grace and peace through Jesus and His Holy Spirit. Communion is a guaranteed place to encounter Jesus' power and presence.

Communion is a place of *forgiveness*! When Jesus was here on earth He was famous for eating with the wrong people, and enjoying the company of sinners.[4] Aren't you glad He still eats with sinners? Every time we take communion, Jesus eats reminds us that He still eats with sinners, His mercies are new every day. Read Matthew 26: 27-28 with fresh eyes, *"Then he took a cup, and when he had given thanks, he gave it to them, saying, 'Drink from it, all of you. This is my blood of the covenant, which is poured out for many for the forgiveness of sins.'"*

Communion is *covenantal*. This is where we renew our baptismal vows to God.[5] Yes, I affirm Jesus as my Savior and Lord, yes, I will follow You all the rest of my life, and be faithful and loyal to You and no other.

Communion creates *anticipation*. This meal is given to prepare us, and to point us to the last and greatest of meals that we will have with Jesus face to face in the new heavens and new earth, what is called the marriage supper of the Lamb.[6] One day we will never take Communion again because we will be united and eat with Him face to face. Did you know in Greek the word Eucharist has the same root as joy, thanksgiving and grace? Communion is a meal of joyful thanksgiving!

Communion also reminds us of forgiveness, and is a great symbol of the defeat of Satan, the flesh, and death through resurrection! It is a place of thankfulness where we are reminded that God called us, Jesus bought us, and the Holy Spirit holds us, comforts us, intercedes for us, convicts us and assures us. That's why it should be a place of such joy and celebration.[7] That's why communion should be a moment where we, like the Psalmists, cry out: *"Enter his gates with thanksgiving and his courts with praise; give thanks to him and praise his name"* (Psalm 100: 4).

There is one last place of guaranteed encounter I must mention. It is the place of suffering for the sake of the Gospel. As we live amid the growing storm we will suffer—misunderstanding, false judgments, mistreatment, and even more, if our fellow-Christians elsewhere and through history are any example. For many of us living here in the West, our very comfortable, safe, middle class privileges will be pushed, threatened, and possibly removed. Yet this will provide us the very environment in which to walk with Jesus as so many have before. It's an old road, well-worn path that everything in us wants to avoid. Yet it is also a place of encounter and transformation. That narrow path becomes the place of authentic walking with Jesus the Man of Sorrows, who also is the conquering Lord of all. Listen afresh to the words of those in other times that even now become more relevant in our time. *"To this you were called, because Christ suffered for you, leaving you an example that you should follow in his steps"* (1 Peter 2:21).

Suffering is part of the calling of every believer, and Jesus' suffering is our example. The word *example* used by Peter is very powerful, not just something we copy from a distance. The idea describes a little child carefully tracing out their letters so they can learn fully to read and write. Oh church, follow carefully in the footsteps of Jesus Christ, including His passion and suffering. Jesus said, *"I have told you these things, so that in me you may have peace. In this world you will have trouble. But take heart! I have overcome the world"* (John 16:33).

Testimony to the truth of what Jesus said was recorded by the first Christians and has echoed constantly down through the centuries. James wrote, *"Consider it pure joy, my brothers and sisters, whenever you face trials of many kinds, because you know that the testing of your faith develops perseverance"* (James 1:2-3). When Paul wrote to the Philippians near the end of his life, after having known Jesus better than most, third heaven and all; listen to what this older pastor leader says: *"I want to know Christ—yes, to know the power of his resurrection and participation in his sufferings, becoming like him in his death, and so, somehow, attaining to the resurrection from the dead"* (Philippians 3:10). This suffering is not to be tearfully endured but seen as calling. Our genuine suffering for Jesus is a guaranteed place of encounter between Jesus and his people.

The Gospel, Scripture, Spiritual disciplines, Spiritual gifts, worship, communion, baptism and Suffering for Jesus—salvation is not earned by these acts or habits though they are all guaranteed places of ongoing encounter. When understood, they build right expectation for the church community. But, just because you meet God in an ongoing way does not mean fire, angels, or profound life-changing moments. It means He is there. This is like going to gym, or doing an activity over a long period of time! It leads to real change and when people come to all of these places knowing who is there, faith grows more and more. And why does this matter? Because all of these environments and actions translate into all cultures; they are globally Christian. They can be and must be the center of any ministry no matter the size or makeup. They can be used in different styles of church or ministries, numbers are no barrier, money is not the center, and Jesus is always present! And so let us meet Him, build our ministries around Him and lead people to Him. That is why our whole discipleship model at Sanctus is based and programmed around theses ongoing places of encounter.

There are moments in history that define what comes next. We stand at the threshold of a new reality whether we know it or want it. The impending storm of competing worldviews will try to diminish us, eject us from the conversation, shut us down and even lock us up. But we dare not build our church like a fortress, going into hiding in an attempt to wait out the storm, while pining for ages long past. We dare not hunker down in an effort to just survive. This is the time to "take heart!" Jesus has overcome the world!

We must choose to thrive. Convergence offers a way to what God has promised, a way for the Body of Christ to thrive no matter the style of church, the resources we have, our size, or our location. It's more deeply rooted, more significant and more powerful than the right leader, the right strategic plan, or the right model of church in any season. And it happens when three unexpected things come together: Spiritual gifts, spiritual disciplines (or practices), and unusual works of the Spirit (revival). When they converge they bring strength, confidence, hope, and real power to form the authentic Christian life and build the Church.

Convergence can happen anywhere. It can translate from a tiny, isolated village in Peru to the boundless, global energy of New York City, from the slums of Calcutta and Nairobi, to basements in Riyadh and high rises in Hong Kong, from Toronto to Tokyo, Manchester to Moscow, from the jungles in Thailand and Brazil to the steppes in Tibet. There hope for the Church in all its forms, from free to liturgical, from cathedrals to house churches, from the mega-church to the 1000's of neighborhood churches. Though it is not sexy or powerful by the world's standards, and it does not guarantee safety, it is heaven-promised and heaven-empowered! A light is piercing through the darkness of the storm to tell us God is at work, and we discover and understand that same light has been reflecting across twenty centuries since Jesus walked on earth. Convergence is where unlikely streams of God's work unexpectedly come together to unleash the unstoppable force Jesus set in motion.

I see churches looking more like the church of Antioch day-by-day (Acts 13), flourishing all around the world through strong teaching, the exercise of all 21 spiritual gifts, mentorship, the spiritual disciplines, mutual submission, strong leadership, growing cultural diversity, serving, and sensitivity to the Spirit's leading. This is the type of church we must be and we pray for God to grow us wider, deeper and longer, to be a place of influence for the kingdom in our own region and beyond.

Jesus is not just our Savior and Lord; He is our model. In Him and through history, though under many different names, we see convergence happen again and again, with world-changing results. Now is the time to return to the only place of guaranteed power, of guaranteed transformation, and guaranteed life change–the place where the world truly is changed and where the kingdom comes on earth as it is in heaven. Lord hear our prayer, and make us like this. Amen.

End Notes

CHAPTER 1

1 G. K. Chesterton, *Orthodoxy,* (Wheaton: Harold Shaw Publishers, 1994), p.47. The exact quote is, "Tradition means giving votes to the most obscure of all classes, our ancestors."

2 Charles Kraft, *Appropriate Christianity*, (Pasadena: William Carey Library, 2005) p.100.

3 Charles Kraft, *Confronting Powerless Christianity*, (Grand Rapids: Baker Publishing Group, Chosen Books, 2002), p.103, 121-122. I am indebted to Professor Kraft for this framework in understanding God's plan.

CHAPTER 2

1 Karl Barth, *Church Dogmatics* (Peabody, Mass.: Hendricksen Publishers, 2010), Vol 1, page 301.

2 Marshall Shelley, *Christian Theology in Plain Language*, (Waco, Tx.: Word Books, 1985), p. 143.

3 Gordon Fee, *Philippians*, IV New Testament Commentaries (Downers Grove: InterVarsity Press, 1999), p.95.

4 Eugene Peterson, *The Message*, (Colorado Springs: Nav Press).

5 N.T. Wright, *Climax of the Covenant*: Christ and the Law in Pauline Theology (Minneapolis: Fortress Press, 1993), p. 84).

6 R.T. France, *Matthew:* An Introduction and Commentary, (Grand Rapids: Wm. B. Eerdmans Pub. Co., 2007), p.99.

7 Alan Cole, *The Gospel According to Mark: Introduction and Commentary* (Grand Rapids: Wm. B. Eerdmans Publishing Co. 1961) p. 109.

8 Charles H. Kraft, *Appropriate Christianity* (Pasadena: William Carey Library, 2005) pp.108-109

CHAPTER 3

1 J. Robert Clinton, *Spiritual Gifts* (Traverse City:Horizon Books Publishers, 1996). I've tried to credit Mr. Clinton when I have quoted him directly, but want to acknowledge how much his work has shaped a lot of my thinking and language in discussing Spiritual Habits and Gifts.

2 Richard Foster, *Celebration of Discipline* (San Francisco: Harper & Row, Publishers, 1978).

3 Dallas Willard, *The Spirit of the Disciplines* (San Francisco: Harper & Row, Publishers, 1988).

4 Charles Kraft, *I Give You Authority* (Ada, Michigan: Chosen Books, 1997), p.51

5 Willard, p. ix.

6 R.T. France, *Matthew:* An Introduction and Commentary, (Grand Rapids: Wm. B. Eerdmans Pub. Co., 2007), p.449.

7 Dallas Willard, *The Divine Conspiracy* (San Francisco: Harper & Row, Publishers, 1998), p.301.

8 Richard Foster, ed., *Renovaré Spiritual Formation Study Bible*—NRSV (San Francisco: Harper & Row, Publishers, 2009), p.2297.

9 Charles Kraft, *Appropriate Christianity* (Pasadena: William Carey Library, 2005), p.258.

10 Dallas Willard, *The Spirit of the Disciplines* (San Francisco: Harper & Row, Publishers, 1988), p.186.

11 Walter Trobisch, *Martin Luther's Quiet Time* (Downers Grove: InterVarsity Press, 1975).

12 Dallas Willard, *The Spirit of the Disciplines* (San Francisco: Harper & Row, Publishers, 1988), p.205.

13 Richard Foster, ed., *Renovaré Spiritual Formation Study Bible*—NRSV (San Francisco: Harper & Row, Publishers, 2009), p.2298.

14 Richard Foster, *Celebration of Discipline* (San Francisco: Harper & Row, Publishers, 1978), p.84-85.

15 Scott McKnight, *Fasting: The Ancient Practices* (Nashville: Thomas Nelson Publishers, 2009), pp.xxiii.

16 Michael J. Wilkins, *Matthew*, The NIV Application Commentary (Grand Rapids: Zondervan Publishing, 2004), p. 281-282.

17 Richard Foster, ed., *Renovaré Spiritual Formation Study Bible*—NRSV (San Francisco: Harper & Row, Publishers, 2009), p.2308.

18 Dallas Willard, *The Spirit of the Disciplines* (San Francisco: Harper & Row, Publishers, 1988), pp.173-174.

19 McKnight, p. xxi.

20 McKnight, p. 151.

21 John Piper, *A Hunger for God: Desiring God Through Fasting and Prayer* (Wheaton :Crossway Publishing, 2013), pp.17-18.

22 Richard Foster, ed., *Renovaré Spiritual Formation Study Bible*—NRSV (San Francisco: Harper & Row, Publishers, 2009), p.2296.

23 Richard Foster, *Money, Sex, and Power* (San Francisco: Harper & Row, Publishers, 1985), p. 109.

24 Wagner-Modified Houts Questionaire, Charles E. Fuller Institute of Evangelism and Church Growth, 1990.

25 Richard Foster, ed., *Renovaré Spiritual Formation Study Bible*—NRSV (San Francisco: Harper & Row, Publishers, 2009), p.2314.

26 Calvin Miller, *A Hunger for the Holy* (New York: Simon & Schuster, Howard Books, 2003), p. 133).

27 Dallas Willard quoted in *Christianity Today,* October 10, 1980.

28 Dallas Willard, *The Great Omission* (San Francisco: Harper One Publishers, 2003), p. 109.

29 Dallas Willard, *The Spirit of the Disciplines* (San Francisco: Harper & Row, Publishers, 1988), p.259.

CHAPTER 4

1 J. Robert Clinton, *Spiritual Gifts* (Traverse City: Horizon Books Publishers, 1996), p. [p.55]

2 Clinton, p. [p.56]

3 C. Peter Wagner, *Discover Your Spiritual Gifts* (Grand Rapids: Baker Publishing Group, Chosen Books, 2012), p.19.

4 Bruce Bugbee, *What You Do Best in the Body of Christ: Discover Your Spiritual Gifts, Your Personal Style, and God-given Passion* (Grand Rapids: Zondervan Publishing, 2005), p, 38.

5 I'm indebted to J. Robert Clinton for this helpful classification of the gifts into Love, Word, and Power gifts. While other classifications have been used, these groupings seem to make practical sense as I watch the gifts in operation. Also, the number of gifts varies between various students of Scripture, but 21 seems to be a reasonable total.

6 Gerald Bray and Thomas C. Oden, *Romans*, Ancient Christian Commentary on Scripture: New Testament VI (Dowers Grove: InterVarsity Press, 1998), p. 311.

7 Paul Brand and Philip Yancey, *Fearfully and Wonderfully Made* and *In His Image* (Grand Rapids: Zondervan Publishing)

8 Craig Blomberg, *Preaching the Parables: From Responsible Interpretation to Powerful Proclamation* (Grand Rapids: Baker Academic, 2004), p.199.

9 *The Amplified Bible*, (Grand Rapids: Zondervan Publishing, 1987).

10 Brian Stiller, *Preaching the Parables to Post-Moderns* (Minneapolis: Augsburg Fortress, 2004), p.160.

11 Stiller, p.165.

CHAPTER 5

1 Gordon D. Fee, *The First Epistle to the Corinthians*, Revised Edition (Grand Rapids: Wm. B. Eerdmans Publishing Co., 1987), p.640.

2 Craig Blomberg, *First Corinthians*, The NIV Application Commentary (Grand Rapids: Zondervan Publishing, 1995), p. 243).

3 Craig Blomberg, *First Corinthians*, The NIV Application Commentary (Grand Rapids: Zondervan Publishing, 1995), p. 215).

CHAPTER 6

1 J. Robert Clinton, *Spiritual Gifts* (Camp Hill: Christian Publications/Horizon Books, 1985).

2 Wayne Grudem, *Systematic Theology* (Grand Rapids: Zondervan Publishing, 1994), p.1027

3 J. Robert Clinton, *Spiritual Gifts* (Camp Hill: Christian Publications/Horizon Books, 1985), p.88.

4 Bruce Bugbee, *What You Do Best in the Body of Christ: Discover Your Spiritual Gifts, Your Personal Style, and God-given Passion* (Grand Rapids: Zondervan Publishing, 2005), p.49.

5 J. Robert Clinton, *Spiritual Gifts* (Camp Hill: Christian Publications/Horizon Books, 1985), adapted from a list found on p.89.

6 J. Robert Clinton, *Spiritual Gifts* (Camp Hill: Christian Publications/Horizon Books, 1985), p.90.

7 Bruce Bugbee, *What You Do Best in the Body of Christ: Discover Your Spiritual Gifts, Your Personal Style, and God-given Passion* (Grand Rapids: Zondervan Publishing, 2005), p.61.

8 C. Peter Wagner, *Discover Your Spiritual Gifts* (Bloomington: Chosen Books, 2012), p.149.

9 Clinton, p.71.

CHAPTER 7

1 Again, I became aware of these categories through the work of J. Robert Clinton.

2 Clinton, p.55.

3 Clinton, pp.54-56.

4 Wayne Grudem, *Systematic Theology* (Grand Rapids: Zondervan Publishing, 1994), p.1058.

5 Clinton, p.63.

6 Leslie B. Flynn, *19 Gifts of the Spirit* (Wheaton:Victor Books/SP Publications Inc., 1974), p.87-88.

7 Clinton, pp.63-64.

8 Flynn, p88.

9 Clinton, pp.75-77.

10 C. Peter Wagner, *Discover Your Spiritual Gifts* (Bloomington: Chosen Books, 2012), pp.145-146.

11 J. Rodman Williams, Renewal Theology (Vol. III), (Grand Rapids, MI: Zondervan Publishing House, 1982), page 170-71.

CHAPTER 8

1 Wagner, p.148.

2 Bugbee, p.61.

3 C. Peter Wagner, *Your Spiritual Gifts Can Help Your Church Grow* (Grand Rapids: Baker Books— Regal, 1979), pp.162-163.

4 Clinton, p.146.

5 C. Peter Wagner, *Discover Your Spiritual Gifts* (Bloomington: Chosen Books, 2012), pp.145-143.

6 Gary Powell

7 Attributed to Lyle Schaller by C. Peter Wagner.

8 Flynn, p.57.

9 Clinton, p.49.

10 Flynn, p.58.

11 Wagner, pp.180-181.

12 Quoted in Wagner, p.185.

13 Adapted from Clinton, pp.78-79.

CHAPTER 9

1 Clinton, p.144.

2 Grudem, p.1052.

3 Bugbee, p.161.

4 Clinton, p.

5 Clinton, p.165.

6 Clinton, p. 165.

7 Fee, p. 655-658.

8 Grudem, p.1072.

9 Grudem, p. 1072.

10 Gordon D. Fee, *The First Epistle to the Corinthians*, Revised Edition (Grand Rapids: Wm. B. Eerdmans Publishing Co., 1987), p.682.

11 Fee, p. 691-692.

12 Wagner, p.263.

13 Richard Foster, *Prayer* (San Francisco:HarperOne,1992), p.191.

14 C. Peter Wagner, *Prayer Shield* (Grand Rapids: Baker Books—Regal, 1992), p.54.

CHAPTER 10

1 Wagner, p.147.

2 Elizabeth Elliot, *Safe in the Everlasting Arms* (Grand Rapids: Baker Publishing Group, Revell, 2002), p.94.

3 Wagner, p.147.

4 Flynn, p.141.

5 J. Robert Clinton, *Unlocking Your Giftedness* (Barnabas Publishers, 1993), pp.157- 158.

6 Various accounts of this event have circulated, among them Steer, Roger Steer *George Müller: Delighted in God.* (Tain, Rosshire: Christian Focus Publications, 1997).

7 Wagner, p.146.

8 Clinton, p.68.

9 Wagner, p.146.

10 Clinton, p.67-68 includes an overview.

CHAPTER 11

1 Charles Kraft, *I Give You Authority* (Ada, Michigan: Chosen Books, 1997), p.51.

2 J. Robert Clinton, *Unlocking Your Giftedness* (Barnabas Publishers, 1993), p.153.

3 Clinton, p.155.

4 Wagner, p.147.

5 Bugbee, p.61.

6 Wagner, p.239.

7 Clinton, p.159. These clues are adapted from his observations.

8 Wagner, p.239.

9 Wagner p.149.

10 Grudem, p.1062.

11 Clinton, p.161.

12 Clinton, p.161-162. Adapted from his suggestions.

CHAPTER 12

1 *Revival is Christ* (November, 2001), Herald of His Coming
http://www.heraldofhiscoming.com/Past%20Issues/2001/November/revival_is_christ_centered.htm

2 R.T. France, *Matthew:* An Introduction and Commentary, (Grand Rapids: Wm. B. Eerdmans Pub. Co., 2007), p.647.

3 J.C. Ryle, *Matthew:* (Wheaton: Crossway Publishers, 1993), p.150.

CHAPTER 13

1 Flynn, p. 87-88.

1 John MacArthur, :New Testament Commentaries (Chicago: Moody Publishers, 1994), p. [p.175]

2 Gordon Smith, *A Holy Meal:* The Lord's Supper in the Life of the Church (Grand Rapids: Baker Academic, 2005), p.38.

3 Smith p. 57.

4 Smith p. 67.

5 Smith p. 91.

6 Smith p. 99.

Other Convergence Materials

For access to an 8 Week Video Series, Study Guide, and all other Convergence material, please go to http://ThriveWithConvergence.com

Made in the USA
Columbia, SC
28 December 2021

52900453R00171